General Lewis B. Hershey
and Conscientious Objection
during World War II

The American Military Experience Series

John C. McManus, Series Editor

The books in this series portray and analyze the experience of Americans in military service during war and peacetime from the onset of the twentieth century to the present. The series emphasizes the profound impact wars have had on nearly every aspect of recent American history and considers the significant effects of modern conflict on combatants and noncombatants alike. Titles in the series include accounts of battles, campaigns, and wars; unit histories; biographical and autobiographical narratives; investigations of technology and warfare; studies of the social and economic consequences of war; and in general, the best recent scholarship on Americans in the modern armed forces. The books in the series are written and designed for a diverse audience that encompasses nonspecialists as well as expert readers.

General Lewis B. Hershey
and Conscientious Objection during World War II

Nicholas A. Krehbiel

UNIVERSITY OF MISSOURI PRESS
COLUMBIA AND LONDON

University of Missouri Press, Columbia, Missouri 65201
Printed and bound in the United States of America

5 4 3 2 1 15 14 13 12 11

Cataloging-in-Publication data available from the Library of Congress.
ISBN 978-0-8262-1941-1

∞™ This paper meets the requirements of the
American National Standard for Permanence of Paper
for Printed Library Materials, Z39.48, 1984.

Designer: Kristie Lee
Typesetter: K. Lee Design & Graphics
Printer and binder: Integrated Book Technology
Typeface: Palatino

To Cathia . . .

Thank you so much for your part in one of our "somedays."

. . . and to Duncan . . .

May this aid in understanding some of your heritage.

Contents

Acknowledgments

★ ★ ★ ★

This book has its origins in a 2002 seminar on the history of the American West under Raymond Wilson at Fort Hays State University. Under Ray's tutelage, I wanted to examine a curious program called Civilian Public Service (CPS) that I had heard about from my family, as my maternal grandfather was a conscientious objector during World War II, serving in soil conservation and forestry camps and in a guinea pig unit. I was raised in the Church of the Brethren with a strong connection to the Mennonite ancestry on my father's side of the family, so I had always been curious about CPS and conscientious objection. While I worked on that paper, I became intrigued by the man who oversaw CPS and dealt with objectors during the war–Lewis B. Hershey, director of Selective Service. The idea that the chief of conscription was sympathetic to the problems of conscience and religious rights during wartime fascinated me., When I learned that Hershey came from Mennonite ancestry, I was hooked. As my father, who is of the Vietnam generation, succinctly put it to a friend while I was writing my dissertation, "He's finally realized that General Hershey is WAY more important than General Patton." I happen to agree (with deep apologies to the doctrinal brilliance and significance of George S. Patton, Jr.).

This book began as my Ph.D. dissertation at Kansas State University in Manhattan. Mark Parillo, my major professor, will always have my gratitude for everything he did for me in my years at K-State. He guided me in the conceptualization of this project, helped me through my coursework and exams, and read numerous drafts of questionable quality. Over the years he has become a good friend whom I will always value.

It is my distinct pleasure to know the following scholars and to offer my thanks for their assistance in this project: Robert Linder's seminars in the history of American Christianity provided a forum for developing some of the ideas I present in the pages that follow. His attention to detail concerning my understanding of the Historic Peace Churches has been instrumental. Dale Herspring, Michael Ramsay, Robert Schaeffer, and Sue Zschoche all offered helpful comments on early drafts of the manuscript. Albert Hamscher's advice during our all-too-infrequent golf rounds got me through some of the drudgery. Dave Stone and Mark Jantzen provided information about the nature of the publishing industry. Scott Bennett read the manuscript, made excellent suggestions for improvement, and has offered a wealth of information, particularly regarding the secular side of conscientious objection.

The time I spent in archives would have been wasted were it not for the wonderful people I met and worked with during my research trips. Wendy Chmielewski and Anne Yoder of the Swarthmore College Peace Collection, John Thiesen and James Lynch of the Mennonite Library and Archives, Richard Sommers, David Keough, and Rich Baker of the Army Heritage and Education Center, and Richard Bolyan of the National Archives were all of great assistance. James Zimmerman of Trine University, Hershey's alma mater, went above and beyond the call of duty in providing me with access to Hershey's personal papers and photographs and giving me a tour of Steuben County emphasizing the places of interest in the life of Hershey and his family. Finally, the staffs of the Franklin D. Roosevelt Library, the Harry S. Truman Library, the Brethren Library and Archives, and the Mennonite Church USA Archives—Goshen were of great help in directing me through the collections or sending me photographs I requested.

I also thank Clair Willcox of the University of Missouri Press for listening to my initial proposal and taking on this project as a part of the press's American Military Experience series. Thanks to Sara Davis, Lyn Smith, Beth Chandler, and Jennifer Gravley for their efforts in the publication and distribution of this book.

Portions of chapter 7 appeared as an article in the March 2011 edition of *War and Society,* and I thank Maney Publishing for granting me permission to reprint some of that article here.

I should also take this opportunity to thank my family. My parents, Bruce and Geneva, have always supported my work on this book. My siblings, Lindsay, Beth, Jeffrey, and Scott have been helpful as well, whether they knew it or not. Jeffrey's wife, Elizabeth, also has my gratitude for spreading the news of my work to her family and friends in the Church of the Brethren. Thanks go to my grandparents, Larry and Barbara Krehbiel and Eulalia Sanger, for their love and support over the years, and to my mother-in-law, Teresa Bailey, for aiding in childcare during the winter break to allow me to finish my revisions. The inspiration for my study of conscientious objection, my grandfather Merrill Sanger, is no longer with us on this earth, but his spirit will always be a part of those who were fortunate enough to have known and loved him. When I think of the fundamental beliefs in the Church of the Brethren concerning peace and nonresistance, I can think of no better example than his.

My wife, Cathia, deserves her own book full of my gratitude rather than just a couple of sentences in my acknowledgments. I met Cathia while at K-State through my numerous student/mentor meetings with Mark Parillo. She is more to me than I can ever express. She will always have my thanks for everything. In terms of this work, she served as an editor, tolerated my piles of books and documents, and provided a sounding board for ideas and suggestions. I could not have finished the book were it not for her. It is difficult to say what role my young son, Duncan, played in this book. After all, it is not easy for a child of about one year to offer editorial comments or suggest evidence to shore up my arguments. That said, the experience of observing his birth was beyond words, and through him, I am reminded every day of just how fortunate I am to have a wife and child who love me and mean the world to me.

General Lewis B. Hershey
and Conscientious Objection during World War II

Introduction

From 1941 to 1970, the name Lewis Blaine Hershey was synonymous with the U.S. draft. As director of Selective Service, General Hershey was chief administrator of the institution through which the United States conscripted armies for World War II, Korea, and Vietnam. Though Hershey's career in conscription planning and administration stretched back to the years between World Wars I and II, it was during the Vietnam War that he became incredibly controversial in the collective mind of the American public. As the antiwar movement grew, many public demonstrations focused on the draft, and Hershey became a target of the protestors' anger. He was not entirely blameless. As he aged he displayed an inflexible stance on draft classifications and a heavy political hand. His most infamous action during this time was the "Hershey directive," which reclassified any deferred person interfering with the draft, a move aimed at antidraft protesters with whom he vehemently disagreed. Those against the war and the draft viewed Hershey as a member of the establishment responsible for American involvement in Vietnam, and his public image plummeted. With some members of Congress and the American public calling for Hershey's ousting, President Richard Nixon replaced him, hoping to reduce protests on college campuses.[1]

While the public's view of Hershey during the Vietnam years is enduring, it misses the mark. A review of the early years of his career reveals a much more tolerant, nuanced, and sympathetic individual, especially in his dealings with conscientious objectors and their alternative service during World War II. Hershey was responsible for constructing policy on conscientious objection and his beliefs and actions in shaping alternative service during that time established precedent for the remaining years of conscription in the United States. Thus, he was the lynchpin in the American system of alternative service during the twentieth century.

Hershey's approach stood in stark contrast to the decentralized policies of the colonial era, the problematic alternatives during the Civil War, and the abhorrent treatment of conscientious objectors (COs) in World War I. Moving toward a more systematized and sympathetic means of dealing with the problems of conscience during wartime, Hershey accepted input from the Historic Peace Churches (Mennonite, Brethren, Society of Friends) and the National Service Board for Religious Objectors (NSBRO, an organization in Washington representing COs and directed by the Historic Peace Churches) and developed and administered Civilian Public Service (CPS) as the means of providing an alternative form of service for those who had religious objections to serving in the military. Under Hershey's direction there was increased institutional tolerance for conscientious objection in the mid-twentieth century. Although CPS did not remain after the World War II draft, the concept of alternative service remained in place throughout the remaining years of conscription with only one minor exception.[2]

Conscientious objection, alternative service, and the World War II experience are discussed in a rich array of works, but most of them take the point of view of the Historic Peace Churches. They largely celebrate the men of CPS who maintained their religious beliefs and identities even in the face of mandatory conscription and service.[3] The standard work on conscientious objection during World War II paints the federal government, the Selective Service, and Hershey in a negative light.[4] Historians have paid particular attention to Hershey, but conscientious objection is treated as a detail in a much larger portrait of conscription in the twentieth century.[5] This work seeks to rectify the view of Hershey as overly restrictive and place him in the context of creating, administering, and protecting alternative service, thus establishing a precedent that continued until the end of conscription in the United States. In this work, he is not necessarily celebrated, nor is he overly vilified. Instead, he is presented as an advocate of tolerance who was able to effectively balance the desires of the Historic Peace Churches with the requirements of the federal government during wartime. It was a difficult and thankless task but one that Hershey was able to complete, and in doing so, he protected the privilege of objection while preserving the duty of service.

Though he is not celebrated as one of the great military figures of the World War II era along with Dwight Eisenhower, George Marshall, and

Douglas MacArthur, Hershey still stands as significant during that time. He was a military professional in an age in which the professional soldier began to be a part of mainstream American society, moving away from an antimilitarist tradition.[6] While he was thoroughly a military man shaped by his experience in the National Guard and his service in World War I and the interwar army, he also displayed many civilian talents, which led to his successes during World War II. He possessed a keen understanding of the federal bureaucracy, took a well-reasoned approach to the place of conscience and service in American society, and had a particular talent for political negotiation. Hershey's unique set of skills made him the ideal choice to administer conscription and alternative service during World War II, as he was both a professional soldier and government bureaucrat sympathetic to the nuances of religious objection.

It bears mentioning that although Hershey wielded enormous power within the Selective Service, he was not simply a government bureaucrat protecting a personal fiefdom. He truly believed in what he was doing. His beliefs fell under a paradigm shaped by his belief in the duty of service for all eligible men, harkening to the citizen soldier tradition in American history. He believed that those who objected owed an obligation to the state when called. Those thoughts came from his experiences growing up in rural Indiana, his service in the National Guard, and his deployment during the First World War. Administering alternative service also meant protecting it from external forces that sought to eliminate, change, or further restrict alternative service under Hershey's watch. Those who disagreed or argued with Hershey over alternative service included veterans' groups, some members of Congress, strongly patriotic regions of the United States, portions of the American public, portions of pacifist groups like the War Resisters League and the Fellowship of Reconciliation, and even some members of the Historic Peace Churches.

Though unpopular in some quarters, Hershey's actions provided the most tolerant program for COs then seen in the United States, and that fact was not lost on many members of the Historic Peace Churches. Though some members within the churches disagreed with the fundamental concept of CPS, many of the Peace Church representatives expressed their gratitude to Hershey throughout the war, recognizing the uniqueness of his views within the military and the government. Indeed, as both a military professional and a government bureaucrat, Hershey could have acted as an impediment toward alternative service. Instead, he provided a necessary alternative for religious objectors in World War II, thus helping to easethe tension between service and conscience in American history.

In a larger sense, this work is the story of how Hershey provided for a small minority in the American populace while raising a massive army to deal with the largest war in American history. More simply, this work examines how the American government, as viewed through Hershey's actions, deals with the "other" in American history. It reveals how the duty of service to the state during wartime, a central feature of the citizen soldier in the American military tradition, extended even to those who objected during World War II. Hershey fervently believed in the concept (real or imagined) of the citizen soldier, and through his administration of CPS, he extended the duty of service to religious, and eventually secular, conscientious objectors.[7] As a result, alternative service remained in place from World War II until the end of the draft in 1973, seeking to resolve a theoretical contradiction in the American political tradition between a citizen's duty to the state and an individual's liberty of conscience.

Chapter 1

★ ★ ★ ★

An Emphasis on Service

Civilian Public Service and the Citizen Soldier Tradition

A discussion of Hershey's importance to conscientious objection during World War II requires a brief examination of both Civilian Public Service and the concept of the citizen soldier. Hershey firmly believed both in the right of the CO to object and in the citizen soldier tradition. Thus, his concept of alternative service melded the objector's desire to avoid military service with the duty of eligible males to serve during a national emergency or when national interests were at stake. CPS balanced those two dynamics.

Commencing in 1941, CPS marked a significant improvement over the unsatisfactory provisions from World War I. The U.S. draft during that war was a complete failure for conscientious objection. The language in the Selective Service Act of 1917 was much too narrow, allowing only for objection from members of peace sects and it provided no options for alternative service. As a result, COs were sent to military camps and military prisons, where they received extremely poor treatment.[1] Throughout the interwar period, the Historic Peace Churches undertook a number of initiatives to make sure that their peace stance remained relevant and that in the event of future conscription, they would not be caught unprepared. The federal government also maintained a state of preparedness for conscription with the Joint Army Navy Selective Service Committee

(JANSSC, the interwar conscription planning organization), though that agency planned for military manpower contingencies, not conscientious objection.[2] In 1940, with war in Europe raging once again, the federal government sought to arrangefor the possibility of war with the passage of the Selective Service Act in September. An important section of that legislation laid the groundwork for Hershey, the Selective Service, and the Historic Peace Churches to build a program of alternative service in the hope of avoiding the mistakes of World War I. In its final form, section 5(g) of the Selective Service Act of 1940 read,

> Nothing contained in this act shall be construed to require any person to be subject to combatant training and service in the land or naval forces of the United States who, by reason of religious training and belief, is conscientiously opposed to war in any form. Any such person claiming such exemption from combatant training and service because of such conscientious objections whose claim is sustained by the local board shall, if he is inducted into the land or naval forces under this act, be assigned to noncombatant service as defined by the President, or shall, if he is found to be conscientiously opposed to participation in such noncombatant service, in lieu of such induction, be assigned to work of national importance under civilian direction.[3]

That section of the law bound the government to provide an alternative form of service for COs who objected to military service. It did not provide for absolutist objectors who refused any form of service to the state. Although there was now a law providing for conscientious objection, there was no administrative chief for it, nor was there a program for the work of national importance That changed, and Lewis Hershey became centrally important, when President Franklin Roosevelt issued an executive order on February 6, 1941, delegating his authority to the director of Selective Service and placing all matters for determining exactly what constituted work of national importance in that person's hands. This gave the director ultimate control as to what projects fulfilled the requirements of national importance.[4] The power granted to the director of Selective Service provided latitude for a man like Hershey to shape the form and direction of alternative service during the war. As the years progressed into the Cold War, it became clear that the power granted to Hershey had ramifications for the remaining years of conscription in the United States.

Hershey relied on the Historic Peace Churches to help him develop CPS. He made it clear to the Peace Churches that not many people in the federal government had devoted much time to considering a program of alternative service, and he required their input to move in a direction agreeable to all parties. He also asked that they consolidate their efforts to further streamline the process. Out of that recommendation (and an increasing spirit of ecumenism among the Peace Churches during the interwar years) came NSBRO, which worked closely with Hershey and his director of Camp Operations (the division in Selective Service for CPS administration), Colonel Lewis Kosch.

Though Hershey was the primary and most significant figure concerning conscientious objection during World War II, he delegated some authority. Hershey was a bureaucrat and an administrator whose workload prevented him from devoting all of his energies to the daily administration and operation of alternative service. He left that to Kosch and the Camp Operations Division. The programs under CPS were what constituted work of national importance and all of the CPS projects required Hershey's approval before being allowed to commence. It must be mentioned, though, that not all of the wartime CPS programs are discussed in the following chapters. Only those requiring Hershey's active involvement for establishment, beyond his approval, are examined. Nevertheless, Hershey approved or rejected all of the programs presented by NSBRO to the Selective Service, even when he did not work on a daily basis to secure a specific program in CPS.

This work is not concerned with all of the specific programs undertaken by CPS during World War II, but it is necessary to understand CPS and the projects it encompassed during the war to highlight the wartime dynamic between Hershey, the Peace Churches, the federal government, and the individual CO. When an objector appeared before his local draft board, he could receive two classifications, provided his board granted him the CO status. The first classification was I-A-O, meaning he was available for military service, but only as a noncombatant. The other was IV-E, meaning he was not available for military service, but instead was to be assigned to work of national importance. During World War II, all CPS assignees were IV-E.[5]

The earliest manifestations of the work of national importance had a distinct New Deal flavor to them, as the Selective Service created CPS work camps in old Civilian Conservation Corps camps. There were two types of camps–soil conservation and forestry. Many men worked in soil conservation at some point during their CPS tenure. CPS historians estimate that one in six days worked in CPS was in soil conservation efforts. Some of the men in these camps also worked with the Farm Security Administration and the Bureau of Reclamation. They built dams and fences, dug ditches, planted ground cover, and built irrigation systems. Much of this work was wearisome, dreary, and monotonous, facts not lost on the assignees. Some assignees did not mind the monotony of the work, but others claimed there was nothing "nationally important" about it, maintaining that those projects were nothing more than make-work programs that isolated them and provided them few opportunities beyond digging in the dirt.[6]

The forestry work (which also included a few camps in the National Park System) was often equally monotonous. Each forestry camp usually held a few hundred men, and their efforts constituted the general maintenance of America's forests. The men built firebreaks, roads, and trails. They cleared flammable growth and rotten logs. They also served as fire watchmen, surveying the forest from towers spaced across the land. In addition, they also improved the communication infrastructure by building and repairing telephone lines throughout the forests. There was one major exception to the repetitiveness of the forestry efforts. The most exciting job in all of CPS was that of a smokejumper, who parachuted into remote locations to fight forest fires. Beginning in 1943, select CPS men received specialized training in firefighting and parachuting to become smokejumpers . Despite the danger involved, hundreds of assignees volunteered for the duty. Overall, a quarter of all CPS work days were in the prevention and fighting of forest fires.[7]

While soil conservation and forestry camps utilized the largest number of men during the years of CPS, there were also many other projects. The other programs constituted the so-called detached services. Men could volunteer for detached services after serving for a set amount of time in the work camps. One such program was in the realm of agricultural production. Due to labor and production shortages on farms during the war, agriculture provided an opportunity for CPS assignees to do what they considered to be more meaningful work. By 1943, CPS assignees were working in different agricultural projects, whether it was for independent farmers and dairymen, laboring as dairy testers, or assisting in agricultural experiment projects. Furthermore, some men could gain furlough from their work camp if there was a dire need for farm labor in a county and the camp was fifteen miles or less from the area in question. However, this program was somewhat controversial among the Peace Churches because the local county agricultural agent could seemingly declare an emergency to commandeer labor from the nearby CPS camp.[8]

Another voluntary project in CPS was the Guinea Pig Units, so named because the men volunteered to be human scientific test subjects. Administered by the Office of Scientific Research or the Surgeon General's Office, the Guinea Pig Units helped study such varied subjects as nutrition, disease and illness, dehydration, lice infestation, and hypothermia. There were many projects, with some of them using methods that are at least questionable by today's ethical standards. The unit at the University of Indiana in Bloomington studied the physiological effects of clothing, wrapping men in wet sheets and leaving them in rooms with cold temperatures to see how long they could sleep. The unit at the University of Minnesota Laboratory of Physiological Hygiene studied starvation and nutrition under famed nutritionist Dr. Ancel Keys, who developed the K ration. At one point, the men in this experiment looked similar to emaciated Nazi concentration camp survivors. Other units infected men with typhus, malaria, or hepatitis to study the causes, effects, and best treatments of the diseases.[9] Though much value came from the findings in the experiments, the methods were barbaric when viewed through the lens of the present. Dr. C. Everett Koop, who would become surgeon general during the 1980s, participated in administering one test and commented in recent years that many of the men did not know the risk to which they exposed themselves. As he stated in an interview for the documentary *The Good War and Those Who Refused to Fight It*, "It couldn't happen today. Internal Review Boards would not permit the use of a live virus in human subjects unless they really understood what was going to happen to them. And I doubt that even if they knew what the risk was, that an Internal Review Board in any academic institution would consent to that kind of experimental work."[10] Koop also admitted that he was not proud of his actions in helping with the testing in the Guinea Pig Units.[11]

CPS assignees could also work in mental hospitals as a part of their alternative service requirement. Between the draft and the lure of better-paying jobs in defense industries across the United States, mental hospitals began to feel the pinch of a smaller labor pool. This provided an opportunity for COs to perform their service obligation in work they found to be much more meaningful. Beginning in 1942, CPS assignees began working in mental hospitals around the nation. It was a popular volunteer program, and by the time CPS ended, forty-one hospitals across twenty states had used COs as hospital staffers. More than two thousand men worked in the hospitals at one point during their service commitment. The duties performed by the men in these hospitals included basic patient care, grounds maintenance, and custodial and food service. It was in the arena of patient care that the men of CPS produced one of their most enduring legacies. The CPS men took great care to improve the hygiene and comfort of patients. Through their use of nonviolent techniques in ward administration, the CPS assignees helped to change the manner in which hospitals cared for America's mentally ill. Though not every assignee avoided the use of violence in the hospitals, enough of them did to bring about lasting changes. As Alex Sareyan, a World War II CO and postwar mental health advocate, wrote in 1994, "The Civilian Public Service mental hospital experience triggered the most significant crusade on behalf of the mentally ill that has occurred in this century."[12] The most recent work done on the mental hospital units comes from Disability Studies professor Steven J. Taylor. His arguments are similar to Sareyan's, such as when he states, "Their [CPS assignees] efforts prompted major psychiatric and mental hygiene organizations to acknowledge the failures and deficiencies in how states cared for the 'mentally ill' and 'mental defectives.'"[13]

The work done by CPS in soil conservation, forestry, Guinea Pig Units, farm labor, and mental hospitals constituted the largest portion of alternative service programs for the conscientious objector in World War II. However, there were some projects instituted on a smaller scale in other areas throughout the United States. One such example was the construction and installation of privies in Florida to combat the spread of hookworm,a project lauded by a Selective Service official inspecting the men's efforts. CPS also established a unit in Puerto Rico, seeking to improve public health and continue the mission of the New Deal's Puerto Rican Reconstruction Administration, which suffered from a lack of funding once the war began.[14]

Civilian Public Service lasted from 1941 until 1947. During World War II, there were 34.5 million men drafted, and fifty-two thousand of those claimed they were conscientious objectors. Out of that fifty-two thousand, approximately twelve thousand men objected to military service and served in CPS. [15] These men constituted a small minority in the larger picture of the American experience in World War II, but the development of CPS had long-standing ramifications. The program did not survive the era of World War II, but the idea it represented (alternative service) remained in place in the United States following the war. With the exception of a brief deferment period just prior to the Korean War, the federal government required COs to perform some form of alternative service in lieu of their military duty until the end of the draft in 1973. The alternative service precedent firmly established during World War II, manifested in CPS and built and maintained by Lewis Hershey, continued throughout the remaining years of conscription in the United States.

As stated earlier, an examination of the citizen soldier tradition is required as well. In American military history, the concept of the citizen soldier is one of the most enduring ideas throughout the nineteenth and twentieth centuries. It holds that the nation's and the citizen's interests are similar and therefore, citizens make the best defenders of the nation. The principles of the concept also prevent the military from gaining too much professional power, as its soldiers are simultaneously citizens. However, for this concept to work, it requires large-scale participation in times of national crisis. During World War II, that large-scale national participation came in the form of conscription. The rights of conscientious objectors created a question on the issue of conscription and religious freedom, namely what balance must be struck between a citizen's duty to the state during wartime and his rights as a member of a religious minority. Conscientious objection has been a troublesome issue throughout American history, particularly during wars in which the American state used conscription as a means of raising troops. Of all the wars in U.S. history, World War II was the pivotal conflict in terms of COs and conscription because it established the precedent of alternative service and the privilege of religious-based objection, regardless of Historic Peace Church membership. Although World War I had provisions for COs and, eventually, for alternative service, the results were far from positive for all involved, and there was not enough time to implement an effective alternative service program. Therefore, World War II represented the watershed moment in the relationship between the CO and the state.

As a fundamental part of the American military tradition, Allan Millett and Peter Maslowski point out that "...American defense policy has traditionally been built upon pluralistic military institutions, most noticeably a mixed force of professionals and citizen soldiers. These pluralistic institutions reflect the diverse attitudes of professional soldiers, citizen soldiers, and antimilitary and pacifistic citizens about the role of state-sponsored force in the nation's life."[16]

That definition describes almost perfectly the nature of conscientious objection and alternative service during World War II. It was a pluralistic operation between the professionals such as Hershey in the Selective Service and the Historic Peace Churches and their constituency, who represented the "pacifistic citizens," creating the cooperative administrative and operational roles that defined conscientious objection. While Millett and Maslowski are speaking of the ways in which the pluralistic military institution fought throughout American history, the concept applies to another facet of American military history–conscientious objection–due to the professionals in the Selective Service administering alternative service.

The concept of the citizen soldier represents a core American value of the egalitarian distribution of a duty of service during times of crisis, placing this work further into a discussion of the nature of American social, political, and military dynamics. Since early in their history, American citizens expressed a fear of a standing professional army. Drawing on historical examples such as Oliver Cromwell and his New Model Army or the redcoats of English King George III in the republic's earliest years, Americans traditionally view professional armies as separate from the state, therefore representing a threat to its very existence. A professional army can easily become a tyrannical force that infringes upon liberty. Therefore, the best defenders of the nation are those who have the most interest in its fortunes–its own citizens. In the American tradition, the citizen soldier blurs the line between military and civilian society. The two are not separate. Their interests are intertwined as society seeks to protect itself with its own military.[17]

Some of the best work done on the concept of the citizen soldier comes from military theorist Eliot Cohen. Cohen posits that there are a number of different arguments on how to define the citizen soldier. If he exists as a way to prevent tyrannical control of the government by a professional force, then he is not simply "a soldier who can vote," he is more of a "civilian-soldier." By that idea he means that, "…it is necessary that the bulk of the armed forces consist of men whose main pursuits are pacific, who are fresh from their civilian lives and look forward to their swift return to those lives, whose main identity is as citizens and not as soldiers, whose loyalty lies with home and community, and not with the military as a corporate body."[18]

Cohen also argues that in liberal-democratic states (like the United States), the concept of the citizen soldier is a bit more understated and calls for citizens to control the military, not just serve in it: "According to this view the most proper as well as the most effective defense of a country rests with those who have the largest stake in it; there is something mean or degenerate in a community that relies on hired members of the lower classes to fight its great battles."[19]

Based on that line of reasoning, the American military tradition is rooted in a duty of service by its citizens. Granted, during the years of conscription millions of young male citizens had no choice about whether they served, but they were citizens, nonetheless, and they voted (except for the 18–20-year-olds) and elected the men who passed conscription laws. After their military service ended, most of them returned to their civilian lives. As conscientious objection and alternative service came to be defined by Lewis Hershey during World War II, a similar dynamic emerged. Because every able-bodied American male, in theory, was required to serve his nation in time of war, this meant that conscientious objectors must serve as well. This reflected Hershey's fervent belief in the concept of the citizen soldier, and from that dynamic came alternative service. Though Cohen does not agree with him, Hershey argued near the end of World War II that the militia system in the United States was the "ancestor" of the Selective Service and that the two resembled each other closely.[20] Hershey also admired the work of General John McAuley Palmer, the twentieth century's foremost proponent of the citizen soldier as the backbone of the military.[21] Hershey's attitudes toward service, the citizen soldier, and conscientious objection, along with his other beliefs and background are discussed in detail in chapter 2.

The preceding pages serve as an introduction to two significant components of this book: Civilian Public Service and the concept of the citizen soldier. Hershey's belief in the duty of all eligible males to serve the United States held profound ramifications for conscientious objectors as they found themselves in remote work camps, mental institutions (as laborers), on farms, and serving as scientific test subjects during World War II. It bears mentioning that even if one regards the concept of the citizen soldier as flawed logic, it was something that Hershey strongly believed in, and that belief influenced his shaping of alternative service. He wanted to make the sacrifices of the COs similar to those of the men in the armed forces, minus, of course, the armed conflicts. That desire was the result of his belief in the citizen soldier tradition in American military history. Coupling that desire with the requirement that all eligible men during World War II perform national service of some sort, it becomes clearer that Hershey's actions during that time provided a form of alternative service that further defined the concept of the citizen soldier, extending some of its tenets to those who objected to serving in the armed forces.

Chapter 2

★ ★ ★ ★

Background and Beliefs of Hershey

Some of Lewis Hershey's beliefs about and attitudes toward conscientious objection and national service developed well before he became director of the Selective Service. Comparing his early life experiences to his later musings on the nature of the conscientious objector and alternative service reveals that his background and life experiences were critical influences. Through his Mennonite ancestry and familiarity with Christianity, Hershey had an understanding of Christian ethics that applied to conscientious objection. His service in the Indiana National Guard shaped his attitudes toward the merits of conscription. His personal experience as the embodiment of the citizen soldier early in his military career helped develop his sense of duty to the state. His formative years growing up on a farm in northeastern Indiana instilled him with a sense of rural America that helped lead to an emphasis on decentralization in the draft. Overall, an examination of Hershey's life before he became director provides insight into his developing attitudes toward conscientious objection and national service. Hershey firmly believed in national service by all eligible males and in decentralization of the draft. He also believed that sincere religious objectors should perform some form of alternative service. As a result of his early years, he displayed a nuanced and sympathetic understanding of conscientious objection, and it shaped his development of alternative service during World War II.

Though not the primary motivation for his protection of conscientious objection, Hershey's religious background provided him with both a basic knowledge of the Historic Peace Churches (or at least the Mennonites) and some common ground with the Peace Church membership. He was not a practicing Christian, but his formal education included six years of Latin and a heavy reading of the Bible. While he had religious training and was familiar with Christian ethics, he did not care for the specific structure and theology of Christian churches, and he expressed particular disdain for those who overtly professed their Christianity. He possessed what his biographer terms a "personal creed which reflected equal parts Greek stoicism, humanitarianism, American individualism, and deism."[1]

One portion of Hershey's religious background is quite intriguing. His ancestors were Mennonites. He was a descendent of the Hersche family of Appenzell, Switzerland, an area of significance for the beginnings of Anabaptism.[2] His family came to Lancaster, Pennsylvania (another strong center of Mennonite heritage), in 1708. However, his grandfather was not actively religious by the time he moved to Indiana in 1849, a characteristic passed on to Hershey.[3] Yet he seemed to be quite proud of his Mennonite heritage. His birthplace, Steuben County, Indiana, had a large Amish population, and on occasion he referred to himself as the "Mennonite General."[4] He had the heritage and early background analogous to a typical conscientious objector, but he, himself, was most definitely not a CO or practicing Christian.

Hershey's religious beliefs were noteworthy in view of the way CO policy unfolded during World War II. The provisions for conscientious objection shifted dramatically from World War I to World War II. In the First World War, COs had to be members of an established peace church, but in the Second World War, a CO's objection needed to be based only on "religious training and belief." Therefore, a person did not have to be a member of one of the Historic Peace Churches to be classified as a CO. Of this dynamic, Hershey was quite supportive, but he emphasized that a CO's reasoning needed to be grounded in religion and the belief had to be personal.[5]

The other portion of Hershey's ideology shaped by his early years was his concept of service. From 1916 to 1918, Hershey served first as a National Guard recruiter, then on the Mexican border during the tensions surrounding the Mexican Revolution and, later, in World War I. These experiences led Hershey to strongly believe in the duty of every eligible male to serve his country when asked. His view toward national service came in large part from his time as a National Guard recruiter based in New Albany, Indiana. Hershey's successes as a recruiter during 1916 were limited at best; his biographer notes that he gained only four recruits from the end of August to early October. Discouraged and unsettled, Hershey believed that a generation of men was emerging with no concept of the importance of their duty to the state. In part, he blamed the War Department, as sending guardsmen home after one month did not provide an incentive to join for adventure, travel, or active service. After one particular fruitless attempt, Hershey wrote of a man who seemed not to care about whether he even held a job: "It is more than I can conceive what some people have in the way of an idea about this old world anyway. This young man seemed to have absolutely no idea of personal responsibility toward anybody or anything."[6]

As Europe and other parts of the world fell deeper into the abyss of World War I, Hershey grew disillusioned by many Americans' reluctance to get involved or to serve. He commented in his diary, "The people that really believe that something should be done are for the most part altogether too willingly to let someone else do it! As a friend writes me, 'I wish you success in the recruiting business, but I cannot sign.' More and more the feeling grows on me that America, as did Germany in 1815, will some time be awakened by a national degradation. I firmly believe that we [should] prepare to maintain peace than fight to regain."[7]

Though Hershey was by no means a warmonger (he expressed his dislike for war in a number of private conversations with NSBRO executive secretary Paul French), he was a realist, and he believed that the best prospects for peace came from preparedness. That meant that men had to serve in the military for the United States to be prepared against any menace that threatened its interests.

American involvement in World War I also had a profound effect on Hershey's concept of service, his views concerning peace, and what he perceived as complacency. Hershey elucidated his beliefs on preparedness not long after the United States declared war on Germany. His diary entries make it quite clear that he hated the prospect of war but believed it was a necessary sacrifice, apparently accepting much of President Woodrow Wilson's rhetoric with his calls to "make the world safe for democracy." Men marrying quickly to avoid the draft particularly irked Hershey: "The horror of war is felt at the very mention of the name. Yet in that dire need we stand of its stimulatory effect. How tardy indeed is our nation from the legislator down. To a sad pass has come this 'beacon light' of the Western Hemisphere when provisions have been made to prevent whole droves of young men of military age from marrying to shirk their duty."[8]

From this entry, we see that Hershey was disappointed in a nation that espoused spreading freedom across the globe but made exceptions for men who, in his mind, married for no other reason than to avoid the draft. The passage suggests that Hershey would not support conscientious objection in his later years. But bear in mind that Hershey made it clear that *sincere* objectors were to be given full protection. His problem lay with those he regarded as irresponsible shirkers of their national duty.

Hershey also believed that reversing an American trend of anti-interventionism into foreign wars would be difficult, even though he wrote, "Personally, I am a strong believer in the ultimate good that shall arise from the war, no matter how long it may be prolonged." He was also concerned about the complacency he perceived in Americans during peacetime. He believed in preparedness to ensure peace but regarded the notion of peace in perpetuity as a false hope. War was a part of the human condition and like it or not, it would never go away.[9] The best way to preserve the American lifestyle and freedoms was to remain vigilant. Beyond rejecting intervention in foreign wars, it also meant the service of all eligible males in some form.

Hershey's stance toward conscientious objection was multifaceted, and it was clearly built around a concept of service and decentralization that came, in part, from his upbringing and early years in the military. Those beliefs remained with him, and by the time of the Second World War, some of those ideas became intertwined with his stance on individual conscience and objection. In early 1941, Hershey publicly outlined his overall ideas for classification of the CO. His description is an excellent example of both his belief in the individualism of conscience and the decentralization of conscription. When asked to define a CO, he answered, "It is not possible to pronounce such a definition. Conscience is an undiscernable [*sic*] something hidden in the heart and head of a man. Each case must stand on its own foundation. The law has given the local boards (and the boards of appeal when appeals are perfected) the power and function to decide this unusual issue in each case. They are the judge and the jury. Those of us in National Headquarters and also in State Headquarters should be careful not to encroach upon their peculiar province."[10] He added that the role of the policymakers was to provide a framework for the local boards to make their classifications. According to Hershey, it was up to the local boards "to locate the conscience and then measure the extent of its objection to the military service."[11]

On the surface, this dynamic seems to make local draft boards the central institution in the tale of conscientious objection in World War II, but the reality lies a bit deeper. Scholars have noted that the draft boards tended to be inconsistent in granting CO classification. Some boards were quite lenient while others denied all CO classification requests.[12] This inconsistency was definitely a part of the CO experience during World War II, and it was a direct result of Hershey's desire to have a decentralized mode of conscription. His delegation and his desire to have a Jeffersonian model of conscription led to this dynamic. While he may not have directly classified objectors (in all fairness, he was the national director, and classification was a job he had to delegate), his passing of the responsibility to local boards was incredibly significant in the way conscientious objection unfolded in World War II.

Also within his belief structure toward a decentralized draft was the "necessary man." To Hershey, that man was one who held a job significant to the war effort, such as working on a farm or in a vital industry. This important point reflects the primary mission of the Selective Service —to raise an army without disruption of the economy or production on the home front. Hershey made this quite clear in the middle of 1941 when he wrote, "The primary purpose of the Selective Service System is to procure men for military training, but these men must be obtained in a manner which will cause minimum interference with our national life and especially that part of it engaged specifically in providing means for national defense."[13] In short, the goal of the Selective Service was to help win the war. It was to identify men fit for military service and keep the "necessary man" in industry or agriculture if he was too important to production on the home front.[14] He left the classification of these men to the local draft boards with guidance coming from his national office. Hershey emphasized this point throughout the war: it was the job of the Selective Service to select the people who could be spared for military service with the purpose of building an army to fight in a modern, industrialized war. The Selective Service's primary mission was not to provide for or administer conscientious objection, but Hershey's role in that dynamic was still pivotal.

Hershey's reasoning for decentralizing conscription reveals a pragmatic approach with an eye for the real-world applications of his regulations, a skill that remained with him for the rest of his life. During a 1975 interview, his views were discernable despite some rambling:

> You think you can write a dozen books that would cover all of the cases that you have [in regards to conscientious objection]. Because in the first place, outside of the Mennonites and the Brethren, who happen to [be] pretty well drilled, but the Quaker and anybody else that you can think of is an absolute individualist. He probably doesn't agree

with anybody in his group. I can take a bunch of Quakers and have them sit down here and you'd be surprised at what they would tell you. "Would you go in the Armed Forces?" "I would if I had to. I wouldn't tell anybody, but I would go in. Because in the first place, I've got to go somewhere and I'll go that way." "How about you?" "Oh, I wouldn't go near the place." "Would you take work of national importance?" "No, not under any circumstances...." Now, you just start out trying to write up, so that the local board when they get a hold of the guy can listen to what he says [meaning heavy centralization makes classification nearly impossible].

I'd rather trust the folks that are out there, especially those that work for nothing, and a guy who's working for nothing on a local board is in much better shape than a guy who's getting paid.[15]

What this signifies is that Hershey believed that nobody knew the situation of the CO better than those who lived in the CO's community. Therefore, to his mind, no single person was better qualified than the local draft board to determine the CO's sincerity or his classification. He believed in the importance of American locales to classify draftees for some from of national service. It may have made for inconsistency, but it was the system in place, it affected conscientious objection, and Hershey fought for it throughout his career.

Above all else, most important to Hershey was the concept of national service. In October 1941, Hershey responded to a CO who complained that the government could not coerce him into working or serving. His reply provides one of the best insights into his beliefs concerning service and minority rights. In his letter to L. Taylor Krawczyk (Louis Taylor), the CO in question, he consistently argues that if the majority of citizens in the United States shirked their duty to the state and society, the entire structure could fall apart. He viewed CPS in particular and the idea of alternative service in general as a privilege for minorities that allowed them to avoid military service but did not allow them to avoid any service whatsoever. He wrote,

As a member of society you daily throughout your life have accepted privileges made possible entirely by efforts of others. So long as you participate as a member of society and accept its common privileges, society must reserve the right to require and compel services from you. Military service is basic because its objective is the preservation of the life of the organization. By grace, our government permits alternate service for those opposed to bearing arms. This alternate service is not the right of citizens. It is an indulgence extended to a few. Whenever this privilege becomes a common request, it must be denied or the nation perishes.[16]

Hershey believed that this stance actually benefited conscientious objectors. If COs were allowed to avoid all service, the resulting backlash could bring about a system even "less favorable" than the current structure of conscientious objection.[17] This letter signifies a foundation of CO policy as administered by Hershey during World War II and offers a major insight into the definition of the citizen soldier in the United States. During wartime, it was the duty of every citizen to protect or otherwise serve the interests of the nation. Whether one toiled in the fields, labored in the factories, served in the military, or objected to war, everyone must serve. Society and the structure of civilization demanded it. Therefore, even one who objected to military service could not avoid service altogether. The duty to the state and society must be fulfilled by alternate means.

It bears mentioning that although Hershey is the focus of this study, and he was the central figure for conscientious objection in World War II, he was but one man. The Selective Service was a bureaucratic institution, and its official role as the arbiter of policy needs must be understood. The best record for the Selective Service during World War II is the *Reports of the Director of Selective Service.* Though it is an institutional governmental report, it reflects the personal views of Hershey filtering through to become a matter of institutional policy. For example, in the chapter on conscientious objection, there appears the subheading "The Individual Conscience in a Free Nation." The text in that section meshes perfectly with the personal beliefs and attitudes of Hershey put forth in the preceding pages. It reads, "It is part of those larger and human conceptions of human liberty and human personality which are at stake in this war, that the judgment of individual conscience opposed to the national will, should be given consideration and allowed a form of cooperation consistent with its judgments, if they are the results of religious training and belief. Judgments that are merely economic, or political, or social in its grounds, are in the areas where the State imposes its will."[18] In other words, the rights of the individual to object should not be trampled on, and the central reason for the objection had to be religious in nature. If the objector's reasons were secular, the state could rightfully force him to serve in the military as a combatant. It bears mentioning that conscience can indeed be secular, but the Selective Service and Training Act of 1940 did not provide for it, and Hershey did not believe in secular objection. This was a source of conflict between Hershey and secular pacifists during the war.

Also in the report is a discussion of service for COs. The Selective Service was quite blunt on this point: "The [Selective Service and Training

Act of 1940] ... does not recognize the right, nor grant exemption from service to the Nation in its time of peril." Conscientious objection was absolutely not a way of avoiding service altogether. Instead, if a CO was eligible for service, his beliefs came into play, and either he was drafted into the army as a noncombatant (Class I-A-O) or placed in Civilian Public Service (Class IV-E).[19] Those who objected to any form of *military* service qualified for CPS. A similar statement appears in the early portions of the official history of conscientious objection and the Selective Service. It reads, "*The philosophy of Selective Service,* as embodied in its basic law of 1940, was that no militarily liable citizen had the right of exemption from service to the Nation in time of emergency, whatever his religious training or affiliation, and whatever his personal beliefs and opinions."[20]

Therefore, of his earliest ideological manifestations, Hershey's belief in the importance of national service to the state as one of the foremost duties of Americans was pivotal in his stance toward conscientious objection. Also playing significant roles were his Mennonite heritage and belief in decentralization. His early years definitely played a role in shaping those facets of his character and his ideology, as a discussion of those years will show.

Lewis Hershey was born on September 12, 1893, to Latta and Rosetta Hershey in Steuben County, Indiana. Northeastern Indiana, near Angola, was Hershey's home until he graduated from high school. Rosetta died in 1898, and her sister, Alma, helped to raise young Lewis.[21] Hershey worked on the family farm and in later life had a romantic attachment to the years he spent there, though he never wanted to make farming a career. Hershey often recalled how his upbringing in rural Indiana helped to shape his character. He stated in an interview with biographer Richard Seiverling, "First, we all believed in work—hard work—and long working hours. Second, we learned early in life how important it is to rely on a person's word. We would never take a man's note if you couldn't trust his word. We took our neighbor's word at face value, because we knew his background and we believed there was validity to his word."[22]

He began his education in one-room schoolhouse in 1899, and from the first he proved to be an exceptional student. He went on to Fremont High School at a time when most of his peers quit school after the eighth grade, graduating in 1910. His aptitude was apparent when he continued on to Tri-State College (now Trine University) in Angola, from which he graduated with honors in 1914. While there, he displayed particular talents in mathematics, the humanities, and athletics. He played intramural baseball and varsity basketball in addition to serving as deputy sheriff of Steuben County, working for his father when the citizens of Steuben

County elected Latta as their sheriff. He also coached the women's basketball team at Tri-State and was a member of debating clubs.[23]

After graduating from Tri-State, Hershey found employment as principal of Flint High School in Steuben County. Hershey proved to be an outstanding high school principal, displaying qualities that would eventually serve him well as the director of the Selective Service. He endeared himself to the local population in Flint with his optimistic nature, paternalistic demeanor, and organizational skill. In addition to his duties as an administrator, Hershey also taught a broad range of subjects alongside four other teachers. He was so popular that parents who normally sent their children to larger schools pulled them out and sent them to Flint so Hershey could educate them. When his National Guard duties called him away in 1916, many of his students threatened to quit if he left.[24]

Hershey began military service when he enlisted in the Indiana National Guard in 1911. He saw service in the Guard as an opportunity for career advancement, something he felt would elude him if he remained in the Angola area as an educator or farmer. He advanced quickly, becoming a corporal in 1912 and a sergeant a year later. His imposing physical stature (he was six feet tall) and his talent for organization, which had been so valued by the citizens of Flint, again served him well. He was an exemplary Guardsman who valued drill and punctuality. His company eventually elected him second lieutenant in 1913 and fellow Guardsman and eventual Selective Service subordinate Lewis Kosch served as his campaign manager for the post. Thus began a long association between the two men that had a significant impact on conscientious objectors in World War II.[25]

That same year, the federal government called Hershey's unit to active duty, and he deployed to the U.S-Mexico border as a part of the U.S. incursion into Mexico to stem Pancho Villa's raids. It was during this tour that he began to develop his philosophy about the United States and its level of military preparedness. During his deployment along the border he experienced the squalid camp conditions and generally poor military decorum of an army lacking decent training. He came to believe in conscription and rejected the practicality and workability of an all-volunteer force. He also realized that if he wanted to advance through the military ranks, his best opportunity would be in the regular army. However, prior to the First World War, an appointment was unlikely. Yet, he served on active duty for the U.S. Army from June until December 1916 and chose to remain in the National Guard after his unit was released from federal service, also serving for a time as a recruiter in the New Albany area. He failed to recruit many men, and that low number reinforced Hershey's conviction that using volunteers was not a feasible basis for raising an army prepared for the needs of modern warfare and international dynamics.[26]

After his release from active duty in December 1916, Hershey began a graduate degree at the University of Indiana in Bloomington. When the United States entered the First World War in April, Hershey found himself working at the headquarters of the First Battalion, Third Infantry of the Indiana National Guard to prepare it for commissioning in the U.S. Army. When Congress passed the Selective Service Act of 1917, he approved and went back on active duty in August, Shortly afterward his regiment became the 137th Field Artillery in the 38th Division of the National Guard of the United States. In May 1918, he received a promotion to captain, and that summer he became the division personnel officer.[27]

Hershey's writings on the eve of World War I reveal a man who frequently thought about the role of the United States in the world. He believed that much good would ultimately come from American participation in World War I, and he chided those of his countrymen who did not support preparedness or intervention. He believed that sectors of American society had become lazy and focused too closely on their own problems rather on than those of the world. He contended that many pacifist leaders, who called for strict neutrality before World War I, seemed to change their minds quickly, yet their followers were not as wont to get involved. He did not feel that America adequately prepared for its role in the future of the world and hoped World War I would change the public's thinking from a local viewpoint to an international one. He wrote in his diary, "Many of these conditions had a great deal to do with the noticeable lethargy that had hold of the people as the outbreak of the present war so far as America was participating. Our people unused to thinking in national terms, let alone international, could grasp ... slowly our interest in the outcomes of the conflict."[28]

Before his embarkation for France as a part of the American Expeditionary Force (AEF), he still believed in the mission of the United States to aid in the cause of the Allied Powers. He thought that, ultimately, the war would solve some of the problems of inaction and superfluity that he saw pervading American culture. He did not believe that the war would fix everything, but it could "...remove many of the superficial things that have overcrowded our existence." To his mind, the men who served saw firsthand what difficulties life presented to people. Regardless of their wealth or social standing, military life allowed soldiers "to live like men," and "Countless numbers are by sacrifice finding out what real life is like after all."[29]

In late September 1918, he embarked overseas as a part of the AEF but never saw action, as the belligerents signed the armistice exactly one month after he landed in France. He remained there, serving in an administrative role until September 1919 as a transportation officer at the AEF Headquarters in Brest (where Kosch secured a transfer to join him), and he organized the transportation for thousands of doughboys returning home.[30]

After the war, a pessimistic Hershey believed that there would be a future need for a strong military because the peace made at Versailles would not last, so the United States had to be prepared. This was another reason he sought a commission in the regular army, along with being prodded to do so by his wife, Ellen. Hershey remained in the Guard until he accepted an officer's commission in the regular army in 1920, training as an artillery officer. From 1923 to 1927, Hershey bounced around the United States. He graduated from the Field Artillery School at Fort Sill in 1923. After his training at Fort Sill, he taught Military Science at Ohio State University from 1923 to 1927 while serving as an ROTC commander at Camp Knox in Kentucky during the summer months from 1924 to 1926. In July 1927, Hershey became the commanding officer of an artillery battery at Fort Bliss, Texas. During these years, the tall, athletic Hershey also displayed a talent for polo. However, in November 1927, this affinity led to a serious setback for his advancement as an artillery officer when a polo mallet struck his right eye during competition. He lost the use of his eye, but he did not let his disability hinder his success in the army.[31]

Hershey attended the army's Command and General Staff College at Fort Leavenworth, Kansas, graduating in 1933. His first assignment following graduation was as a quartermaster in the Arkansas Civilian Conservation Corps. As a part of the New Deal, President Franklin Roosevelt had the military provide officers to establish and supervise the CCC work camps. This was only a temporary assignment for Hershey, though, and afterward he was able to gain admittance into the Army War College. He performed serviceably, if not glowingly. Interestingly, his War College evaluation noted that Hershey was "qualified for duty with civilian components." Next, he became the assistant to the G-4 at Fort Shafter, Hawaii, and gained a promotion to major in July 1935.[32]

In 1936, Hershey received orders to report to the personnel branch of the War Department in Washington, D.C.[33] With this appointment began a long and storied career in national manpower policy, which lasted until the early 1970s. He served as secretary of the Joint Army Navy Selective Service Committee in 1936, which led to his appointment as the assistant director of the Selective Service under Clarence Dykstra in 1940. He became director after Dykstra's resignation in 1941, a position he held for nearly three decades, serving under six presidents.

A cursory examination of the background of Lewis Hershey reveals the foundation that led to his opinions on the nature of conscientious objection and national service during World War II. From his years growing up on a farm in northeastern Indiana, Hershey was a man who remained tied to his roots believing in a Jeffersonian model of conscription that emphasized decentralization in classification of draftees. That decentralization was of great significance for conscientious objectors as that was the first step for them in gaining legal recognition on a personal level. Furthermore, his Mennonite heritage provided him with some sense of identity in which he could relate to the objectors. At the very least, Hershey's Mennonite background provided him with a certain knowledge of the stance of religious conscientious objectors. Finally, and by far most significantly, his years as a recruiter for the National Guard, his service on the Mexican border, and his experience in World War I shaped the concept of service that led to his insistence on alternative service for all objectors. Every draftee was to serve in some capacity, as it was his belief that all eligible men were duty-bound to serve their nation when called upon. This belief tied conscientious objectors to the tradition of the citizen soldier in American history. All matters of conscience in the draft went through Director Hershey's office. For that reason, his views were of the utmost importance. The foundation laid during his early years, such as an emphasis on service and a belief in decentralization, provided the necessary basis upon which he built his nuanced and sympathetic ideology that shaped alternative service during World War II.

Chapter 3

★ ★ ★ ★

History and Demands of Manpower and Conscientious Objection

The United States has a long-standing history of conscientious objection to military service. Its earliest roots come from the Quakers, who arrived in Britain's North American colonies in the mid-seventeenth century. Although conscientious objection has been a part of the American military experience from the colonial era, the lack of uniformity in dealing with COs meant that there was no firm precedent in 1940 for how to treat objectors with the advent of peacetime conscription. This had to do partly with the changing nature of warfare and the differing needs of the military from the seventeenth through the twentieth centuries and partly with the changes in federal power during that time and the state's abilities to muster armed services in wartime. The localized dynamics of the colonial era and the Revolution meant that laws differed from colony to colony, though all colonies had some sort of provision for COs. Commutation and the practice of hiring substitutes in the Civil War offered COs methods to avoid conscription, but those methods were problematic for some members of the Peace Churches. World War I saw the first truly national draft intended to raise an army through conscription, but there was no precedent for dealing with COs in a conscripted army, and the result was a disaster. As a result, by World War II, there was no frame of reference for the treatment of and provisions for conscientious objection as a matter of federal policy. While the federal government made some accommodations prior to World War II, they differed over time and were not firmly established as federal law. Furthermore, many of those accommodations were problematic for the Historic Peace Churches, who did not wish to compromise their beliefs. This is why World War II and General Hershey's role in developing and supporting the legislation for conscientious objection and alternative service are so important. Indeed, Hershey's actions during the war represented the first systematized institutional effort to provide an alternative form of service for religious objectors as the government sought to avoid repeating the mistakes of World War I.

It is impossible to understand conscientious objection during the colonial era of United States military history without a working knowledge of the militia tradition, because, as military historians Allan Millett and Peter Maslowski state, "The most important response to the dangerous military realities was the creation of a militia system in each colony."[1] The militia emerged in the American colonies for a number of reasons. In the English tradition, it was part of a legacy that hearkened back to the late-twelfth-century reign of Henry II and was then further cemented with the Instructions for General Muster in 1572 during the Elizabethan Era.[2] The many dangers of the frontier, including the constant threat of attack by natives, combined with the expense of maintaining a professional fighting force made the militia an attractive option for defense in all of the American colonies. While it was a diverse institution and varied from colony to colony, each militia shared a number of similar traits.[3]

The militia laid the foundation for the tradition of the citizen soldier in American history. While that particular dynamic did not really emerge until the early national period in the United States, some trappings reach all the way back to the early colonial era. A militia-based defense force assumed that all able-bodied males in the settlement held the responsibility of defense. With the exception of Pennsylvania, where Quaker control did not require military service, every British colony instituted some form of a militia early in their settlement. It was common practice for a colony to declare that all able-bodied men within a certain age range were responsible for service. The range was usually from sixteen to sixty, but there were always exceptions. In some places the upper age limit dropped to forty-five, while in others, the lowest age might be eighteen or twenty-one. In keeping with the theme of individual responsibility for defense, members of the militia were responsible for arming themselves.[4]

Because of its structure and purpose, the militia was most definitely a community-based organization. The earliest militias defended their own areas and could not aid their neighbors without opening themselves to attack. However, as colonial society began to mature and expand inland, the militia system began to change, and in some ways, it became obsolete. The threats of Indian attack were inland, away from population centers along the coasts. For larger settlements, the militia became more of a ritualistic and cultural organization than an actual legitimate form of defense. During a time of war, the colonial legislatures reorganized these units into the fighting entities that served in battle. As the colonies matured, the militia served as a device for training for larger conflicts and expeditions rather than a large-scale local defense force. Rather than maintain a large active militia, the militia districts added men to the ranks during a conflict or expedition through volunteering, drafting, substitution, and hiring.[5]

The dynamic described above was the primary means of fighting some of the early conflicts in colonial America, such as the Pequot War (1634–1638) and King Philip's War (1675–1676). As France and Spain became the primary enemies of England and, consequently, of the English colonists, the means of military manpower procurement shifted, yet the legacy remained, and the militia still played a role. At home, it was still a duty that all eligible men shared, and sometimes men left their homes to fight in battle. Militiamen fought in King William's War (1689–1697), Queen Anne's War (1702–1713), the War of Jenkins' Ear (1739–1742), King George's War (1744–1748), and the French and Indian War (1754–1763). Although the militiamen fulfilled their duty, the British regulars had a particular disdain for them, at best seeing them as poor soldiers.[6] However, the militia in the early years of American colonization played such a significant role that it took on a legacy of its own, evolving into the citizen soldier tradition that marked service in America's armed forces throughout their existence.

For the purposes of this study, conscientious objection during the colonial era meant objection to service in the militia. The first conscientious objectors in the American colonies were the Quakers, or Society of Friends, who arrived on America's shores in the latter part of the 1650s following the emergence of Quakerism in England under the leadership of George Fox. They settled in the colonies of Massachusetts, Plymouth, New Hampshire, Rhode Island, New Netherlands, Maryland, Virginia, and the Carolinas.[7] Eventually, their largest centers of population were in Pennsylvania, New Jersey, and Delaware, thanks to the efforts of William Penn, who established Pennsylvania in 1681. Throughout the colonial era, only Pennsylvania had a blanket deferment for Quakers from military service, but that lasted only until the advent of the American

Revolution. All the other colonies required service in the militia, usually for those males aged 18 to 50. Beyond service in the militia, Quakers also faced the possibility of impressment into the Royal Navy, which happened on occasion. [8]

Throughout the colonial era, the official stance of the Society of Friends was complete exemption from military service. Persecution for this stance came almost as soon as they arrived in the colonies. The first documented examples were in Maryland in 1658, where Quakers were attacked, fined, and had some possessions taken from them for their refusal to serve in the militia. In some cases, the Quakers' positive relationship with Indians created much animosity toward them by colonial executives and resulted in those executives publicly denouncing the doctrine of pacifism.[9] Other colonies, such as New York, Massachusetts, North Carolina, and Virginia invoked punishments similar to those in Maryland.[10] Outside of Pennsylvania, the most liberal of the colonies for treatment of COs was Rhode Island, which is understandable given the proclivity for religious liberty of the colony's founder, Roger Williams. The Rhode Island government passed legislation in 1663 that promoted religious liberty and ten years later, passed a provision in a militia act that exempted all people (not just the Peace Churches) from militia service whose conscience could not allow them to take up arms. This effectively created some of the first CO legislation in the American colonies along with a similar act in Massachusetts, albeit with reservations, after Rhode Island's 1663 act but before the militia exemption. The Rhode Island legislation stemmed from more than just the beliefs of Williams, it was also the result of a government in which a large number of Quakers served. Furthermore, this Quaker-dominated legislature rejected bills that took advantage of Indians, choosing instead to live in harmony with their native neighbors.[11]

Pennsylvania was the other colony that had significant legislation protecting the rights of the conscientious objector. Much as Rhode Island's religious dynamic was a result of the influence of Roger Williams, Pennsylvania's was the product of one of the most famous Quakers in history, William Penn. After experiencing persecution at the hands of the English government for his religion, Penn eventually received a colony charter and founded the colony of Pennsylvania in 1681 with religious liberty and freedom of conscience as its core values. Penn sought to create a colony that reflected the values of his Quakerism. So deep was the Pennsylvanian commitment to pacifism that the colonial legislature did not create a militia until the French and Indian War, which began in 1754.[12]

That conflict produced the most tension in traditionally Quaker-friendly Pennsylvania. Previous conflicts in colonial America, such as the War of

Spanish Succession, and the War of Jenkins' Ear, led to the continuation of Quaker persecution for their refusal to serve. Beyond their refusal of military service, many also refused to labor in any capacity that the military required, such as building forts or digging ditches. But the call for military action became louder during the French and Indian War. On the Pennsylvania frontier, settlers (most of whom were non-Quaker) called for increased defenses against the French-backed Indian attacks on their settlements. With additional pressure from the English government, the Quaker government of Pennsylvania turned away from an official stance that reflected the values of the Society of Friends and passed legislation providing money for military expenditures. This marked the end for the "holy experiment" of the Quaker government in Pennsylvania.[13]

In colonies other than Pennsylvania, the French and Indian War meant a reemergence of Quaker persecution. Needing men to augment the British Army to face the French and Indian threat, the English government pressured the colonies to improve the numbers in recruitment and take an active role in requiring men to serve in the militia.[14] However, there were examples of tolerance. Perhaps the best example comes from a colonel in the Virginia militia whose name until the Revolution was synonymous with an embarrassing surrender at Fort Necessity: George Washington. Under his command, Washington had seven Quaker draftees, each of whom absolutely refused to hold a musket, pay a fine, or hire a substitute. Washington proved to be more than accommodating in this instance, as he eventually agreed to grant them their freedom from service.[15]

During the colonial era, the Quakers represented the largest peace group in the colonies, but there were other Christian sects that refused to serve in the military. Though quite small in number during this time, the Rogerenes, the Brethren, and a few individual Baptists repudiated military service based on their religious beliefs. More numerous, but lacking the extensive documentation of the Quakers, were the Mennonites. Coming to Pennsylvania and Virginia in 1683 and still speaking German, the Mennonites practiced nonresistance and hence, refused to serve in the colonial militia. Their practices differed from those of the Quakers in that they were willing to pay fines instead of personally drawing the sword against their fellow man. However, they, like the Quakers, rejected hiring substitutes, seeing that practice as little more than sending another man to kill and shed blood in one's place, making them complicit in taking another life. Because of their settlement in Pennsylvania, the Mennonites did not face much difficulty when it came to militia service, especially when compared to the Quakers in other areas. Interestingly, Mennonites in Virginia also encountered few difficulties, owing to their willingness to pay fines in lieu of military service.[16]

The militia continued as a part of the American military tradition during the early days of the American Revolution. The militias filled their ranks through both draftees and volunteers, resorting to conscription only when manpower was inadequate for the situation at hand. As had been the case during the colonial era, the overwhelming trend during the Revolutionary years was that citizens saw their duty as protecting the interests of their locales. All eligible adult males were responsible for local defense, but the duty of colonial defense fell to the volunteer militia. In practice, the volunteers were much more pertinent, because community-based defense was not as important as colonial or regional defense.[17]

The creation of the Continental Army imparted a new dynamic to military service in the colonies. Now, one military organization represented all of the colonies. The Continental Army represented the national identity of the fledgling United States. As the fortunes of the army went, so went the fortunes of the United States. Throughout its existence, the Continental Army's biggest problems were manpower and supply. The ideology of the Continental Congress created a major roadblock for raising the needed number of troops. The Congress did not wholeheartedly support a standing army, and because of that reluctance, supplying the army with adequate numbers of men and supplies was a constant headache for General George Washington. According to Revolutionary War military historian E. Wayne Carp, there was a "localist worldview and deep distrust of the military" in the early American political dynamic. For example, in 1776, an enlistment drive for a twenty-thousand-man Continental Army fell woefully short, forcing Washington to resort to militia enlistments, a proposition that he definitely did not favor.[18]

Some of the states resorted to mandatory military service to solve the manpower crisis, though the legislatures did so reluctantly. Massachusetts was the first in 1776, and eventually the Continental Congress established a quota for each state to send to the army, which was then divided among the militia districts. This was not a complete and total draft, as men could hire substitutes or pay commutation fees, practices that continued through the Civil War.[19]

For the main peace sects in the colonies/states, the American Revolution represented a new dilemma, yet most of them remained true to their peaceful convictions and refused to serve. Many of them believed in the ideology of the Revolution, but they could not support a violent revolt.[20] The biggest problem for the Brethren, Mennonites, and Quakers was universal military obligation. There were statutes for conscientious objectors in the colonies with large populations of pacifists, but there were eventual problems with substitutions and/or commutation fees.[21]

As stated earlier, a man could avoid military service by paying a fee or finding a substitute, but this posed a particular problem for the Quakers. They refused both options because they renounced war and military service in all forms. Hiring someone to do their killing for them or paying a fee that would be used to help make war was impossible for them as a group. As a result, the Quakers suffered the harshest treatment of the three peace sects during the American Revolution. Quakers refused to pay war taxes, use paper currency (because they believed it was issued only to help make war), help construct fortifications, and perform other military labors. In return, the government confiscated their land as a replacement for their service. While some individual Quakers aided the military in one form or another, these members found themselves shunned from their meetings.[22]

The Revolutionary experience was a bit different for the Mennonites and the Brethren. They did not absolutely reject substitutions and commutation fees in the same way that the Quakers did. The Mennonites and Brethren argued that substitutes or fees were a part of their duty to the state and thus did not compromise their peace witness. While this was their official stance, they did not enter into this relationship without some trepidation. Mennonites viewed the hiring of substitutes as more problematic than the paying of fees. In fact, most Mennonites did not support hiring a substitute. The Brethren were leery of substitution as well, but they eventually adopted the practice.[23] Because the Mennonites and the Brethren were more willing to provide an alternative form of service, their wartime experience was much less harsh than that of the Quakers.

Once the United States gained its independence, conscientious objection was a part of the discussion in forging a new system of government. There was talk for protection of conscientious objection in the Bill of Rights. When James Madison brought the Bill of Rights into the House of Representatives during the First Congress (he was a representative at the time), he called for protection of conscientious objectors from militia service.[24] His original wording was, "The right of the people to keep and bear arms shall not be infringed; a well armed and well regulated militia being the best security of a free country: but no person religiously scrupulous of bearing arms shall be compelled to render military service in person." Though the provision passed in the House after much contentious debate, it failed in the Senate. This debate, which was part of the larger issue of a standing army's threat to liberty, continued through 1790, when North Carolina and Rhode Island, both with significant Quaker populations, sought to protect conscientious objection with amendments from their ratifying conventions that allowed for the hiring of substitutes in one case and complete exemption from a draft "except in the case of national emergency" in the other. Congress struck down both of the possible amendments, establishing the precedent of conscientious objection as a privilege granted by the federal government rather than a right protected by the Constitution. [25]

During the first half of the nineteenth century, the United States participated in a number of different conflicts that once again provided moral dilemmas for conscientious objectors. The War of 1812 was the first major conflict of the era to use American armed forces on a large scale. It was also the first chance for the federal government to incorporate a national draft. Military defeats in the first two years of the war and troop shortages led to economic incentives to bolster volunteers to the U.S. Army, but the ineffectiveness of that policy led to discussion of a national draft. When the British formally invaded the United States in 1814, the manpower situation became critical, and President James Madison called for a national draft. Political divisions between Federalists and Democratic-Republicans, along with refusals to cooperate between the House and the Senate, led to the bill's death in December 1814. By then the manpower needs were not as pressing, since American forces kept control of the Great Lakes, and the end of the war was in sight.[26]

Further compounding the issue of pacifism and war, during these years a number of secular pacifist groups began to emerge.[27] Because this study is concerned primarily with the Historic Peace Churches and their relationship to the American state through the lens of General Hershey, the secular pacifist organizations will not be discussed in great detail, but they do bear a passing mention because they illustrate the growing complexity of the American Peace Movement and the doctrine of pacifism. It was during the antebellum era that peace activists established the first national peace organization, the American Peace Society. Pacifism also became closely aligned with the Abolitionist Movement led by William Lloyd Garrison, who did not support the American Peace Society because he believed it did not go far enough. Though by the late 1850s he would come to be more accepting of bloodshed to eradicate slavery, Garrison initially drew upon Christ as an example, repudiating violence and advocating a nonviolent approach to peace reform and the abolishment of slavery. While abolitionists undertook used nonviolent methods to protest slavery, Garrison also called for pacifists to challenge military service laws through civil disobedience, but with no national draft law during the Mexican War, the chance for their efforts to challenge that conflict dissipated.[28]

Throughout the first half of the nineteenth century, the issue of compulsory militia service continued to be problematic for the Historic Peace Churches, particularly for the Friends. The Friends' issue lay with complete and total objection to any form of military service, including the hiring of substitutes or the paying of commutation fees. They continued to be quite vocal about their disdain for military service, as demonstrated by their petition to the Virginia Legislature in 1810 asking for complete immunity to service in the militia.[29]

As was the case during the colonial era and the Revolution, the Mennonites and the Brethren had little trouble with governmental authority regarding military service, given their willingness to pay their commutation fees and go on about their business. As time progressed, the Quakers began to soften their stance on absolute objection. While a small number of Quakers had been willing to pay the fee, the official stance of the group called for no cooperation. However, as Quaker society moved into the 1830s, leaders found the absolutist stance becoming more difficult to maintain. More Quakers were willing to pay the fee and cooperate, moving toward the stance of the Mennonites and the Brethren.[30]

The first instance of comprehensive conscription legislation came during the Civil War. Faced with the end of the one-year enlistment terms and the South's weakened stomach for war, the Confederacy needed soldiers. In April 1862, the Confederate Congress, with President Jefferson Davis's support, passed a conscription act that declared all white men ages eighteen to thirty-five eligible for the draft, which had a service period of three years. In addition, the government extended one-year enlistments for another two years of service. However, as would be a recurring theme in the Civil War draft, a number of exemptions existed. Men could hire substitutes from the ranks of those ineligible for the draft, and there were certain occupational deferments, such as for those working in the civil service, railroads, river transportation, mining, various industries, medicine, religion, and education.[31]

The problem was that such exemptions opened the door to fraud. Unlike its Federal counterpart, the Confederate draft did not allow men to pay a commutation fee, so the price of substitutes skyrocketed. A man could join as a substitute, desert, then sign up again to collect what was becoming a huge bounty. Men so abused the substitution system that the Confederate government abolished the practice only twenty months after the passage of conscription. Another issue was dishonest self-representation in an attempt to gain an occupational deferment. It seemed as though there was a newfound emphasis on education in the South, as many locales established new schools. Illegitimate apothecaries appeared throughout the South. Governors who did not support conscription vastly expanded the civil service in their states, hoping to undercut the draft. Some men attempting to evade the draft calls simply avoided the authorities.[32]

Overall, conscription was one of the most unpopular and divisive pieces of legislation in the Confederacy, particularly after September and October of 1862, when the Confederate Congress extended the age limit to forty-five but granted exemptions to one white man per each plantation with a slave population of more than twenty. This prompted the time-honored, resentful phrase, "A rich man's war but a poor man's fight."[33]

The first piece of legislation in the North concerning conscription was a militia quota in 1862. Under the terms of this statute, President Abraham Lincoln could call up the state militias for service terms of not more than nine months. By 1862, the initial surge of volunteering had wavered, and the North faced a shortage of men needed to fight a much longer war than anticipated. While this act established a draft of sorts, its intent was to improve recruitment and increase the numbers of volunteers. It was not a national draft in the same sense as the draft adopted by the Confederacy in the same year. It was successful as the numbers of volunteers did increase. There were areas, though, where volunteering did not meet the quotas, and the federal government used the draft to fill the ranks. In addition, there were violent protests against it in eastern Pennsylvania, Ohio, Indiana, and Wisconsin.[34]

The first complete form of conscription in the North came in 1863 with the Enrollment Act, passed in March. By this time, the pool of men who volunteered out of patriotic fervor, a sense of adventure, or a sense of duty were already in the service, and recruitment had dropped again. Now, the control of recruitment moved to the national level, establishing an important precedent that continued through to the twentieth century. The harsh realities of the Civil War battlefield and a bustling wartime economy meant that most men had jobs, and few wanted to fight in the army. As was the case with the earlier militia draft, this was an attempt by the North to prod people into volunteering. Actually, the North drafted few men under the Enrollment Act. It covered all male citizens and immigrants who applied for citizenship from the ages of twenty to forty-five. It exempted men who were unfit mentally or physically or who had dependents for whom they were the only source of support. Any man who did not qualify for exemption could still pay a fee of three hundred dollars or sign up a replacement to avoid military service. Of the 207,000 men drafted, only 46,000 ended up serving in the army, with the rest hiring substitutes or paying commutation fees.[35]

Numerous problems and inconsistencies plagued the draft in the Civil War. As James McPherson writes, conscription in the Civil War was meant to increase the numbers of volunteers by threat of a draft and "[a]s such it worked, but with such inefficiency, corruption, and perceived injustice that it became one of the most divisive issues of the war and served as a model of how *not* to conduct a draft in future wars."[36] One need only look to the New York City Draft Riots of 1863 to see just how unpopular and divisive the issue could be.[37] Corruption was rampant among local officials throughout the North, who sought to pad their numbers and increase their pay while making lackadaisical effort. Men could bribe physicians, provide falsified documents claiming dependents, or fake afflictions that would give them an exemptions. The practice of hiring substitutes caused controversy in some circles, yet the long-standing precedent reached back to the colonial era. As in the South, men became bounty jumpers, taking the substitution payment, joining the army, then deserting and going through the process many times over for additional financial gain. The fact that many of the substitutes kept deserting and rejoining meant that they did little actual fighting, providing an insignificant contribution to the Northern war effort. Furthermore, the commutation fee became the target of visceral hatred, because it evoked an image of the poor fighting for the rich. Though McPherson and Eugene Murdock, a Civil War draft historian, challenge the actual class distinctions in the Northern draft, the issue was so unpopular that Congress ended the commutation fee in July 1864.[38]

Viewing the draft as an instrument of gaining manpower through its own legislation is problematic when examining the Civil War. Conscription acts during the Civil War were never meant to fill the ranks of the army with draftees. Instead, those acts were a means of encouraging volunteering through negative reinforcement. As McPherson points out, conscription was a ham-fisted "carrot and stick" approach to improving recruitment and volunteering.[39]

This is the overwhelming theme in the scholarship on the draft in the North. Murdock, author of *One Million Men: The Civil War Draft in the North,* argues that the Northern draft was a "semidraft," and its main goal was to encourage men to volunteer. Although that was its purpose, it also inspired some unscrupulous practices, such as bounty jumping and deserting.[40] Overall, only 7 percent of men drafted actually put on a uniform in the North. Totaling all of the Northern draft calls, 46,000 men went to war as draftees, and 74,000 hired substitutes, while 800,000 volunteered. Therefore, the draft in the Civil War did what it was intended to do: encourage voluntary enlistments, a sentiment echoed by James W. Geary, a Civil War historian who claims that the addition of volunteers driven to enlist by the draft with those actually conscripted accounts for about 13 percent of the total number of men added to the Union army from March 1863 to April 1865.[41]

Also of profound importance was that a national draft established a precedent of the federal government demanding military service in wartime, further defining the role of federal power in the U.S. political system.[42] In terms of manpower procurement, the draft in the Civil War was an excellent example of what worked and what did not, providing an important reference point for those who implemented national conscription with the Selective Service in 1917.

During the Civil War, once again the Historic Peace Churches made up the central population of COs.[43] The Quaker experience is the most enlightening for several reasons: the Quakers were the largest of the Historic Peace Churches in the United States, they were more active in the society as a whole (they did not actively seek to remove themselves from worldly dynamics in the way that the Brethren and the Mennonites did), and they kept better records from which we can study their actions. What is more, they had the most distinctive response because most still claimed the absolutist stance and refused to pay the commutation fees or hire substitutes. For others, though, this was changing.[44] The morality of the Civil War was an issue for objectors since many of them were active in the Abolitionist Movement. To serve or not serve in a war to end slavery (after the Emancipation Proclamation in 1862) presented a profound moral dilemma for those objectors who despised the peculiar institution. A number of men from the Historic Peace Churches did sign up to fight and faced punishment from their local congregations or meetings.[45]

Both President Lincoln and Secretary of War Edwin Stanton possessed somewhat of a sympathetic view toward conscientious objection. They freed most COs from prison if they had knowledge of them.[46] Lincoln had an understanding of their position, and there was a mutual respect between the Friends and Lincoln. However, Lincoln did not push Congress to pass legislation protecting conscientious objectors. Stanton's views were similar to Lincoln's in his sympathy for COs. He even ordered three drafted Quakers to be released in October 1862 with no fine or penalty. In December 1863, he ordered that all conscientious objectors forced into the military and detained be paroled until explicitly recalled by the federal government. He also attempted (at the request of the Provost Marshal General James B. Fry) to gain commutation fee exemptions and other pro-CO legislation in late 1863 and early 1864. Congress possessed sympathetic elements toward COs, though this was by no means a universal inclination.[47] Stanton also persuaded Congress to allow for alternative service in military hospitals or helping freed slaves. COs could also pay the three-hundred-dollar fee into a fund for "sick and wounded soldiers," but when some of the objectors balked at this arrangement, Stanton relented and ordered that all absolutist COs should be paroled.[48]

The exemptions in the Northern draft law were not necessarily satisfactory to the Peace Churches. The Quakers, though more willing than in the past to pay commutation fees, did not agree with the lack of legal differentiation between those who paid a fee based on conscience and those who merely wished to avoid service. The Mennonites and the Brethren, given their overwhelmingly rural population, objected to the high price because few of their members would be able to afford it. Stanton's actions liberalized the 1864 provisions for COs, but the tension remained.[49]

The discussion of conscientious objection in the South is a bit thinner because the records are less detailed than Northern records, and the records were not well preserved. Furthermore, COs in the South had less interaction with their government than COs in the North. One area that presented a problem for COs was the attitude of Confederate President Jefferson Davis. He relegated all matters of conscientious objection to his assistants and did not discuss his personal views on the matter to the level that Lincoln did. Davis told a group of Quakers visiting him in 1862 that he was disheartened to discover that there were people in the Confederacy who were not willing to defend or fight for their country and, if necessary, die for it.[50] From Davis's viewpoint, this is an understandable reaction, as he had an extensive background in military affairs.[51]

COs in the South faced more difficulty than those in the North because most of them were opponents of slavery. A number of officials did sympathize with their stance (particularly Assistant Secretary of War John Campbell), and those officials fought to gain exemptions for the COs acceptable to the objectors, but for the first eighteen months of the Confederate draft, the only way to avoid military service was through occupational deferments or the hiring of substitutes. The Historic Peace Churches detested hiring substitutes, and given the skyrocketing price of substitution in the South, most of the Peace Church members could not afford them.[52]

Eventually, the government officials with the authority to do something about conscientious objectors came to the conclusion that the limited exemptions for COs worked reasonably well given that the Peace Churches were small and did not threaten the war-making capability of the state. Some of the military brass, such as Thomas "Stonewall" Jackson of the Confederate army, echoed this sentiment.[53]

If the Civil War established what not to do in administering a national draft, the First World War established what not to do with conscientious objectors. The treatment of COs in World War I was reprehensible at best and bordered on torture at worst. This abhorrent treatment grew out of both the fervent wartime nationalism in the United States combined with the distinct lack of adequate provisions for the concept of conscientious objection and the lack of alternative service for those who received the CO classification. Though there were definite abuses of COs during this time, most mistakes concerning classification and the lack of alternative service came about as a result of inexperience within both the federal government and the Historic Peace Churches.

The involvement of the United States in the First World War produced many changes at home for Americans. One of these changes was an increased federal presence that managed production, procurement, and other elements that went into fighting a modern, industrial war. The strong federal state that typified the governmental structure of the United States during both world wars was, in John Whiteclay Chambers's words, "created by a desire for efficient coordination and legitimated by popular consciousness and a sense of political participation by and benefit to the citizenry."[54] A legitimated state, such as the one that emerged from the Progressive Era, coupled with the rising tide of nationalism in the United States created the conditions for conscription administered by the federal government. Beyond that social dynamic, the federal government also allowed for some measure of local control with local draft boards. This provided a seemingly decentralized structure that played to the sympathies of the American citizenry, while the federal government could maintain control over a system pivotal to any chance of success on the battlefields of Europe in 1917. The emergence of a strong federal state and the changes brought by World War I created the conditions for a nationwide draft that would be reluctantly accepted, though not celebrated, by a majority of the American people.[55]

This description of the years leading up to and including World War I begs the question, "What does this have to do with conscientious objection and the two World Wars?" In a word: everything. The rising tide of nationalism in America, the need for large numbers of able-bodied men, and the increasing power of the state made it much more difficult to be a CO than in the previous wars of America. To be a CO during a period of nationalism-fueled patriotic fervor was to be labeled a traitor or a coward. Now that the draft was completely a federal endeavor meant to raise troops (rather than encourage enlistment) with no provisions for substitution or commutation, COs faced a new set of circumstances. Granted, objectors were few enough that replacements could easily be found, but that lessened neither the hardships COs endured nor the hostility they faced.

As the cataclysm of World War I saw the nations of Europe systematically destroying one another, the U.S. government faced a predicament. From 1914 to 1917, the United States remained officially neutral, though it sent supplies across the Atlantic to the Allied Powers. This "neutrality" eventually morphed into a general declaration of war against the nations making up the Central Powers, of which Germany was the most prominent. As described in detail earlier, the United States had reached a point where a massive industrial army could be conscripted, trained, and sent to fight, but those things took time, and Americans had no experience raising an army in circumstances like the present. The military was not yet large enough to fight, nor was industry large enough to supply the army that would be required. As military historian Allan Millett argues, creating a modern army and placing it on the moonscapes of the Western Front where it would face off directly against the Prussian military tradition of the German Army was no small task: "[President Woodrow] Wilson and his advisers did not misunderstand the implications of this commitment: the United States would have to form a mass army virtually from scratch and send it into a type of warfare breathtaking in its complexity and scope."[56]

In the form that it eventually took, with General Enoch Crowder as the director of the Selective Service and the draft boards executing policy at the local level, the Selective Service Act of 1917 had conscripted a total of 2.8 million men by the end of the war. However, the Selective Service Act allowed for a number of deferments. Men who held important jobs in industry or agriculture could be exempted from service if their local draft boards agreed that they were vital to production. Conscientious objectors could also be exempted, though their position was much more tenuous. Under the provisions of the draft, about 64,700 men claimed to be COs, though nowhere near that many actually were granted official status.[57] An overarching theme throughout all of this was a fear within the federal government of the perceived inequity of conscription. Even the perception that certain groups were favored could produce a fair amount of backlash among the general public. President Wilson and Secretary of War Newton Baker believed that there could be accusations of unequal draft eligibility, along with the possibility that COs would hinder the mobilization of the army. For that reason, the eventual exemption for COs was initially limited to members of the Historic Peace Churches.[58]

The Selective Service Act of 1917 did have a distinct clause that allowed for conscientious objection. It read as follows:

> … nothing in this act contained shall be construed or compel any person to serve in any of the forces herein provided for, who is found to be a member of any well-recognized religious sect or organization at present organized and existing and whose existing creed or principles forbid its members to participate in war in any form and whose religious convictions are against war or participation therein in accordance with the creed or principles of said religious organizations; but no person so exempted shall be exempted from service in any capacity that the President shall declare to be non-combatant….[59]

The Act did not provide for any form of secular objection, which proved to be a problem as conscription and the war raised dissent and conscientious objection from both religious and secular quarters. Furthermore, as it read, the CO provision was problematic for the Peace Churches. By not allowing for any religious objector to serve in a role other than a noncombatant (meaning support roles that did not carry weapons, such as medics), the federal government excluded and infuriated the absolutists. The absolutists did not wish to serve the government or military in any capacity, and noncombatantcy did not mesh with an absolutist belief structure.[60]

What the wording of the Act ultimately meant was that COs would be subjected to military authority. On April 12, 1917, Mennonite representatives went to Washington to try to get COs completely exempted from military authority. On that same day, Lillian Wald, Jane Addams, and Norman Thomas, three prominent pacifists, appealed to Baker to allow for the absolutists to be exempt. Although Baker heard their appeals and told the Wald/Addams/Thomas group that he would do what he could to protect COs from oppression and maltreatment, the pacifist contingent's efforts were to no avail as Baker, President Wilson, and members of Congress refused to institute exemptions or quickly initiate alternative service. They only supported noncombatantcy. In fact, Congress inserted the limitations on CO qualifications based on peace sect membership into the language of the bill upon a recommendation from Baker. On August 8, the government announced that all who had been drafted were required to report at the times established by their local draft boards, and on August 11, it announced that COs had to report to the military camps, firmly establishing military authority over COs.[61]

One of the many problems with the government's policies toward COs was the ambiguous instruction the draft boards received pertaining to what constituted a Peace Church (referring to the "religious sect or organization" language). Because of the lack of communication within that realm, local draft boards tended to be quite arbitrary in granting CO status. The Selective Service failed to inform the local draft boards in regards to the nature of the Peace Churches.[62] Additionally, the fractured nature of the Peace Church denominations made it very difficult for the draft boards. For example, Mennonite is a denominational term that covers all of the various groups in the Mennonite tradition. Yet, the number of groups involved could make a draft board member's head spin. Various names of Mennonite groups are the Evangelical Mennonite Conference, the Conservative Mennonite Conference, the Fellowship of Evangelical Bible Churches, the General Conference Mennonite Church, the Mennonite Church, the Old Order Mennonite Church, and the Church of God in Christ -Mennonite, which illustrates just how confusing denominations could be for a person sitting on a draft board who might or might not have even been familiar with the term Mennonite.

Another problem faced by COs was the lack of alternative service or specific definitions of noncombatantcy. Many months went by before Wilson and Baker addressed the issue. About twenty thousand COs who had already received their official CO classification had been inducted and had reported to training camps in the interim, until the government decided what it should do with the objectors.[63] As it turned out, placing COs in military camps proved to be one of the worst things the government could have done.

Historian David Kennedy writes, it "was undoubtedly the most callous feature of the government's policy." Three and a half months after the first registration, Baker ordered that COs were to be separated from the rest of the camp's population and advised in the importance of serving in the armed forces, hoping they would cease their objection to government authority and military service. Baker hoped humane treatment in camp would sway objectors, and they would choose to serve in the army. But ordering that officers should give the COs "kindly consideration" in their attempts to get them to change their minds did not result in such consideration in practice. From the government's point of view, this policy was successful, as only four thousand COs refused to take up arms throughout American participation in the war; however, many objectors were the subjects of beatings, hosings, taunting, teasing, public humiliation, and hazing designed to force them to take up arms to fight for the flag.[64]

Treatment of the COs varied from base to base. In some cases, lower-level officers who lacked empathy for the COs were inflexible, or lacked the skills needed to deal with a difficult problem were responsible for the mistreatment. Some of them believed that the best way to test the sincerity of a man's objections was to subject him to harsh treatment and relentless badgering. CO handling differed among commanding officers as well. At Camp Upton, New York, Major General J. Franklin Bell was somewhat liberal in his treatment of the COs under his command and convinced a large majority of the men to renounce their objection and take up arms (but there was an instance of a CO being beaten mercilessly at Camp Upton for a refusal to follow orders). Such was not the case at Camp Funston, Kansas (connected to Fort Riley), under the command of Major General Leonard Wood, who went on record as saying that conscientious objectors were "enemies of the Republic, fakers, and active agents of the enemy." His observations and temperament toward COs undoubtedly led to the deplorable conditions at Camp Funston, in which upward of seventeen COs died as a result of their treatment.[65]

One example of the harsh treatment under the command of General Wood comes from the correspondence between Ivan Sussoff, a Russian Molokan objector, and his wife. He wrote,

> When we got here, they began to torture us again. They dragged me like an animal with a rope around my neck. That peeled the skin off my neck. They shaved my head, they cut my ears. They put a sabre to my neck. They tore my shirt in pieces and wanted me to put on a uniform. They threw me into an ice-cold bath. I did not count how many times they beat me. Once in one of those ice-cold baths I fainted and they took me out and tortured me again. They pulled the hairs off my feet like feathers. I was motionless. I only prayed to God to take me away from this world full of horrors.[66]

Sussoff's recounting of his treatment at the hands of military officers at Fort Riley provides but one personal example of how bad the situation could be for COs assigned to military instillations.

It is not difficult to see the inherent problems in placing the objectors in military camps. Aside from the desire of the COs not to be there, their separation immediately labeled them as "different," and once other conscripts learned just who those separated men were, COs were met with anger and ridicule. Simply stated, conscientious objection was definitely not popular, and placing the objectors in the camps only exacerbated tension with those who had to pick up rifles and fight. Secretary Baker eventually extended the CO exemption in December 1917 to provide for secular objectors who opposed all wars, but he did not yet allow for alternative service, which would have allowed for removal of the men from camp and avoided headaches for the government in dealing with either secular or religious objectors. Instead, men would be required to serve in the military in noncombatant roles, which would be defined later in the spring.[67]

It was not until March 1918 that President Wilson, after considerable lobbying by the National Civil Liberties Bureau (later the American Civil Liberties Union) to the War Department, outlined the policy for noncombatant service that the Selective Service Act called for almost a year earlier. Under this policy, conscientious objectors could serve in the Medical, Quartermaster, or Engineering Corps instead of fighting, even though those fields still supported the warmaking capacities of the army. However, those already inducted and in the camps had to face a federal Board of Inquiry that determined the validity of their beliefs. Although that board was not sympathetic to the plight of the COs, and it ridiculed many men who stood before it, it did affirm the CO status of a large number of those who still held firm to their beliefs. For the men who consented to government authority, two approved options permitted furlough and service in an alternative capacity. In the spring of 1918, a farm furlough plan was implemented for COs in the camps, who were to serve with limited pay after being chosen for the program. Service in the farm furlough was not universal for COs as the board determined who served. Assignees received the normal wage in the assigned area, kept what amounted to an army private's pay and subsistence, then were required to donate the rest of the money to the American Red Cross. However, it still fell under military control, making it problematic for the Peace Churches and other pacifists who rejected military service. The other project was in the American Friends Service Committee's relief and reconstruction efforts overseas.[68] Though it was quite limited, this was the first attempt at alternative service from the federal government. It did not have the extensive administrative network of Civilian Public Service, and it came too late in the war to do much good. The mistreatment in the camps and in the prisons was already occurring, which is the dynamic that dominates the narrative of the First World War and conscientious objection. The late inception of a very limited alternative service plan magnified the problems of dealing with COs, and pressed the government to seek solutions when the draft returned in 1940.

Although the federal government now had a policy that specifically defined the work COs could do under the aegis of noncombatantcy, a major problem remained: the absolutists. The men who refused to submit to any governmental or military authority faced court-martial. Before the 1918 reforms, forty objectors were court-martialed, much to the dismay of the National Civil Liberties Bureau. The court found almost all of the men guilty and sentenced them to terms in military penitentiaries. Three military prisons held conscientious objectors found guilty at courts-martial: Fort Jay, New York; Fort Leavenworth, Kansas; and Alcatraz Island, San Francisco Bay, California. The conditions under which they were imprisoned were detestable. Guards chained most of the COs to the bars or grates in solitary confinement cells for hours at a time. One of the best-known examples of mistreatment in the military prisons is the tale of the Hofer brothers. The Hofers belonged to the Hutterites, a communal sect from the Anabaptist tradition. Sentenced to prison, they found themselves in solitary confinement in a cold, damp cells in Alcatraz. Kept in manacles while in their cells, guards promised that they would remove the shackles if the brothers consented to wearing military uniforms. Eventually transferred to Leavenworth and kept in solitary confinement, they contracted pneumonia and died. As a final insult, the body of one of the brothers was sent home in a military uniform.[69]

The overall numbers for the COs during World War I are as follows: 64,700 men filed for CO status; draft boards granted the status to 56,800 of those men. Ultimately, the army drafted 20,873 of those COs, and 16,000 renounced their objection and chose to take up arms. Of the remaining objectors, 1,300 chose noncombatant service, and another 1,300 managed to gain off-base civilian work assignments in one form or another. Nine hundred forty COs remained in the camps for the rest of the war, and 450 went to federal prison for refusing to serve.[70]

Inexperience and hostility toward conscientious objectors caused the main problems with the federal government's CO policy during World War I. As Chambers and Millett both note, the United States had not needed to raise an army of this size prior to the First World War. That inexperience meant the administrative bodies used trial-and-error methods, leading to a lengthy process for solving glaring problems. Granted, there was a definite hostility toward COs, and a lack of understanding existed, but the federal government had also never previously dealt with COs this extensively. This is what makes Hershey and World War II so important. Not only was he sympathetic to the CO, but he also sought to learn from and avoid the mistakes of World War I. In particular, this meant keeping men who objected to military service out of the armed forces and providing them with an alternative form of fulfilling their obligation.

The Historic Peace Churches' experience during World War I also requires some explanation. There was not much centralization within the churches, which contributed to the lack of coordinated lobbying by the churches themselves. They did not take a unified stance toward conscription, preferring to approach the matter singularly and leave the choices up to the members who were eligible to be drafted. The lack of a definitive code of behavior from the churches for the COs also led to much confusion and frustration. A quote from one of the objectors stationed at Camp Funston illustrates this. When asked by his superiors in the military what he could and could not do, he replied, "We don't know how far to go because our church hasn't defined our privilege."[71] Both the government and the Peace Churches failed in their efforts to provide adequate programs or present a clear stance on the issue. A failure to communicate effectively, sectors of hostility toward COs, and the lack of experience in dealing with conscientious objection at the federal level are what led to the poor treatment of COs and the lack of explicit legal definitions for objectors during World War I.

Because of a hostile Congress and an American public that rejected the idea of conscription, the military did not push again for draft legislation until after World War II had begun in Europe. Though the plan was not popular in the government or among the American public, the army began to prepare for a draft administered by the Selective Service during the interwar period. It drafted legislation to present to Congress when it would be feasible and trained a few hundred officers as "selective service specialists" to provide a draft infrastructure when the need arose. This began with the creation of the Joint Army Navy Selective Service Committee (JANSSC), founded in 1926. Ten years later, Lewis Hershey, then a major, became involved in matters of conscription and the American citizen when he received an appointment as the secretary of JANSSC.[72]

By 1940, it had become clear that the United States needed to bolster its armed services, given the events in East Asia and Europe. Although the War Department did not support it, President Franklin Roosevelt and Congress believed that manpower mobilization was necessary to alert Americans that U.S. participation in a second global conflict was a distinct possibility. The War Department did not support the idea because there were not enough regulars or equipment to mobilize on the scale envisioned. Yet through the incorporation of 300,000 National Guardsmen and another 600,000 draftees from the passage of the Selective Training and Service Act of 1940, along with officers from the reserves and new volunteers, the U.S. Army's manpower swelled to 1.2 million in mid-1941.[73] War clouds were on the horizon, and the U.S. was preparing, though it would not be ready when Japanese planes attacked the U.S. Pacific Fleet at anchor in Pearl Harbor on December 7.

A number of geographic and economic factors helped to shape how the United States fought World War II. At the core of the American experience in the war was industrial production. The United States was in a unique position. It was far removed from the threats of invasion or strategic bombing. This meant that American industry could produce war materiel without the threat of enemy bombing or attack (with the exception of the Battle of the Atlantic and shipping losses). It also had an almost entirely self-sufficient economy, meaning that nearly everything needed for industrial production existed within U.S. borders. Because of its distance from the fighting and its capacity for producing unparalleled amounts of war materiel, the United States could afford to expend machines rather than men.[74]

This industrial and geographical dynamic allowed the United States Army to wage war with the "ninety division gamble." The army planners initially thought they needed two hundred divisions, but General George C. Marshall, Roosevelt, and his cabinet steadily whittled this number down to a goal of one hundred, and even that was never reached. The idea that a ninety-division army would defeat Japan and Germany may have seemed shortsighted, but there were other circumstances that led the United States to field a smaller army.[75] There was a general understanding among the Allies that the greatest asset of the United States was its capacity for industrial production. During the war it became apparent that there was no way to get to two hundred divisions and fulfill the needs of U.S. industry, the other armed services, and support troops within the army. All told, the U.S. raised eighty-nine army divisions. Because of American air and sea power, coupled with the size and might of the Soviet Army that was pushing back Germany, the U.S. did not need a massive army, but its total still paled in comparison to the three-hundred-division German Army. Yet, the American Army still could have used more men. One reason for the shortage was Americans' desire to have their soldiers serve under relatively comfortable conditions. As esteemed American military historian Russell Weigley writes,

> Making allowances for the proportionately lesser need for combat soldiers owing to mechanization, the conclusion seems inescapable that the effort to maintain an approximation of the American standard of living in the Army and even in the combat zones diverted an excessive amount of manpower away from the essential combat units of the Army. On one hand, the War Department and the General Staff very nicely calculated and mobilized nearly the precise number of combat troops needed to win the war. On the other hand, it might have been better–if a way could have been found–to pay more heed to the maxim that in war not economy but an excess of means is desirable.[76]

The army of World War II was not a lean fighting force. But the number of divisions also suffered from the needs of industry and agriculture on the home front.

Each of the main allies in the war played a distinct role in defeating the Axis powers. Great Britain stood alone in late 1940 and early 1941, refusing to capitulate, and later served as a staging area for the invasion of France. The Soviet Union bore the brunt of ground combat and defeated the German Army. The United States was the arsenal of the Allies. To play this role effectively, the United States had to produce materiel on an unprecedented scale. Not only did it produce massive numbers of planes, tanks, trucks, and amounts of fuel, it also manufactured medicine, communication devices, electronic countermeasure systems like radar and sonar, navigational equipment, and countless other items used to fight the war. The geographic isolation that protected United States' industry also presented a problem. Vast amounts of tonnage to ferry the goods across the Atlantic and Pacific Oceans to the theaters of combat were necessary. If this was to be a war of machines, a system was needed for shipping the machinery of war. Until 1943, building a merchant marine and antisubmarine escorts was the highest priority for U.S. industry. In response, the Kaiser shipyards on the West Coast and Henry Kaiser's methods of modular construction substantially reduced construction times for liberty ships and victory ships.[77]

Overall, this industrial dynamic required many people to staff the factories that produced these goods. The draft in World War II was not one of complete and total conscription, hence the term *Selective Service.* One of the largest problems faced by the United States was balancing the manpower needs of industry with those of the armed forces. The Selective Service was to choose, or "select," the men best suited to serve in the armed forces without disrupting industrial or agricultural production. Its goal is apparent on the headlining banner of its monthly newsletter, *Selective Service.* The artwork of the banner consists of a citizen plowing his fields, three men in military uniform bearing the flag, and a machinist at work.

To defeat the massive industrialized might of Germany and fight Japan at the same time, the U.S. needed to strike a delicate balance between the number of men it could put in the field, at sea, and in the air while having enough to ramp up industrial production to the levels required. However, at the beginning of 1941 it was becoming painfully apparent that the draft affected industrial production. There was, of course, consideration given to the industrial situation, but in practice, the government was more concerned about disrupting the American family than the American factory. Local draft boards did not want Washington interfering in their deferments for individuals, and from the industrial side, managers sought to protect their entire workforce, and organized labor did not support conscription. There were also threats of drafting workers who went out on strike, something supported by Secretary of War Henry Stimson. However, both Hershey and President Roosevelt disliked the idea of using the draft for industrial manpower management, though local draft boards continued to use the draft as a threat to striking workers throughout the war.[78] Therefore, the draft was not to be used as a dictatorial force for industrial control. Congress did not support a law that decreed national control of the economy through federal manpower planning, that is, having men drafted into specific jobs and being forced to work there. Another reason that this did not happen was the rejection rate of the draft. Overall, 47 percent of industrial workers received a IV-F classification and returned to their jobs without having to worry about military service.[79]

This was the dynamic at the feet of Hershey, the Selective Service, and the Peace Churches at the beginning of World War II. The history of conscientious objection up to the Second World War reveals that there was no systematic precedent for dealing with COs at the national level. It is for that reason that Hershey's actions and support during World War II were so critical and represented such a watershed. Hershey was sympathetic to the CO and wanted to avoid the mistakes of previous wars, particularly World War I. Thus, the Second World War was really the pivotal point for the relationship of the CO to the state in American history. It firmly established alternative service as the apparatus that provided for conscientious objection in the United States. In so doing, it further defined the concept of the citizen soldier by outlining the duty of all eligible men to serve. The recent history of World War I made it clear that alternative service was necessary to provide for conscience, but it was not immediately clear how that was going to happen.

Chapter 4

★ ★ ★ ★

The Early Agents of Objection and Conscription

The Historic Peace Churches, the Interwar Years, and the Selective Training and Service Act of 1940

Prior to the passage of the Selective Service Act in September of 1940, entities involved in provisions for conscientious objection began to mobilize for the possibility of conscription. The efforts of the Historic Peace Churches were the most prevalent during this time as peace and nonresistance were central features of their doctrine and identity. However, secular groups, such as Congress and the Joint Army Navy Selective Service Committee, operated in ways that affected conscientious objection once conscription became law in the United States. Though the issue eventually ran through General Hershey, the legislation for conscientious objection in the Selective Service Act was the result of a multifaceted effort on the part of the Historic Peace Churches, the American Civil Liberties Union (ACLU), pacifist groups like the Fellowship of Reconciliation and the War Resisters League, Congress, and the War Department. During his congressional testimony as a member of JANSSC, Hershey revealed his tolerant attitude, and once the federal government established the Selective Service, his belief structure had far-reaching consequences throughout the war. Hershey began to stand in opposition to some members of the military and the federal government who did not belief in providing legislation for conscientious objection. In stark contrast to some of his colleagues, Hershey called for provisions that protected conscience in the face of conscription, illustrating his sympathy for the plight of the sincere conscientious objector in American society.

Understanding the Historic Peace Churches' essential role in the development of CO legislation in 1940 requires a background of their experience and beliefs. The first element must be a definition of nonresistance, central to the doctrine of the Historic Peace Churches, and how it is separate from pacifism. Based on the biblical principle of separation from worldly evils and numerous passages in the New Testament, particularly Jesus' Sermon on the Mount, nonresistance holds that violent actions by Christians are prohibited. As nonviolence scholar William Robert Miller states, "[I]t is a way of maintaining righteousness in the face of danger that is not only physical but also moral in that it invites the possibility of evil in the act of resistance."[1] The idea of Christians separating from the world around them is an important facet of the belief system in the Historic Peace Churches, mainly among the Mennonites and the Brethren. The simplest way to describe it is that Christians should live *in* the world, but not be *of* the world. The Society of Friends, on the other hand, has been much more socially active, operating in the world around them to achieve social and political change.

Within the realm of what has been termed pacifism, groups differ in their views on the meaning of a rejection of war and violence and a commitment to peacemaking. Pacifism and nonviolence are not the same. Furthermore, Christian pacifism possesses similarities to both pacifism and nonresistance but is distinct in its own right. As a member of the church put it, pacifism is "a societal technique prudentially calculated to resolve conflict situations ... it becomes a means of manipulating society." Nonresistance is more of an all-encompassing interpretation that, in the words of Brethren scholar Dale Stoffer, "refers more broadly to a lifestyle of defenseless love in the face of evil ... rooted in Jesus' own teachings and example."[2] In fact, many Mennonites did not support the notion of pacifism because it invoked the rhetoric of struggle or resistance against war, which violated the tenets of nonresistance.[3] Christian pacifism, though, is more in tune with the Quaker peace witness (living one's life with a visible commitment to peace) throughout their history. As described by religious scholar Myron Augsburger, Christian pacifism is an "evangelical and biblical" peace witness that promotes "living by the way of love, a spirit of brotherhood and reverence for life." As he writes, "Ours is to be an active penetration into society with the redeeming love of God." Christian pacifism, though similar to nonresistance, calls for a more active participation in the world than do the strictest of nonresistant beliefs.[4]

The oldest portion of the Historic Peace Churches has its roots in Anabaptism. According to church historian William R. Estep, Anabaptism originated in Zurich, Switzerland, beginning in 1525 in reaction to Ulrich Zwingli's Reformation in that canton.[5] Anabaptism is best described as part of the Radical Reformation, with Martin Luther's and John Calvin's followers making up the larger mainstream Protestant Reformation. Disagreements over the rights of baptism began to emerge between Conrad Grebel and Zwingli from 1522 to 1525. Grebel, a student of Zwingli with humanist leanings, did not agree with Zwingli concerning the nature of baptism in the Bible. Grebel claimed there was no scriptural basis for the baptism of infants. The two men came to disagree vehemently, and that split led to Grebel becoming the earliest Anabaptist leader and adult, or believer's, baptism became a core practice of the Anabaptists. Grebel's importance to the early movement is undeniable due to what Estep terms "a crusading zeal that knew no rest until his death."[6] His leadership was short-lived, though, as he died just a year and a half after performing his initial baptisms.[7]

A distinguishing point of Anabaptism was the movement's lack of a singular guiding scholar or leader. Minor differences in biblical and theological interpretation marked Anabaptism and made it distinct from other groups in the Protestant Reformation. Lutherans had Martin Luther and Calvinists had John Calvin, but early Anabaptists had no such singular, dynamic leader. Later men such as Menno Simons, Jacob Ammann, and Jacob Hutter organized sects under their leadership. The closest to an early Anabaptist leader was probably Grebel; however, a large number of other evangelizers, preachers, and writers contributed directly to the growth and spread of Anabaptism throughout Europe. An incomplete list includes Felix Manz, Michael Sattler, and Balthasar Hubmaier, all of whom died for their Anabaptist beliefs. The persecution of Anabaptism did not end with their deaths as there would be many more Anabaptist martyrs.[8]

It bears mentioning that the Anabaptists are a difficult group to typify. There were only a few points on which all Anabaptists agreed; indeed, one of the identifying features of the movement was its splintered nature. Though there are many differing degrees of shared beliefs, scholars point to a few in common that define Anabaptists: the authority of the Bible, the brotherhood of believers in Christ-centric living, adult baptism, strict congregational control, and Jesus' Sermon on the Mount as the foundation for behavior, and nonviolence. In short, the Anabaptists sought to establish what they saw as the true church utilizing the teachings of Jesus and an affirmation of faith through both belief and deed.[9]

Another unifying belief among the Anabaptists was the brotherhood of all believers. That belief is tied to adult baptism. Anabaptists viewed baptism as an adult choice to be made by those who wished to accept Christ as their savior. To their minds, children were protected until they reached an age where they could choose to accept Christ and be baptized. Baptism was the public act of acknowledging faith and was an adult's choice to make, not something to be done at an age when the person did not really understand what was happening. This is where the term Anabaptist comes from, as their detractors called them this, drawing from Greek for the terms to re-baptize or re-baptizers.[10] This believer's baptism was the clearest delineation between Anabaptists and other reformers of the Protestant Reformation.[11]

Because of their radical beliefs, Anabaptists bore the brunt of Protestant and Roman Catholic persecution in the sixteenth century. The established state churches viewed Anabaptists as heretics and blasphemers because both Catholics and other Protestants held that the church and state were inseparable. When Anabaptists declared themselves as the people establishing the "true" church, they seemingly undermined the official, state-sanctioned churches and thus broke the law. To diverge from and offer an alternative to the state churches as the Anabaptists did was a treasonous and revolutionary act. The result was the persecution, capture, and/or execution of most Anabaptists. Followers were imprisoned, and methods used to torture them in an attempt to eliminate the movement included imprisonment, ripping of flesh using red-hot tongs, drowning, execution by sword, locking them in a burning building, and burning them at the stake.[12] In the words of Radical Reformation scholar George H. Williams, Anabaptists were "the gravest danger to an orderly and comprehensive reformation of Christendom."[13]

Such persecution, and the resultant martyrdom, kept the Anabaptists from becoming a mass movement in Europe. Granted, the faith did attract a large number of followers and spread throughout Europe, but it never enjoyed the large following or the widespread acceptance of other churches. Anyone who dared to preach or practice the tenets of Anabaptism risked unspeakable torture followed by certain death if captured.[14]

Because of their major leadership efforts in the peace witness in the National Service Board for Religious Objectors during World War II, the Mennonites must be discussed at length. Under the leadership of Menno Simons, a Dutch Catholic priest who renounced his faith over the issues of infant baptism and transubstantiation, the Mennonites became the most important group of the Anabaptists to emerge after the early actions and deaths of Grebel, Manz, and Sattler, among others. There were two distinct groupings. The first were the Dutch Mennonites, under Menno. Emerging in the mid-1530s, Menno and his followers experienced severe persecution. In addition to their focus on the New Testament as the authoritative work and their practice of adult baptism, Mennonites also adopted the doctrine of nonresistance because Jesus taught it in the New Testament. Mennonites from the Low Countries (presently the Netherlands) eventually moved to the North German States, Prussia, and Russia to escape persecution and develop the land there at the invitation of state leaders. They eventually found a religious haven in North America when thousands emigrated from Russia in the 1870s to the Dakota Territory, Kansas, and parts of Canada. The largest Mennonite organizations to emerge from the Dutch tradition were the General Conference Mennonites, the Mennonite Brethren Church of North America, and the Krimmer Mennonite Brethren. [15]

The other main Mennonite group to emerge from Anabaptism was the Swiss Mennonites. In contrast to the Low German dialects of their Dutch cousins, the Swiss Mennonites spoke High German, and they had differences in clothing and actions. The largest groups to emerge from the Swiss Mennonites were the Mennonite Church and the Amish. The Amish, who organized under the leadership of Jacob Amman in the 1690s, had immigrated to the American colonies by the early eighteenth century. Also emerging from the Swiss tradition was the General Conference, a cooperative organization formed in the mid-nineteenth century consisting of Mennonites from Pennsylvania, Ontario, and Iowa. Many of the Dutch Mennonites who immigrated to the central United States affiliated with the General Conference, making it an amalgamation of both the Dutch and Swiss Mennonite heritages.[16]

The Mennonite principle of nonresistance was the foundation of the sect's conscientious objection. Mostly due to their emphasis on the New Testament, Mennonites focused on living their lives based on the teachings of Jesus. That focus called for Christians to love their enemies and turn the other cheek in the face of violence. Also factoring into the nonresistance of the Mennonites was the concept of the Two Kingdoms. As described by Mennonite historian James Juhnke, Anabaptism held that "Both the state and the state churches belonged to the evil kingdom; the new community of regenerated believers was part of the kingdom of Christ." The state, though it provided order, must never supersede the kingdom of Christ. For Anabaptists, and eventually Mennonites, this restriction on a Christian's allegiance to the state meant no participation in war, no state-administered oaths, and no holding of political office.[17] Upon this belief structure, the Mennonites built their principle of nonresistance.

Nonresistance was a central feature of Anabaptist/Mennonite doctrine from its earliest days. As Conrad Grebel stated in 1524, "True Christians use neither the worldly sword nor engage in war, since among them taking human life has ceased entirely, for we are no longer under the Old Covenant.... The Gospel and those who accept it are not to be protected with the sword, neither should they thus protect themselves." Menno Simons echoed Grebel's sentiments, writing, "The regenerated do not go to war, nor engage in strife. They are the children of peace who have beaten their swords into plowshares and their spears into pruning hooks, and know of no war.... Spears and Swords of iron we leave to those who, alas, consider human blood and swine's blood of well-nigh equal value."[18] The words of Grebel and Simons reveal more than a call to their believers to renounce war. They also emphasize a regeneration of spirit, and they implore followers to restore the Christian church of the New Testament.

The next group established was the Society of Friends, or Quakers as they are commonly known. The Friends grew out of what religious historian Sydney Ahlstrom describes as "left-wing Puritanism," which meant moving away from the hierarchy and structure of the Church of England's practice of Christianity.[19] The sect began in 1652 with George Fox and his followers in England, who emphasized a personal relationship with Jesus Christ. Out of that emphasis came the defining feature of the Quakers, the Inner Light, a concept to be discussed momentarily. They emphasized social and gender equality and became social activists. In the United States, they were among the first abolitionists. They pressed for freedom of assembly, worship, and speech. They refused to take court oaths, objected to state-appointed clergy, taxes, and war, and disagreed with the idea that a person must attend church, seeking instead to emphasize a personal relationship with Christ. Because of their egalitarian nature (and other unpopular practices), English authorities viewed them as a threat to the stability and strength of society and the state. As a result, the Friends experienced heavy persecution and began to immigrate to the American colonies in the 1650s.[20] After meeting resistance from Puritans in Massachusetts, the Friends found a home in religiously tolerant Rhode Island. However, it was not until William Penn gained his royal charter for Pennsylvania in 1681 that they truly found a haven (as did the Mennonites and Brethren). Under the control of the

Friends, Pennsylvania became ethnically and religiously diverse due to the open-minded ideas central to its establishment.[21]

The core of Quaker religious thought lies in a personal experience with Christ. In emphasizing personal experience, Quakers were noncreedal, holding the idea that creeds can simply be repeated and become void of any real meaning.[22] Also growing out of the importance of personal experience was the concept of the Inner Light, the idea that God is manifest in every human being. They drew this idea from the Gospel according to John, where John states in 1:9, "That was the true Light, which lighteth every man that cometh into the world." [23] The Inner Light is an all-encompassing connection between Jesus and all of humanity. Friends scholar D. Elton Trueblood explains it best when he says, "The Light which strives to reach every man is not some vague general light, but the present continuation of the Light which shone in Jesus as he called men by the Sea of Galilee."[24]

The Society of Friends also has a long-standing tradition of social activism and service, which stems from its interpretation of the New Testament and the purpose of the early Christian Church. According to Trueblood, "The more carefully we read the New Testament, the more we come to realize that the Christian Church, in its first phase, was essentially a missionary movement."[25] As stated earlier, Quakers were advocates of freedom of speech, worship, and assembly in England. Also, though divisions emerged over how to confront the issue, they were directly in the middle of the antislavery effort in the United States before the American Civil War. In 1917, during World War I, they consolidated their service efforts and peace witness with the founding of the American Friends Service Committee (AFSC). The AFSC's efforts included war relief and rehabilitation, peace studies and education, and justice and reconciliation.[26] Successful in many of its endeavors, the AFSC won the Nobel Peace Prize in 1947 for its international relief and rehabilitation work.[27]

Though Quakers have long been identified as pacifists, the centrality of the Quaker peace testimony in their early years has recently come under closer scrutiny. For example, in the early days of the movement, there were Quaker soldiers alongside pacifists among the group, suggesting that the peace witness was not all-encompassing among early Quakers. Pacifism as a central tenet became firmly established from 1660 to 1661 when Fox made a number of firm public statements that a true Christian must be nonviolent and love his or her enemies.[28] In 1661, Fox and Richard Hubberthorne issued a declaration to King Charles II that firmly established the Quaker pacifist stance. The most important part read,

"All bloody principles and practices as we to our own particular do utterly deny, with all outward wars and strife and fightings with outward weapons for any end or under any pretense whatsoever; and this is our testimony to the whole world."[29] For the Quakers, "war is intrinsically wrong and evil," in the words of Trueblood.[30] By following the teachings of Jesus, Quakers turned to social activism rather than killing as a means of resolving conflict and achieving justice in the world around them.[31]

The last major peace group established was the Brethren, which began with baptisms in a river near Schwarzenau, Germany. It was there in 1708 that a group of five men and three women, led by Alexander Mack Sr., baptized one another with a threefold immersion, thus initiating three centuries of a community of believers whom outsiders referred to as a "peculiar people." The Brethren grew out of the convergence of three European religious movements: Reformed Protestantism, Radical Pietism, and Evangelical Baptism. Most of the original Brethren came from the mainline German Reformed Church, a group with a Calvinist heritage. This background in the German Reformed Church explains the Brethren's acceptance of many traditional Protestant beliefs. The Brethren never became numerous in Europe, the sect's growth limited by intolerance and persecution. Within twenty-five years, members began to immigrate to Pennsylvania, searching for religious tolerance. [32]

However, it was Pietism, along with the Anabaptists, that most influenced the Brethren. Today, the Brethren are classified as a Pietist denomination. Pietism was a religious movement within Protestantism during the late seventeenth and eighteenth centuries. Because it was a convoluted and widespread movement, Pietism had many different tenets and was nuanced from group to group, but some distinct beliefs and actions did emerge. One was the effort to restore the "True Church" as outlined in the New Testament. Another was the reemphasis on the Bible (particularly the New Testament) as the authoritative work. Most of all, Pietism attempted to combat nominalism, or spiritual deadness, in the churches and reinvigorate religious fervor and spiritual belief.[33]

Out of Pietism arose a distinct branch of radicals who sought to break away and form their own groups rather than reinvigorate their churches from within. They are referred to in the scholarship, not surprisingly, as Radical Pietists. It was from this milieu that the Brethren emerged. Radical Pietism combined elements of mysticism, universal restoration, noncreedalism, communalism, and, in some cases, celibacy. Overall, there was a distinct emphasis on *experiencing* God on a personal level. The Thirty Years' War (1618–1648) also helped pacifism or nonresistance gain a foothold within Pietism, because the extreme destruction and loss of life from that war had a long-lasting impact on Europeans.[34] The influence of Pietism is apparent throughout the theology and practices of the Brethren.

In North America the Brethren began to expand and establish communities along the eastern seaboard. The first settlement centered around Germantown, Pennsylvania, and within a few years, the Brethren began to spread into the south-central parts of that colony. During these years, the first split among the Brethren occurred with the formation of the Ephrata Cloister under the leadership of Conrad Beissel. Beissel was a German immigrant who came to the colonies with a desire to break from the sect and go out on his own. In 1728, he and followers formed the Protestant monastery named Ephrata. This offshoot from the mainstream Brethren would not be the last to break away and create a new church.[35]

The largest split, and the one with the furthest-reaching effects, occurred among the Brethren between 1881 and 1883. Growing out of the modernization of the United States and the introduction of modern society to some of its communities, the Brethren split along three major lines: the Old Orders, who wished to preserve the traditional Brethren ways; the Progressives, who wished to move forward quickly with modern ideas; and the Conservatives, who fell in between the other two groups. Acrimonious debates and tensions emerged over such things as Sunday Schools, education, mission work, ministerial pay, and style of clothing. However the biggest controversies erupted over the place of the Brethren in modern society, where authority in the church would lie, and the manner of gaining new membership. It was over these matters that the Old Orders broke away and called themselves the Old Order German Baptists. The Progressives chose to form the Brethren Church, and the Conservatives that remained called themselves the German Baptists, eventually changing their name in 1908 to the Church of the Brethren. Over time, other, smaller divisions would break away from the church, but this was the by far the largest in its history.[36]

For the most part, the beliefs of the Church of the Brethren fall in line with those common to mainstream historic Protestantism, meaning a belief in the Holy Trinity and an emphasis on the priesthood of all believers. The latter point is of particular importance to the Brethren, as there is a distinct emphasis on the church as a community of believers, and with that comes members' sense of kinship and identity with one another. Drawing from Anabaptist tradition, members of the church addressed one another as "brother" or "sister" (hence the term *Brethren*). Also of profound importance to the Brethren is the emphasis on personal spirituality and an individual relationship with God, though not to the extent of the Friends. According to Brethren scholar Dale R. Stoffer, the emphasis on personal spirituality came from Pietism, as did the stance against creeds. The Brethren sought to move away from papal dogma and creedal restraints to develop a more individualized interpretation of scripture. In the words of Stoffer, the Brethren thought that the personal elucidation allowed "the Holy Spirit [to] be free to shed new light upon God's word."[37]

The best-known defining feature (and for the purposes of this work, the most important) of the Brethren belief structure is the emphasis on nonresistance. Many times, the Brethren are mistakenly labeled a pacifist church. While they do refer to their community as a Historic Peace Church, that term did not come into use until 1935, and then it was used only to describe its relation to the Mennonites and the Friends. The emphasis on nonresistance came from a literal interpretation of the teachings of Jesus in the New Testament, coupled with the belief that individuals are accountable to God above all else (nonconformity). Nonconformity and a literal interpretation of the teachings of Jesus led the Brethren to adopt a nonresistant stance, which was similar to that of the Mennonites.[38]

These three groups—Quakers, Mennonites, and Brethren—led the way in preparing for conscientious objection when conscription became law in the United States in 1940. As Hershey said then, no person in the federal government had given much thought to the issue. Though Hershey was the person in charge of conscientious objection and did the most to shape alternative service, he relied heavily on input from the Historic Peace Churches because of their long-standing traditions of nonresistance or Christian pacifism. Conscientious objection was a part of their identity, and they began to discuss the issue in real-world terms between the world wars well before a public discussion on conscription was an issue.

An increasing spirit of ecumenism and cooperation among the Historic Peace Churches marked the years between the two world wars. The first incarnation of this collaboration was in the early days of U.S. participation in World War I in May 1917, when representatives of the Brethren, Mennonites, and Society of Friends met, though little of substance actually came out of the gathering. The first major Peace Church conference came after the war in 1922 at Bluffton College, a General Conference Mennonite school in Ohio. Given the awkward and lengthy title of National Conference of Religious Bodies Who Hold That Peace between Nations Can Be Maintained by Following the Teachings of Jesus, it outlined its purpose as follows,

> A number of these groups have been sadly misunderstood during the past six years. Because of their isolation they have frequently had no knowledge of what other like-minded groups were doing. Not infrequently one or the other of these groups or individual members of them have suffered more or less persecution.... The thought of their inability to prevent war or even utter an effective protest against it, was so overwhelming that they either compromised or suffered in isolated silence. Under these conditions these groups have not been able to effectively demonstrate that love, as it was revealed in Christ Jesus, is capable of meeting such situations as arose in 1914 and 1917. [39]

The conference sought to bring together groups that had the peace witness as a major part of their beliefs in order to discuss ways to spread the message beyond the denominations represented.[40]

Participants reacted positively, and the conferences continued throughout the 1920s and early 1930s. There were nine conferences from 1922 to 1932 (counting the meeting at Bluffton), with varying levels of attendance, discussing ways for the Peace Churches to explore the peace witness in the modern world. However, the economic abyss of the Great Depression meant that the Peace Churches did not meet again until 1935.[41]

In 1935, the most significant of any conference during the interwar years took place in Newton, Kansas. This conference, called by Henry P. Krehbiel,[42] a prominent Mennonite in the area, continued the recent themes of seeking to develop plans for a more effective peace witness among the Peace Churches in the modern world. At the gathering, Peace Churches made more substantive agreements than at previous meetings, and their efforts in Newton helped shape their strategy for approaching Washington when conscription came in 1940. The conference lasted for three days and chipped away at barriers between the liberal peace sects and some of their conservative counterparts.[43] For example, the conservative Mennonite Church never supported the term pacifism. Members believed it was of the modern world and belonged with modern liberal thought, not the Mennonite peace witness. So, to compromise and attract as many peace sects as possible, Krehbiel coined the term Historic Peace Churches, and it is used to this day to describe collectively the Brethren, Mennonites and Society of Friends.[44]

One of the important decisions reached at the Newton conference was the issuance of a formal statement, codifying the beliefs of the Historic Peace Churches. The statement contained eight affirmations: the Peace Churches' stance being "rooted in Christ and his Word," the desire to love all of mankind (including enemies), "the value of human life and personalities," the superiority of "sacrificial service, love, and goodwill" in society over "the spirit of hatred, ill will, and fear," a rejection of violence, the sinful nature of war, allegiance to God, and the desire to adhere to those principles in their lives.[45] With this statement, the Peace Churches effectively outlined their ethos and doctrine regarding their peace stance.

However, as discussed earlier, the stance of the Selective Service was much different, and, ultimately, Hershey and his organization's view won out. The biggest disagreement was over allegiance. For Hershey and the Selective Service, every citizen, regardless of religious creed, owed a duty of service to the state in a time of national emergency. There were to be no exceptions. The loyalty of the Historic Peace Churches ultimately lay with the Kingdom of God. Compromise took the form of alternative service, which avoided violence for the Peace Churches and fulfilled a citizen's duty for Hershey and the Selective Service. Alternative service, though, did not come until conscription became law in 1940.

The conference in Newton did much more than establish a codified peace stance for the churches. Of utmost importance was the decision among the churches to establish an ongoing cooperative relationship for matters of peace and conscientious objection in dealing with the federal government. Documentation from the conference suggested that a joint committee formed from representatives of the American Friends Service Committee (AFSC), the Mennonite Central Committee, and the Peace Committee of the Church of the Brethren should plan a course of action in regard to peace activities. The AFSC would be responsible for calling the first meeting. In case of war, the conference adopted a plan to present a united voice for conscientious objectors to the federal government. The platform called for reinstructing the membership on the Historic Peace Churches' traditional stance toward war, pressuring the membership to resist service to the military or anything controlled by or contributing to it, providing counseling in matters of peace to those members who might be wavering, rejecting funding the war, and providing a support network (both financial and spiritual) for conscientious objectors affected by the draft, among other things. The conference unanimously adopted these provisions.[46]

The decision to form a joint committee proved to be insightful and productive. Recall that one of the major problems during World War I was the lack of a united voice from the Historic Peace Churches for conscientious objectors. To rectify that mistake and be prepared in case of another war or draft, creating a united front was important to the leadership at the conference. Indirectly, the cooperation between the Peace Churches led to the creation of the National Service Board for Religious Objectors

(NSBRO). Created at the behest of Hershey, NSBRO was the primary voice for conscientious objectors during World War II and beyond (it exists today as the Center for Conscience and War). It dealt with Hershey on matters of CO policy, draft status appeals, and varied issues that arose throughout the war. NSBRO was the voice of the Peace Churches in World War II, and its roots are in the 1935 Newton conference. Though the Peace Churches created NSBRO at the urging of Hershey in 1940 (to be explored in the next chapter), this increase in Peace Church cooperation between the world wars allowed for a more seamless creation of a cross-sect representative body.

After the 1935 conference, but before the passage of the Selective Service Act of 1940, the Historic Peace Churches remained proactive in making their views known and attempting to secure exemptions for conscience in case of another war of conscription. Church members cooperated with one another in communicating their stance toward war and conscription to President Franklin Roosevelt. Representatives met with Roosevelt in 1937 and again in 1940. At the second meeting, on January 10, 1940, they outlined their beliefs and purposes, revealing many of the central advances that they hoped to gain throughout the development of CPS as well as roots of many of the arguments they later had with Hershey and Kosch over the matter. In case of conscription, they wished for three main provisions for conscientious objection. They asked for a civilian board appointed by the president and serving under a member of the cabinet to determine CO sincerity, classification, and assignment to civilian projects. They wanted draft boards to send all conscientious objectors to this civilian CO board, assuring civilian control over COs at all times. Finally, they called for the Peace Churches to set up and administer work projects to which the COs could be assigned, such as war relief and reconstruction (along with domestic relief and reconstruction), refugee resettlement, land reclamation or forestry work, farm labor, and health services. They closed their statement to Roosevelt by saying that while they represented the Historic Peace Churches, they hoped their arguments would be considered for all individuals who conscientiously opposed conscription.[47]

What is apparent in the Peace Church meetings with Roosevelt is that they wished to retain civilian control over matters of conscientious objection, and they lobbied hard for it during the summer of 1940. Though they were unsuccessful in their efforts, their attitudes toward civilian control were thus firmly established well before the Selective Training and Service Act of 1940.

Not long after the Historic Peace Churches' second meeting with Roosevelt, the draft became a reality. The first peacetime conscription act in the history of the United States came about in response to events in Europe, culminating with Germany's invasion of Poland in September 1939. Conscription was still a contentious issue in the United States, and nobody proposed legislation in Congress until the middle of 1940, as there was still a strong anti-interventionist sentiment in the United States even after Adolf Hitler's aggressive action during the first year of the war. The German invasions led lawmakers to increase the strength of the regular army, which had a measly 188,000 soldiers in its ranks, along with about 200,000 in the National Guard. What soldiers there were were woefully undertrained and had obsolete equipment as well. The poor level of preparedness and the events of Europe from 1939 to 1940 led to increases in the American military, but progress occurred at an alarmingly slow rate.[48]

It was becomingly increasingly clear that the possibility of confronting the German war machine would require many more men than would probably volunteer, yet President Roosevelt, General George Marshall, and members of the Joint Army Navy Selective Service Committee (of which Hershey was the executive secretary) did not think a draft was feasible without a declaration of war. What helped get the ball rolling for the draft was Grenville Clark and his Plattsburg cronies in the Military Training Camps Association. Clark was a Wall Street lawyer with a history of elite influence and an ardent supporter of military service and interventionism. The Plattsburg Movement, occurring just prior to World War I, called for military preparedness and espoused military service as a duty shared by all male citizens. It established training camps for officers (from elite backgrounds) during the war. Clark and his fellow Plattsburgers believed that English civilization needed saving from the "barbarous" Germans, an idea that hearkened back to the days of Woodrow Wilson during the First World War. The best way to help the English, to their minds, was to raise a prepared force through conscription. They lobbied hard through many different channels, supported the nomination of such proconscription officials as Secretary of War Henry Stimson, and worked to spread favorable press and garner support throughout the United States. Through their efforts, they eventually convinced Senator Edward R. Burke (D-NE) and Representative James W. Wadsworth (R-NY) to sponsor their bill.[49] The push from Clark and his elite, nonelected compatriots was bothersome for some people. Initially, Hershey viewed them as "usurpers," and Marshall was very apprehensive about the negative publicity that could arise were word to get out that the War Department approved of the plans put forth by Clark's group.[50]

Marshall and his staff had been working on the idea of conscription through JANSSC since the 1920s. Led by Hershey, in 1939 JANSSC published its plans for conscription should the United States go to war. Its publication, *American Selective Service,* provides a historical overview of manpower and a vision of how conscription should unfold if hostilities arose. Of particular interest to this study are the ideas of service presented. The statements read as if Hershey spoke them. For example, prior to the First World War, manpower procurement was, in JANSSC's words, "wasteful and unsatisfactory." Though there is no discussion of conscientious objection, the concept of service that shaped conscientious objection and alternative service is definitely apparent: "The conception [of a World War I draft] rested upon three propositions. One of these, as old as mankind, is that every citizen is obligated to join in the common defense. The second, not readily agreed upon in the early days of the republic, is that in a National emergency the authority of the National Government over its armed forces is paramount and exclusive. The third proposition is that local self-government is the fundamental basis of American democracy."[51]

The ideas, prevalent among the planners at this time, including Hershey, meant that all had to serve in some capacity, the federal government's word was supreme, and local control of the draft would be preserved.

When conscription appeared closer to actualization, Marshall wanted to coordinate the War Department's efforts with the ideas of Clark's group. Led by Hershey, the War Department limited the age range of service to 21 to 45, restricted training to twelve months, standardized pay, and declared that the draft law would issue no blanket deferments but would rely on case-by-case assessments.[52]

Burke proposed selective training and service in the Senate on June 20, 1940, and Wadsworth put forth concurrent legislation the next day in the House of Representatives.[53] For conscientious objectors, the initial wording of the CO provision in the bill was problematic. It provoked considerable anxiety because it bore a striking resemblance to its World War I predecessor. It read,

> Nothing contained in this act shall be construed to require or compel any person to be subject to training or service in a combatant capacity in the land and naval forces of the United States who is found to be a member of any well recognized religious sect whose creed or principles forbid its members to participate in war in any form, if the conscientious

> holding of such belief by such persona shall be established under such regulations as the President may prescribe; but no such person shall be relieved from training or service in such capacity as the president may declare to be noncombatant.[54]

The convoluted wording in the second half of the provision aside, the most problematic phrase in the section was "member of any well recognized religious sect." This portion of the bill aroused much debate and testimony from numerous groups on the floors of both the House and the Senate.

Drawing on that problem, one of the largest issues during the hearings for the bill was expanding CO provisions beyond the members of Historic Peace Churches. Other problems also became apparent such as the method of classification and the legislating of alternative service. Because in 1917 Congress had not legislated for alternative service, government programs came only after many COs suffered mistreatment in army camps and military prisons. As a result, in 1940 legislators added alternative service provisions. Finally, there was the question of civilian control over conscientious objectors. This was a major issue among the Historic Peace Churches when they addressed the issue with President Roosevelt in 1937 and again in early 1940, well before the introduction of the Burke-Wadsworth Bill.[55]

Hearings began on July 3 in the Senate and on July 10 in the House. They continued through the middle of August, with final passage of the bill coming in September. Most of the testimony concerning conscientious objection came from representatives of pacifist groups such as the Fellowship of Reconciliation, War Resisters League, and The Women's International League for Peace and Freedom, minority-rights advocates such as the American Civil Liberties Union, the Historic Peace Churches, and other Christian denominations. Lewis Hershey, then a major, gave significant testimony on conscription before both the House and the Senate, but he discussed conscientious objection only briefly when prompted before the House Committee on Military Affairs. Appearing before the Senate as the chief executive of the Joint Army Navy Selective Service Committee, Hershey commented on the need for men, even in peacetime. He gave an overview of the efforts of JANSSC and discussed what the Selective Service would look like and how it would operate. He pointed out that there were other models of conscription used by other countries that influenced the committee's plans. Hershey also emphasized civilian control of conscription through the use of local draft boards, an early public display of his long-standing belief in that dynamic.[56]

In his testimony before the House, Hershey reiterated many of the statements he had made to the Senate, provided a relatively extensive discussion of registration, and elaborated on deferments for workers in defense industries and education. During his House testimony he publicly spoke about conscientious objection. Congressman John Sparkman (D-AL) asked if the bill should be changed to allow for an individual's conscience, removing the restriction of "peace sect" membership. Hershey responded, "You are speaking of something that I have a great deal of sympathy with, but I have not arrived at, perhaps, the best solution. Unquestionably if we could find the man and know that he is, in fact, whether he belongs to a creed or whether he does not, a conscientious objector, we should try to the utmost to do something about it." He stated that if they were indeed sincere, they should be accommodated and that the COs he had met were "honest about it." Hershey also said that the problem to his mind was insincere COs, people who were not truly religious objectors but were just looking for a way to avoid the draft. He acknowledged that this was a difficult problem, but it was a problem in need of a solution.[57]

That was the moment when Hershey publicly established his sympathy for the CO. While other men called for restrictive or coercive methods, Hershey stated that if a man was indeed a sincere objector, then he should be accommodated. Hershey held this belief throughout his work in the Selective Service during World War II and, indeed, for the rest of his career. He was in no way hostile to conscientious objectors as long as they were sincere and honest about their objection. What really galled him were objectors who simply did not want to serve or whose objections were not based on a religious worldview.

Hershey's viewpoint concerning the CO stood in stark contrast to those of some of his military colleagues. In testimony before the Senate, Major General William N. Haskell, commander of the New York National Guard, stated that all eligible men should serve in the military, with conscientious objectors receiving an exemption from combat service and nothing more. When asked by Senator Robert R. Reynolds (D-NC) to clarify his position about an exemption from combat service, Haskell replied, "They should be required to do anything that the War Department or the President decides is not combat service.... We had a lot of trouble with conscientious objectors in the last war and it was a racket, to a great extent."[58]

Amos A. Fries, a retired major general in the army, was even more hostile to the CO and made this clear to the Senate committee. He stated,

> I do not believe in making any exemptions for any purposes, whether they be conscientious objectors or what not. I think everyone should take the whole course in military training. I think he should take his full chances in war. If he does not want to shoulder a gun, pull the trigger of a machine gun, all right; but he should go to the front the same as others. He can drive a truck up there; he can drive a tank, he can work on roads; but he should take his chances in being killed as well as the other men. In fact, I think no man should be a citizen who is not willing to defend the country in time of war.[59]

While there were plenty of viewpoints from a number of different groups,ranging from peace organizations to the War Department to the ACLU, the statements by Haskell and Fries support the notion that some high-ranking members of the military did not support conscientious objection or alternative service outside of the armed forces. Hershey's answer before the House reveals a sympathetic stance that contrasted with some of his military brethren.

Hershey's testimony before the House and Senate in mid-1940 also reflects another important point. His primary role as the executive of the Joint Army Navy Selective Service Committee, and later the assistant director, and eventually director, of the Selective Service was not to deal with conscientious objectors but to administer the registration procedures, draft calls, and induction of men eligible for conscription. That does not, however, lessen his importance to conscientious objection. In the development of policy concerning conscientious objection within the larger context of World War II and conscription, Hershey's importance is undeniable, particularly after he was tasked with defining "work of national importance" through Roosevelt's executive order, which will be discussed in the next chapter.

It is critical to note that Hershey was not particularly instrumental in securing legislation for conscientious objection in the Selective Service Act of 1940. He voiced his support for the sincere objectors, but his real importance came after the enactment of the draft, when most of the important decisions shifted to him. Hershey testified before the House and Senate as a member of the General Staff and an expert in the process of manpower procurement. The passages concerning conscientious objection in the 1940 draft bill were largely crafted through the efforts of Howard Beale of the American Civil Liberties Union and Paul Comly French and Raymond Wilson of the Society of Friends. Others spoke in support, but these men represented the central thrust to provide for conscientious objection.

Harold Evans was the first to speak for the Society of Friends. On July 10, he outlined the beliefs of the Quakers and explained why they objected to military service. He said, "They have believed that lasting good can be accomplished not by war and violence but only by service and an appeal to the divine spark in the life of everyman."[60] Evans continued to outline the position of the Society of Friends, comparing the idea of conscription and warfare to the first steps toward dictatorship in the United States, a line of reasoning that brought forth much questioning from Senator Henry Schwartz (D-WY). When Burke stepped in and asked a more pointed question about the Society of Friends' views on the adequacy of CO provisions in the bill, Evans responded that "democracy cannot be preserved by coercion; that modern war annihilates democracy; and that freedom can be maintained only by self-discipline, by contagious enthusiasm for service, by devotion to a great cause." He affirmed that the Friends wished for conscientious objection to be preserved in the bill. He believed that as it stood, it merely mirrored the 1917 Act and wished for something similar to the British model of conscription. He asked for four main provisions: civilian oversight of COs, national registration of COs, absolutist exemption for those who objected to all forms of coerced service, and equal treatment for all religious denominations.[61]

Immediately following Evans' testimony, Paul French took the stand. French presented a signed statement from the Friends General Conference in Philadelphia. The statement argued that the bill as worded was

> a negation of the right of conscience, and a denial of religious freedom. It is a violation of the fundamental concepts of democracy. It tends to a system of life and type of government in which the individual becomes subservient to the State.
>
> We appreciate the duties and responsibilities of citizenship, especially in these times, and are eager to perform constructive service for the community, but are unwilling to grant the right of the State to conscript its citizens for services which they hold to be morally wrong.[62]

French effectively summed up the general beliefs of the Society of Friends to the committee, emphasizing that their objection was not over an unwillingness to die, but an unwillingness to kill. He said, "We are not unwilling to die for America if it will serve any real purpose, but we refuse to kill for any reason because we are convinced that each human being contains a spark of the Divine Spirit and we are not willing to kill the divine in a fellow human being."[63] Furthermore, this statement from French typifies the Friends' belief concerning the Inner Light and warfare.

Beale, a historian from the University of North Carolina, spent the summer of 1940 laboring to secure legislation for conscientious objectors at the behest of the national director of the ACLU, Roger Baldwin. Beale had written numerous times on issues of academic freedom, had been a member of the ACLU since the early 1930s, and had a close relationship with Baldwin. Beale, with support from Baldwin, chose to focus the ACLU's efforts on protecting conscientious objection rather than opposing conscription as a whole. Though both of them had a disdain for the draft, they knew that a battle against the institution of conscription was one they likely could not win. Not everyone in the ACLU supported this stance. The Union had been entirely against a draft as late as 1937, but as the war clouds gathered, Baldwin, and the liberals in the Union who agreed with him, believed that a war to defeat Nazi Germany was probably necessary. Thus, they decided the best course of action was to secure the best possible provisions for conscientious objectors.[64]

J. Garry Clifford and Samuel Spencer, in *The First Peacetime Draft*, point to Beale as the most important person in securing provisions for conscientious objectors. While their argument is slightly misguided (the Historic Peace Churches were instrumental as well), they do offer an insightful comment from Beale, who authored *Theodore Roosevelt and the Rise of America to World Power*. An ardent nationalist and militarist like Theodore Roosevelt would have deplored the idea. Beale said, "I shudder to think what Theodore would think of me if he knew what had taken his biographer's attention from TR himself. How he would denounce me!"[65]

Beale's testimony was not the first on behalf of conscientious objectors, but his was the most detailed and cogent. In his remarks to the Senate, he pointed out that he was not there to oppose conscription but instead to protect "the fundamental rights of liberty of conscience." He argued that the CO provisions in the bill as they stood were "too vague" and resembled too closely the tenets of the 1917 legislation making the criteria for objection much too narrow. Instead, he asked the committee to expand the wording to allow for COs of all religious denominations as well as those who were members of established antiwar organizations such as the Fellowship of Reconciliation. This was a call for a program for conscientious objectors along the British model. Through Beale, the ACLU asked for three classes of objectors: the absolutists who accepted no form of service or control and would not be required to serve in any capacity, civilian servants who accepted a civilian-controlled service program, and noncombatants who could serve in the military but not bear arms.[66]

Beale also attempted to reassure legislators about the possible misuse of CO status by urging Congress to use tribunals to examine the sincerity of objectors, in which the COs could call witnesses to vouch for their beliefs. He continued by pointing out that exempted COs were not desirable in the army but could provide much-needed labor in certain sectors. He concluded, "Gentlemen, does anyone think that men fighting in violation of their consciences and in repudiation of their God as they have honestly conceived Him and believed in Him will make good soldiers? They will make wretched soldiers. At civilian jobs serving their country with the high degree of devotion that the ones I have known among these people have, they are capable of great usefulness to their Nation."[67]

Two weeks later, on July 25, Beale and the Quaker contingent (along with others) appeared before the House Committee on Military Affairs. Beale offered several comments and proposals. He called for extending the provisions for COs to all who objected to military service, not just the Historic Peace Church members. He proposed that Peace Church membership be accepted as proof of sincerity. He urged civilian control of conscientious objection, called for a National Civilian Board of Appeal for COs, and acceptance of all three levels of objector (absolutist, civilian servant, and noncombatant). Finally, he reaffirmed that objectors were not anti-American but were good people who were following their conscience.[68]

After testimony from Amos Horst of the Mennonites, French took the stand to provide his most significant testimony yet. French elucidated exactly what conscientious objectors wished to have in CO legislation. Coming from a member of a long-established peace sect with deep historical roots in the United States, French was definitely an expert on the subject. He was also able to mention the desires of the War Department. The day before his testimony, he had met with staff at the War Department to outline plans for conscientious objection and War Department representatives agreed with the Quaker contingent. After meeting with Colonel Victor O'Kelliher from the Joint Army Navy Selective Service Committee, French testified the Quakers wanted the Department of Justice (therefore, civilian control) to examine those who registered as conscientious objectors and then report to the local draft boards on their authenticity. The Quakers and the War Department agreed that COs should be able to serve as noncombatants, in civilian work of national importance, or they should be sent back to the army if found to be insincere in their convictions. The problem of absolutists, though, still remained. The War Department did not support exempting absolutists from all forms of service, but French still asked the House Committee to consider the issue. Raymond Wilson, a fellow Quaker, followed French and immediately reaffirmed the desire for civilian control of conscientious objection.[69]

While the House continued hearings through August 14, members of the Senate Committee on Military Affairs retreated to discuss the matter among themselves and issued a report on August 5. In their report, the majority opinion sided with the CO lobby in that they agreed to provide for a national registry of conscientious objectors, Department of Justice control and hearings for classification, and noncombatancy or civilian service for those found to be sincere in their objection. Where they differed with the representatives of the Peace Churches and the ACLU was on the matter of absolutist objectors. The committee decided not to provide for those objectors who refused service of any kind.[70] The House committee produced similar sentiments in their report of August 29, providing the same measure of protection and the same methods as the Senate.[71]

By the end of August, it seemed that those who sought measures of protection for conscientious objectors had gotten mostly what they wanted, with the exception of protection for absolutist objectors. However, the final bill passed in September placed authority in the hands of the local draft boards, not the Department of Justice. This was a huge disappointment for the Peace Churches and the ACLU, particularly after they had worked so hard to attain complete civilian control over the issue. So what had happened? At the end of August it seemed as though the Senate and House were in agreement. It was on the floor of the House and in conference committees that things changed.

On September 6, during debate in the House on the Compulsory Military Training and Service bill, Francis Walter (D-PA) called for changes to the provisions for conscientious objectors. The biggest change he advocated was eliminating the role of the Department of Justice and turning classification control entirely over to local draft boards, and in turn, the Selective Service. Jerry Voorhis (D-CA), who supported COs and even contemplated calling for a bill that provided for voluntary national service, vehemently protested on the floor, but the chair ignored him. Chairman Lindsay Warren (D-NC) replied, "I did not hear your objection," a response that was a blatant falsehood. Despite the dissent from Voorhis and the previous efforts of the Peace Churches and the ACLU, the measure passed, placing the authority for CO classification with the Selective Service and its local draft boards."[72]

This sudden and significant change to the bill appeared to stem from a desire in the Department of Justice to avoid becoming overburdened. According to Neal Wherry's official Selective Service history of conscientious objection in World War II, "This amendment in the House apparently arose from a feeling that referring the conscientious objector case to the Department of Justice made for an involved and unnecessary procedure."[73]

French echoed this viewpoint. He believed the Department of Justice simply thought it would be too much work. This left French and the CO lobby worried about the local draft boards being inconsistent, a fear that proved well founded. French continued to appeal to several members of the House Committee on Military Affairs, many of whom did not support the amendments made on the House floor and wanted the Senate wording reinstituted in the final bill.[74]

However, their view did not prevail when the conference committee met to iron out discrepancies between House and Senate versions. In the committee's recommendation, the House measures from the floor debate won out. French responded negatively. "[I]t seems to me it is a legislative compromise of the worst sort." His disappointment (almost certainly shared by other CO lobbyists), showed clearly in statements such as "It is curious how a few minutes can undo the work of a month or more."[75]

However disappointed the Peace Churches or the ACLU might have been in losing true civilian control, the shift from the Department of Justice turned out to be a blessing in disguise in many ways. Eventually, President Roosevelt, through an executive order, placed the authority for dealing with matters of conscientious objection in the hands of the director of the Selective Service. Furthermore, by mid-1941, the new director of the Selective Service would be Lewis B. Hershey. As he established in his earlier congressional testimony, Hershey, though an army officer, had a distinctly sympathetic view of conscientious objectors. He was also not shy in voicing his support to the Peace Churches (or the ACLU). In discussing the matter with Beale and French, Hershey reassured them that if he became the director of the Selective Service, the mistakes of the last war would be avoided and no CO would end up in prison.[76]

The passage of the Selective Training and Service Act in 1940 meant that peacetime conscription was now law in the United States. This presented a dilemma for the Historic Peace Churches and any individual who opposed military service. Fortunately for those who objected based on religious grounds, the new provisions for conscientious objection were much more liberal than those put forth during World War I. As previously stated, to be recognized as a CO in World War I, an objector had to be a member of an acknowledged religious sect that objected to war as a central tenet of its faith. This rule excluded more popular denominations such as Lutherans or Methodists. In 1940, Congress provided CO status to any person who objected to war or military service based on religious grounds, as outlined in section 5(g) of the Act: "Nothing contained in this act shall be construed to require any person to be subject to combatant training and service in the land and naval forces of the United States who, by reason of religious training and belief, is conscientiously opposed to war in any form."[77]

The Act also outlined the ways in which COs could fulfill their service to the state. One method was to serve as a noncombatant, to be "defined by the President." If a CO objected to military service of any kind, then his only outlet was to "be assigned to work of national importance under civilian direction."[78]

The last option proved to be one of the most problematic for the relationship between the Historic Peace Churches and the federal government throughout the war. The fact that the Selective Service administered the camps made it appear that "civilian control" of CPS was a farce. Furthermore, many COs believed that soil conservation and forestry service were little more than "make work" and did not utilize their labor effectively. The problems with civilian direction, work of national importance, and the resulting tension between the Peace Churches and the government will be explored in more depth in the following chapters.

Because of the long-standing tradition of nonresistance among the Brethren and Mennonites and Christian pacifism in the Society of Friends, most early efforts in providing for conscientious objectors came from the Historic Peace Churches. Furthermore, legislating for conscience in the Selective Service Act of 1940 was a multifaceted effort on the part of the Historic Peace Churches, Congress, the War Department, the ACLU, and the Joint Army Navy Selective Service Committee. That being said, Hershey's tolerant attitude that guided him in dealing with COs throughout World War II began to manifest itself publicly, standing in sharp contrast to that of some of his professional colleagues. Though he was front and center in the discussion of conscription in the House and Senate, he was not yet the central figure in conscientious objection. That role soon came.

What was definitely apparent from the summer of 1940 was that the entities involved in creating conscription law were redefining service and the citizen soldier. No man was exempt from service, but the government allowed for a man to perform his service through alternate means if his religious beliefs called him to a peaceful vocation. By providing for conscience through legislation, the federal government embarked on a new direction in matters of service and conscience. What eventually came to cement the relationship between service and conscience was the tolerant attitude and well-developed sense of service of a former artillery officer who became the director of Selective Service.

Brigadier General Lewis B. Hershey in 1942 *(National Archives)*.

Hershey seated at his desk dressed in a familiar style—civilian clothing (*National Archives*).

Hershey receiving the Distinguished Service Medal from President Harry S. Truman in January 1946 (*Harry S. Truman Library*).

Selective Service national headquarters staff. Hershey appears on the second row from the bottom, fifth from the left. Note his rather casual demeanor compared to that of most of his military subordinates (*National Archives*).

The World War II era's first Director of Selective Service, Clarence A. Dykstra. Dykstra, with Hershey's extensive help, provided some assistance to conscientious objectors during the creation of Civilian Public Service (*Franklin D. Roosevelt Library*).

As the executive secretary of the National Service Board for Religious Objectors, Paul Comly French met frequently with Hershey, Lewis Kosch, and representatives from the Historic Peace Churches as part of his work in representing the interests of conscientious objectors (*Mennonite Church USA Archives: IX-13-2-3, Box 2, Folder 3, photo 1342*).

Director of Selective Service Clarence Dykstra (leaning on podium) and Assistant Director Hershey (center, with hand in fishbowl) selecting draft number capsules (*National Archives*).

CO representatives meeting with Colonel Lewis Kosch and General Hershey. Kosch appears at the head of the table facing the camera. General Hershey is at his left, but only his ear is visible. At the end of the table opposite Kosch are M. R. Zigler on the right and Paul Comly French on the left (*Brethren Historical Library and Archives [CPS 10-21]*).

Clarence Pickett (right) of the American Friends Service Committee with his family in 1954. Pickett worked tirelessly for the AFSC during World War II, but his attempts to gain more administrative control for the churches irritated Hershey (*Franklin D. Roosevelt Library*).

The National Service Board for Religious Objectors (back row, right to left): M. R. Zigler, Orie O. Miller, Leroy Dakin, Paul Furnas, Charles Boss, and Arthur Swift; (front row, right to left) Paul Comly French, Harold Row, and Albert Gaeddert (*Mennonite Church USA Archives: IX-13-2-2, Box 1, Folder 2, Photo 6*).

Chapter 5

Hershey and Conscientious Objection during the Peacetime Draft, September 1940–December 1941

Though the Selective Training and Service Act of 1940 established alternative service for the conscientious objector, there were still more questions than answers about the form that service should take. Lewis Hershey, when serving as acting director, deputy director, and, finally, director of Selective Service, did much during the crucial years of 1940–1941 to develop, administer, and shape the direction of conscientious objection and alternative service. Many of his decisions, suggestions, or appointments had lasting effects on conscientious objection. As he began to exert his authority, his personal ideology concerning alternative service shaped the entire dynamic that continued throughout the war. The suggestion for better organization from the Historic Peace Churches, the establishment of Selective Service's Camp Operations Division, and the ongoing negotiations with the churches were but some of Hershey's efforts, both small and large, as the central figure in conscientious objection during World War II.

Hershey was not always at the forefront in these years, though. Seeking to maintain civilian control over the Selective Service, President Roosevelt named Clarence Dykstra its director in October. Though Hershey was not technically the head of the Selective Service, he was definitely the foremost expert on manpower procurement for the military in the

United States, and, for all intents and purposes, he served as the director even during Dykstra's short tenure. That said, there was one significant instance when Dykstra negotiated with Roosevelt over what exactly COs should be doing. Hershey still worked on the issue with Dykstra, and when Hershey took over for Dykstra, it was his show to run. What unfolds in the following pages is the story of how Hershey managed to do it and what his beliefs were considering the nature of Civilian Public Service.

Prior to the Selective Service Act of 1940, interwar planners did not see much need to change the wording of the law or the provisions set forth for the First World War in regards to conscientious objection. However, the deliberations over the issue during the summer of 1940 and the testimony of many supporters of conscientious objection made people realize that something needed to be done. What emerged from the 1940 law were legislated civilian control and an alternative form of service in the arena of "national importance." Though the Act was much more liberal than its World War I counterpart, it was not without its faults. For instance, the Act did not direct who (or what) was to be responsible for administration.[1] Nor did it provide a means of funding or determine the boundaries of jurisdiction and control. Thus, it did not make clear the extent of civilian control, and there was also a question of just how "civilian" the Selective Service really was, as it was both a civilian bureaucracy and a military institution.

As conscientious objection was a multifaceted issue, there were a number of problems to be addressed. One group of COs, the absolutist objectors, presented special problems, but there were no provisions for them in the Selective Service Act. There were precedents overseas for dealing with absolutists, and one example cited by American advocates was the British system. In the United Kingdom, the government determined one's CO status through the use of "independent civilian tribunals." A man could object to war or conscription based on any foundation, religious or secular. There were three options available for conscientious objectors: noncombatant service in the military, alternative service, or complete deferment (for absolutists). According to the CPS historians Mulford Sibley and Philip Jacob, the British system was "the most elaborate and far reaching … in the world."[2] The United States' system was more limited. As Hershey's work shows, he supported neither secular objection nor a complete deferment for absolutist objectors. This placed him at odds with radical pacifists in the United States, such as those in the War Resisters League. They pointed to Britain's system as one the United States should adopt and chastised NSBRO for not pushing harder for it.[3]

It was Hershey's belief that all must serve in some capacity, so he contended that the absolutist either had to serve in CPS or go to prison. Furthermore, NSBRO (which dealt directly with Hershey and is a major focus of this study) saw the absolutists as outside its realm. As M. R. Zigler, chairman of NSBRO and member of the Church of the Brethren said, "We did not feel that it was our responsibility to work for that group. However, we did not work against them on their position. We felt they should organize themselves, as we were, and if the government granted them privilege, okay."[4] Though there would be a few discussions of the absolutists, the overwhelming concern was with civilian servant objectors in Civilian Public Service.

Of the three groups of conscientious objectors, noncombatants had the simplest means of gaining recognition. An executive order issued by President Franklin Roosevelt on December 6, 1940, thoroughly defined noncombatancy and what army jobs fell within its parameters:

> (1) Service in any unit which is unarmed at all times
> (2) Service in the medical department wherever performed
> (3) Service in any unit or installation the primary function of which does not require the use of arms in combat, provided the individual's assignment within such unit or installation does not require him to bear arms or to be trained in their use[5]

He further clarified the issue by stating that noncombatant training was to mirror regular military training with the notable exceptions of "marksmanship, combat firing, target practices, and those subjects relating to the employment of weapons."[6] In practice, this meant that noncombatant COs labored in the quartermaster corps, decontamination units, signal corps, or engineering units until Secretary of War Henry Stimson declared in January 1943 that all noncombatant COs were to serve in the medical corps.[7]

Roosevelt's executive order took care of the noncombatant CO, but left much work to be done for the civilian servant. Indeed, much had been going on for months prior to the noncombatant executive order. Planning for a program of civilian alternative service began almost immediately following passage of the Selective Service Act. On September 17, Harold Evans, Clarence Pickett, Ray Wilson, Ross Murphy, and Paul French of the Friends War Problems Committee visited Hershey and Frederick Osborne (of President Roosevelt's advisory board). Hershey made it clear that he wished to establish an advisory board to deal with conscientious objectors and leave all CO matters to it. There were also discussions among the Friends War Problems Committee about the specifics of an alternative service program, ranging from questions on pay to registration.[8] At this point in time there appeared to be more questions than answers, and it was only through cooperative efforts that anything could be solved.

Clearly, there were problems requiring quick remedies. A memorandum dated September 24, 1940, circulated around the national headquarters of the Selective Service calling for an "informal conference" of a number of "national agencies" such as the Works Progress Administration (WPA), the Civilian Conservation Corps (CCC), and the Public Health Service to outline plans for administering COs in their national service. The earliest planning for alternative service occurred in the Manpower Division of the Selective Service. Administrators in the division decided that the best way to implement programs quickly was to use agencies and projects with infrastructure already in place. The most obvious candidate was the CCC from the New Deal, with its soil conservation and forestry programs. In outlining their plans, there was much cooperation among departments, including the CCC, the War Department, the Department of Agriculture, and the Department of the Interior.[9]

Most of the initiative for institutional development and direction came from Hershey, particularly in his early personal meetings with Paul French, representing the Society of Friends. On September 30, Hershey asked French if the Peace Churches had the capacity to oversee all the civilian servant conscientious objectors. Two weeks later, on October 15, Hershey posed the question again, outlining his view more precisely as he added that "no one in the Government service had given much thought to this problem [civilian servant COs]," and he believed that it was the churches' place "to make concrete and specific suggestions along this line."[10] Hershey also initiated a discussion that led to greater organization among the Peace Churches.

The Selective Service realized that the differing opinions of the Peace Churches involved created even more confusion and difficulties.[11] The first to suggest a more streamlined approach for the Peace Churches was Hershey. The idea for what eventually became the National Service Board for Religious Objectors emerged from a meeting between Hershey and Paul French.

Again representing the Society of Friends, French visited Hershey's office to discuss administrative matters concerning COs, including guidelines for the state directors. Hershey asked French if he spoke for all COs or if Hershey had to deal with each individual church or sect. French's reply was that he "probably represented the feeling of all the religious groups" on the issues of registration invalidation and state director information. Hershey was interested in setting up a civilian board for the explicit purpose of dealing with conscientious objection, but he made it clear that he was unwilling proceed in that direction until President Roosevelt had appointed the head of the Selective Service. French readdressed the point that many of the COs chafed under the idea of government control and suggested that a civilian organization such as the American Friends Service Committee needed to be involved.[12]

It was Hershey's next idea in the meeting that really got things rolling. Hershey put forth the idea that the AFSC administer the CO programs and asked how much money the Friends would need from the government to finance this. French responded that the Friends probably would not accept funds from the federal government, but he could not speak for everyone on that point. Hershey and French went on to discuss the nature of religion, and Hershey asked French exactly what the Peace Churches wanted for civilian service. Hershey reassured the churches, through French, about his sympathy for matters of conscience and religious liberty, saying that "if he [Hershey] was named director [the Peace Churches] would have no difficulty in working out a mutually satisfactory arrangement."[13]

French returned to his colleagues with the message that the Mennonites, Brethren, and Society of Friends needed to cooperate under the leadership of the American Friends Service Committee. The Brethren and Mennonites, however, felt that a more cooperative and equal relationship was in order.[14] On October 5, representatives from the Historic Peace Churches voted in favor of "recommendations prepared by the committee of Friends, Mennonites and Brethren in Washington and presented by Ray Newton regarding a possible continuing set-up in Washington, D.C., to work on behalf of the religious conscientious objector. It is understood that the organization will be composed of the Friends, Mennonites and Brethren, and this organizing committee will determine the policy governing issuance of invitations to other organizations."[15] Those recommendations constituted a twofold approach to conscientious objection. The organization's mission was to keep the church constituency informed and to serve as the voice of conscientious objectors to the federal government. Other religious denominations, churches, and sects could be members, but the organization limited membership to religious groups (in line with the wording of the Selective Service Act, no less). The Historic Peace Churches had the representatives on the general committee and covered the expenses.[16]

Thus, the Peace Churches established the National Council for Religious Conscientious Objectors on October 11. After merging with the Peace Churches' Civilian Service Board on November 26, they named the unified organization the National Service Board for Religious Objectors. The executive board of NSBRO was made up of representatives from the Brethren Service Committee, the Mennonite Central Committee, and the American Friends Service Committee.[17]

The establishment of NSBRO was incredibly significant, and Hershey's role in its formation was pivotal. NSBRO spoke for the COs in Washington, and for the duration of the war any changes in policy or camp operations involved NSBRO in some way. Although the Historic Peace Churches were more cooperative with one another than in World War I because of the interwar conferences, Hershey's suggestion that they present a single voice to him spurred them to establish an interdenominational organization devoted solely to matters of the conscientious objector.

Those working with the Selective Service had a variety of stances toward the concept of service and toward administration of alternative service. Ideas came in from all parts of the spectrum. Some favored service "on an individual basis," with COs working on their own projects,not in regimented work camps. Others wanted much sterner "[g]overnment operated and strictly disciplined camps." A significant and convoluted problem was the individual CO's stance toward service. Because of the varied nature of individual beliefs, the Selective Service faced an impossible task in trying to account for all individual stances. Some COs were willing to labor in defense work so long as they did not have to serve in the military. Others went so far as to refuse to plant a single seed or harvest a single grain if its use was to feed the army. It became clear that most COs would not work in defense industries, so the Selective Service shied away from war work as much as possible. Further compounding dissatisfaction in the earliest stages was that setting up a system for alternative service was taking longer than anticipated. The Peace Churches were leery of anything that smacked of government control. To compromise, the government eventually took over old CCC projects and used the existing infrastructure, working with the Forest Service and the Soil Conservation Service under the Department of Agriculture.[18] Furthermore, Hershey's belief in decentralization of the draft led to more leeway in matters of individual conscience, leaving classification in the hands of the local draft boards.

From the passage of the Selective Training and Service Act until October, Hershey was acting director of the Selective Service. President Roosevelt had not yet appointed anyone as director. Secretary of War Stimson believed the director could be either a civilian or a military officer, but he told Roosevelt that if the director was a member of the armed services then he should be an army officer, as the army had been the most involved in planning for conscription. Hershey had strong support from both Stimson and General George Marshall. If an army officer was to serve, they both felt that having Hershey involved at the highest levels was an absolute must. At the time, Stimson believed that "Hershey should have an active part in it ... but he is rather young and not well known to the people." Stimson thought it might be best to appoint a more senior officer and have Hershey work as an assistant director. That being said, Stimson made it clear that Hershey needed to be a part of the draft administration. He said, "Hershey is very familiar with all the questions of what shall be done in the way of regulations and otherwise, and has taken a great part in the preparation of the bill."[19]

Ultimately, Roosevelt chose to illustrate civilian control of the draft as much as possible, even though most of the men working in the Selective Service headquarters were military personnel. So, instead of appointing Hershey to the post, Roosevelt named Clarence Dykstra, president of the University of Wisconsin-Madison, the director of the Selective Service on October 12. Dykstra had a background in government administration; he had served as the city manager of Cincinnati, Ohio, throughout most of the 1930s. At Stimson's behest, Roosevelt named Hershey deputy director, and Hershey also received a promotion to brigadier general. When Dykstra arrived in Washington, he recognized Hershey's expertise and granted him wide latitude in administrative and executive decisions. Though the decision to appoint Dykstra over him surely disappointed Hershey, the two men worked together adequately.[20]

By the middle of October, there was still no alternative service program in place, and Hershey reiterated to French that the Historic Peace Churches needed to present him with a plan. Questions regarding projects, administration, and funding still loomed. Hershey and French discussed the possibility of medical students working in depressed sections of large cities or in "sharecropper areas," an idea that Hershey supported. Hershey reminded French that the Peace Churches needed to state clearly what they were willing to do, how many units were necessary, and how much money they needed to fund the program. Hershey also recognized that nothing could move forward until the Peace Churches presented him with specific information on their needs. He told French, "You fellows want to make up your minds as to what you want to do and how it ought to be done and we are in a position to talk intelligently about it." He also stated there needed to be a discussion of responsibility for the men. Specifically, would responsibility lie with the federal government or the Peace Churches, or would the two share responsibility?[21]

Finally, on November 12, the National Council for Religious Conscientious Objectors presented its initial plan to Hershey and the Selective

Service, the points of which it had negotiated with Dykstra, Hershey, and a Major Guiton Morgan of the Selective Service. The plan outlined three possible avenues of service for the CO. In the first, COs would work directly with the federal government. These men would be paid, but not more than what their equivalent in the military would receive. The government would directly supervise them, and the camps would receive full government financing. In the second type, they would work in camps for the agencies of the government (such as the Forestry or Soil Conservation Service), but the Brethren Service Committee, the American Friends Service Committee, or the Mennonite Central Committee would administer the camps. The government would pay for the facilities, and the churches would pay for administration and support. Each CO would be able to choose whether to work for free or to receive pay from the government, again at the military scale. The final option was complete control by the Peace Churches, with additional agencies to be approved by the director of Selective Service. This part of the plan gave the churches autonomous control over finance and administration. Furthermore, the Peace Churches already had locations in service ready as alternative service camps for COs.[22]

However, from the point of view of the Selective Service, a number of questions remained, first among them being who was responsible for financing. The Peace Church plan called for dual control, but that did not necessarily assure civilian control if government money were involved. Other concerns included the legality of the entire plan, what specific types of work would be done, where the programs would be located, how many COs would perform alternative service, how the local boards would report those filing for CO status to the Selective Service, what a CO's status would be after one year, and the possibility of parole to civilian service camps for those incarcerated for draft law violations.[23]

A letter from Hershey to French on November 28 reflected these many uncertainties. "In line with our conversation of recent date," he wrote, "it appears that it is not possible at this time to make any definite statements regarding the final plans for a program of work of national importance to which conscientious objectors may be assigned." Hershey spoke for all at the Selective Service when he outlined some of their thoughts on the types of camps, which were not altogether different from those of the Peace Churches. He considered four types of camps: camps run completely by the federal government, camps working for government agencies but financed and administered by "some religious or private agency," camps financed and administered completely by religious groups, and camps run by state and local governments. However, Hershey reiterated that all of these ideas were tentative and subject to government approval, just as were the proposals of the Peace Churches.[24]

By early December 1940, there was finally enough consensus within the Selective Service that those involved decided it was time for President Roosevelt to firmly define "work of national importance." They also urged that authority over an alternative service program be placed in the hands of the director of the Selective Service. Furthermore, the Selective Service wanted the director to coordinate the efforts of the various entities to secure funding, issue regulations and steer the direction of the programs, and establish administration for alternative service.[25]

By late November, at the same time the Selective Service was beginning to come to a consensus on matters, the Historic Peace Churches and the Selective Service were ready to submit a program for alternative service to President Roosevelt. At this point alternative service hit a major roadblock. Roosevelt vehemently rejected the plan during a meeting with Dykstra on November 29. Dykstra told French that the president had "expressed instant and aggressive opposition to the plan." Roosevelt believed that working in soil conservation in the CCC was "too easy for them." Furthermore, he believed that COs needed to be drilled by a military officer, apparently having learned nothing from the embarrassments of the First World War.[26] Dykstra knew that an alternative service program needed to go in a different direction. He began to discuss matters with one of Roosevelt's personal assistants, Lowell Mellett, and changed some of the particulars of the alternative service plan. In a December 5 meeting with officers of the Selective Service, Mellett, and members of the Peace Churches, Dykstra asked if the Peace Churches were willing to pay for CPS. As it stood, Dykstra did not think they could get government funds without going through Congress, and that probably meant there would be no service under Peace Church administration. Furthermore, Roosevelt's opposition to the initial plans meant that paying men in CPS was out of the question. Therefore, the Peace Church representatives decided that if there was to be an alternative service plan under them, they would have to pay for it. They decided the Peace Churches would assume financial responsibility until the end of the federal government's fiscal year, but only on a trial basis.[27]

Roosevelt's view here is both intriguing and perplexing. On one hand, he was a religious man whose views shaped his actions toward the poor, and he had a concern for humanity. On the other, he had somewhat of a military background with his cabinet post during the First World War. That being said, Roosevelt's role in conscientious objection was a small one at best, and his significance was more as a delegator than as an active participant. His eventual appointment of General Hershey as the supreme figure in all CO matters was of profound significance. In certain instances on the matter of conscientious objection (such as his rejection of the initial plan), Roosevelt made his voice heard. His background did not engender a great sympathy toward conscientious objection. He was born into a life of extreme wealth and privilege and gained his education at the some of the best American schools: Groton School, Harvard, and Columbia Law. He began his political career with his election to the New York state senate in 1911 and served as assistant secretary of the navy from 1913 to 1920 in the Wilson administration. Though he lost the 1920 election—running as vice presidential candidate under James M. Cox—he had a bright future before him until poliomyelitis or Guillain-Barré syndrome (sources differ) paralyzed him from the waist down. Undeterred, Roosevelt won the election for governor of New York in 1928. Once the U.S. plunged into the economic abyss of the Great Depression, the popularity of President Herbert Hoover plummeted, and Roosevelt won the election of 1932 in a landslide. Until World War II, Roosevelt's name was synonymous with attempted economic recovery in the form of the New Deal.[28]

Though a man of wealth and privilege, Roosevelt possessed a distinct sense of compassion for those less fortunate. It is in his personal beliefs that a few glimmers of Roosevelt's conceptualization of conscientious objection appear. His belief in Christianity and the teachings of Jesus Christ influenced his concern for humanity, and he saw problems in the government and society as problems of morality. In the words of one author, "[Roosevelt] held religion—his own and that of others—to be a highly personal and sacred matter. People around him of all faiths (and of none) were impressed by his religious sincerity and simplicity."[29] He had a particular disdain for interdenominational and sectarian disagreements on religion. For him, "It [was] between belief and unbelief."[30]

Yet his actions when presented a plan for alternative service do not reflect that religious sincerity. There is little scholarship on Roosevelt's views toward conscientious objection. A recent biography of FDR by Jean Edward Smith does not mention the issue. David Kennedy briefly mentions conscientious objectors in his landmark work *Freedom from Fear,* but again, there is no discussion of Roosevelt's views on the issue. Roosevelt's faith did not inspire in him a true sympathetic attitude or a blanket deferment for COs. According to Albert Keim, Roosevelt's attitude toward the matter was "prickly."[31]

On December 19, Roosevelt agreed to allow for the alternative service plan, with NSBRO and the Peace Churches responsible for administration and finance for the camps. On December 28, NSBRO decided to call the program Civilian Public Service.[32] Once the Historic Peace Churches and the Selective Service worked out CPS's particulars, Roosevelt officially approved the program with an executive order on February 6, 1941. The order placed the power for establishing alternative service in the hands of the director of Selective Service.[33] Once Hershey became director, his authority was usually the determining factor for resolving issues. Roosevelt's executive order of February 6 firmly established that power. It read,

> By virtue of the authority vested in me by the Selective Training and Service Act of 1940 (Pub. No. 783, 76th Cong.), it is hereby ordered as follows:
>
> 1. The Director of Selective Service, hereinafter called the Director, is authorized to establish, designate, or determine work of national importance under civilian direction to which may be assigned personas found under section 5(g) of the Selective Service and Training Act of 1940 to be conscientiously opposed to participation in combatant and noncombatant training and service in the land and naval forces of the United States.
> 2. The Director shall make the necessary assignments to such work, shall determine the agencies, organizations, or individuals that may provide civilian direction thereof, and shall have general supervision and control over such work.
> 3. To the extent that he may deem necessary to carry out the provisions of this order, the Director may utilize the services of the Departments, officers, and agents of the United States: accept the services of officers and agents of the several states, territories, and the District of Columbia, and the subdivisions thereof; and accept voluntary services of private organizations and individuals; and may obtain, by purchase, loan or gift, equipments and supplies from Federal and other public agencies and private organizations and individuals, with or without advertising or formal contract.
> 4. The Director is authorized to prescribe such rules and regulations as may be necessary to carry out the provisions of this order.[34]

Roosevelt led through delegation, and this order was no exception. Now, all matters of conscientious objection came to the desk of the director of the Selective Service. He could decide on the matter or delegate the decision to some other agency, depending on his own interpretation. Thus, once Hershey assumed the director's position later that summer, he had the explicit authority to determine the course of conscientious objection.[35] So it was that the philosophy and beliefs of Lewis Hershey came to shape conscientious objection in World War II and establish precedents that would prevail throughout the twentieth century.

In late January, a couple of weeks prior to Roosevelt's executive order, Hershey and Dykstra traveled with French to Philadelphia for a dinner meeting with other Quaker leaders hoping to discuss CPS. On the train back to Washington, a revealing discussion developed between Hershey, French, and Dykstra. Hershey's Army War College thesis covered fear as a factor in leadership, and he began to discuss a report he had prepared for the General Staff concerning how fear affects soldiers. According to French,

> [Hershey] had developed the fact that human beings are incapable for a long period of time of participating in modern warfare without cracking their nervous systems. His study finished with the suggestion that the real solution of the problem of fear in soldiers was to end war. It was a perfectly fascinating point of view from an Army officer.
>
> Hershey felt that if modern war was continued the result would be that only morons would survive and that all persons of intelligence would rapidly and quietly go insane.[36]

Dykstra listened raptly to Hershey's arguments the entire trip back.[37] This is an excellent example of Hershey's complexities as a military officer. He despised war but championed service. He believed in the universal duty for all eligible men to serve, but strongly defended their right to object. He was a complicated man with a well-reasoned view of the world around him.

It was March 1941 before the Selective Service formally declared five camps ready for "immediate use." That did not translate into immediate action or finalized organization, though. Specific projects needed to be worked out for conscientious objectors in the camps. In a meeting with French, Hershey reiterated that the Peace Churches needed to take the initiative in looking for projects that interested them and submit them to the Selective Service for approval. He reminded French that the director (Dykstra) had ultimate authority, but Hershey instructed the Manpower Division to work with NSBRO on the issue. He also wished to be flexible in searching for projects, not wanting to be bound to any one particular government agency. He told French to keep looking for new projects, because if they did not, CPS men could be stuck working in soil conservation until 1945. He also supported COs working in an urban setting, but he believed this had to be handled in a careful and deliberate manner so as not to rile public opinion against COs or the Selective Service. Hershey also desired to appoint someone whose job it would be to report to him on the operation of the individual camps. Though Hershey hated inspections in the army (in keeping with his distinctly unmilitary bearing), and wanted to avoid that sort of activity with the COs in the camps, he believed that in a relationship requiring cooperation between the Selective Service and the Peace Churches, he needed someone close to him to make sure the churches did not have any problems with the agencies for whom they worked.[38]

In April, a change occurred at the top of the Selective Service that remained in place for the next twenty-nine years. Clarence Dysktra, fighting poor health and problems back at the University of Wisconsin, resigned as director, leaving Hershey as acting director once again. Roosevelt was initially reluctant to name Hershey to the post on a permanent basis. The president preferred to appoint someone with a background in education, but Stimson voiced his support for Hershey, and Roosevelt eventually agreed with him. On July 31, Roosevelt overcame his reservations about a military officer in charge of conscription and named Hershey the director of Selective Service. [39] With that promotion, and Roosevelt's executive order, Hershey's ability to shape the direction of conscientious objection was law. It remained so throughout the war.

On May 8, Hershey made another pivotal decision by establishing the Camp Operations Division within Selective Service. Camp Operations was responsible for all administrative and executive procurement for the alternative service camps.[40] Although the churches were going to pay for the camps and essentially run them, they would do so only with the oversight of the Selective Service. To head the new division, Hershey chose an old friend from his National Guard days, Lewis Kosch. Kosch had served with Hershey in Mexico and France, and they had remained in contact between the two wars.[41] Hershey wanted someone he trusted, and so he brought in Lewis Kosch to lead Camp Operations.[42] The ascendancy of Kosch proved to be a stressful experience for conscientious objectors. Kosch was not as sympathetic as Hershey, but neither was he oppressive in the negotiations with NSBRO. While Kosch may not have been the first choice of many in the Historic Peace Churches, by the end of the war he had proved to be a capable man in this administrative position.

Aside from his desire to place an old army buddy in a position of authority, Hershey displayed a well-reasoned understanding of the new direction the military, the government, and religious groups were heading with the establishment of Civilian Public Service. He thought the Peace Churches and the Selective Service should work closely together "because we were both stepping out in a new path and we would need each other," according to French. Hershey believed that more government control could benefit the camps, as the government might procure items more quickly than the Peace Churches. French expressed the sentiment common among the Peace Churches regarding Hershey's efforts regarding conscientious objection when he wrote, "His whole attitude at this point was excellent and I think we have nothing to fear here."[43]

There were still problems getting men into the CPS camps in April. Speaking for the Peace Churches through NSBRO, French suggested to Hershey that the churches were willing to assume the responsibility of "day-by-day discussions with the various technical agencies of the government in regard to work programs and with the army people on inspections and equipment," hoping to expedite the process. French made it clear they were not criticizing Camp Operations, but the churches believed they could do a better job.[44] Hershey's replied that Camp Operations appreciated any help that the churches offered, but he and the Selective Service wanted Camp Operations to serve as the main liaison among COs, the Peace Churches, NSBRO, and the various government agencies under whom the projects occurred.[45] One can see that stresses between the Peace Churches and the Selective Service, particularly Camp Operations, began to bloom, however slightly, in the spring of 1941.

The first CPS men reported to camp in Patapsco State Park, Maryland, on May 15, 1941. There were fifty men representing fifteen different denominations. The men faced a large contingent of reporters and other officials. In the public comments he made for the opening, Hershey described CPS as more than just a simple alternative service program and expressed his hopes for it: "It is an experiment, an experiment such as no nation has ever made before. Through these camps for conscientious objectors we are going to find out whether our democracy is big enough to preserve minority rights in a time of national emergency. I don't know whether the experiment will work or not, but I hope and pray that it will."[46] Hershey's comments again reflect his well-reasoned approach to the issue, recognizing the new concept of service to the government that he, the Selective Service, and the Historic Peace Churches had developed.

Hershey and the Selective Service continued to choose work projects and campsites during the remainder of 1941. Selecting projects for alternative service was much more complex than simply selecting a form of work that fit the definition of "work of national importance." First, the project had to be important to the federal government at the present and for the foreseeable future. Second, the COs had to be willing to do the work, which could not conflict with the CO stance. Third, planners had to consider public opinion, that is, whether civilians near the camps would tolerate COs or would hassle them to the point that the projects in a given camp would fizzle. Furthermore, the Selective Service wanted to avoid both displacing established labor and arousing any "political controversy." For those reasons, the Selective Service limited the first camps to those under the Department of Agriculture's Forest Service and Soil Conservation Service and the Department of the Interior's National Park Service.[47]

Working with the Department of Agriculture and the Department of the Interior showed great foresight, at least in the early stages. At this time, NSBRO saw the programs in the camps as important, though that stance eventually changed. Both agencies (Agriculture and Interior) had experts in positions of authority, and that made the transition for COs into the camps somewhat smoother. Furthermore, those two agencies were willing to use CO labor, a fact not lost on the Selective Service. That willingness proved helpful because, as Hershey later said when discussing the creation of CPS, "We went begging to find places to put them."[48]

Registration for the draft was the same for COs as for those who did not object; it was only when the men appeared before their local boards that things changed a bit. A man wishing to claim conscientious objector status filled out DSS Form 47, which outlined his background, education, and beliefs concerning peace, violence, and the use of force. The board then made its decision to classify the man according to the criteria. A man willing to serve in the military but not carry weapons received a I-A-O classification, while a man unwilling to serve in the military received a IV-E classification and went into Civilian Public Service. A local board could classify a man fit and available for military service if it found the objector to be insincere or basing his renunciation of war on secular reasoning. Though the board's decision was usually final, there was an appeal process in place through the Department of Justice. The Department of Justice held a hearing on the objector's sincerity, which became the basis for a recommendation to an appeal board. The decision of the appeal board was the final word on a man's classification. Though the objector's appeal had to go through the Department of Justice, the board was not bound by the department's recommendations. Through December 7, 1941, there were 1,960 appeals; 206 cases ended in IV-E classifications, 93 in I-A-O classifications, and 240 were rejected. The others did not meet the Department of Justice criteria because the objectors had not yet received their local boards' classification. The appeal board concurred with the Department of Justice in all but 48 cases. The Selective Service structured an appeal process in this manner because there was a belief that local boards might be somewhat unsympathetic toward conscientious objectors.[49]

As director, Hershey wanted all appeals sent to NSBRO to be referred to him. He was not able to read all of them (that job fell to one of his assistant directors, Colonel John Langston), but he did read a fair amount. He sometimes would override the decision of his appeal board, but mostly he wanted to form a general idea of what was happening in the appeals process. He was even willing to review personally all appeal cases turned down by a hearing officer in New York when there were concerns over that officer's fairness. He also made it clear that there were no absolutes in classifying conscientious objectors. There was no way to satisfy everyone, and sometimes an objector received an incorrect classification (such as a sincere objector receiving no I-A-O or IV-E classification). As French presented Hershey's attitude on the subject in a NSBRO bulletin, "He [Hershey] pointed out, however, that we must realize that while we are all seeking absolute justice we are likely to fall short of the goal, as no judicial system has yet been devised to assure complete justice in every case." French pointed out to his constituents, though, that Hershey was making a strong effort to be as fair as possible and uphold the legal provisions for conscientious objectors.[50] Hershey's approach on this matter reflects his pragmatic attitude toward the CPS experiment. No program would be perfect, but he sought to provide for COs in the best way that he saw possible even as he recognized that there were limitations to the system.

Some trepidation existed within the Selective Service over extending the privilege of conscience to individuals from other religions and denominations besides the Historic Peace Churches, largely because of the pressure this put on the local draft boards. For example, draft boards with veterans or members who did not fully understand the religious stances of the COs may have been unsympathetic. From Hershey's point of view, though, "the Selective Service [did] a fair, conscientious, and understanding job with the conscientious objectors."[51] Eventually, some unhappy objectors or Peace Church administrators came to say that the Selective Service was not "fair, conscientious, and understanding," but there are two problems with that point of view. First, Hershey did the best he could in helping to shape a much more liberal policy toward conscientious objectors. There was almost no precedent for alternative service, and Civilian Public Service represented the best compromise possible at the time. Second, the situation could have been much worse, particularly if the director of the Selective Service had been someone with little tolerance for religious liberty or conscientious objection (as was General Leonard Wood at Camp Funston during the First World War).

The length of service in CPS was initially one year, the same as for men drafted into the armed services. When Congress extended the term of military service to eighteen months, the length of service for CPS men grew to match, though, just like the armed forces, the government released men over the age of twenty-eight.[52] Any CPS man discharged after the age of twenty-eight remained in a reserve to be recalled if the same thing happened in the military.[53] With the terms of service in CPS mirroring those in the armed forces, this was truly service to one's country in an alternative matter just as Lewis Hershey had envisioned. He saw a parallel between those serving in the CPS camps and draftees in military uniform. To him, they were to be treated similarly, whether armed or unarmed.[54]

It must be remembered that throughout 1941, the Peace Churches, Hershey, and the Selective Service still thought of CPS as an experimental program. As such, there was the possibility that alternative service could ultimately go in a different direction. However, Hershey truly wanted CPS to work, had said as much publicly, and he expressed his desire for success to NSBRO as well.[55] The government's treatment of COs during the First World War was also on his mind during this formative time. Hershey's ideas on the subject came out in public statements, personal letters, and in his meetings (both formal and informal). For example, he, Kosch, and French traveled to Lancaster, Pennsylvania, in August to meet with a local Amish leader. After a meal at the man's house, Hershey sat on the back fence and mused on the problems of conscience and service for two hours. After the meeting, Hershey and those accompanying him met with three Lancaster County draft boards. Hershey explained to the board members that he wanted to make sure that matters of conscience were being dealt with in an intelligent and discreet manner to avoid the problems of World War I.[56]

Negative public reactions from certain quarters were also a concern for Hershey. Hershey said at a CPS conference at Winona Lake, Indiana, in early September that a majority of Americans supported the idea of alternative service but that 98 percent probably did not agree with the stance of the Peace Churches. He said there was no way of knowing if support for CPS would last, especially given public opinion. He believed that the CPS projects needed to be carefully thought out to avoid arousing negative publicity. However, he reiterated that he thoroughly believed in the mission of CPS and those administering it.[57] This was not the only occasion on which Hershey spoke of public opinion as he gently reminded the Quakers that they could expect tolerance, but not understanding, from the American public.[58]

By October of 1941, it appeared that the experiment in alternative service was not working as planned. To the Selective Service, the biggest problem was the lack of discipline and order in the camps.[59] A distinct lack of regulation and organization in the Quaker camps troubled Kosch, who had been traveling to various camps for observation. The issue troubled Hershey, too, but Kosch was quite concerned. However, Kosch also tended to be reactionary and intemperate compared to Hershey's calm demeanor and pragmatism. Kosch's response to the situation was to threaten to take complete control of the Quaker camps in a month to six weeks. Hershey agreed something needed to be done, but his approach was less threatening, and he appeared much calmer than Kosch. French and Clarence Pickett, though, agreed to make some administrative changes to improve camp cleanliness and the punctuality of work details (with some help from Hershey when he joined French to meet with other Quaker leaders on November 5).[60] Though the issue did not surface again in 1941, the discipline in the Friends' camps was an issue at times throughout the rest of the war.

One major disagreement between the Historic Peace Churches and the Selective Service during the years of CPS was the confusing issue of administration. Many Peace Church representatives did not care for what they perceived as an increasing dictatorial approach by the Selective Service. This issue reached flash point during the latter part of 1943, but one sees examples of it beginning to emerge in the early days of CPS. For example, during a trip to inspect a CPS camp in Indiana with Thomas Jones, the first director of Friends Civilian Public Service, Kosch listened to Jones muse about the vision he had for the future of CPS. According to Jones, Kosch became increasingly irritated and finally exclaimed, "Who in the hell do you think you are? Don't you know that I am in charge of these camps under Selective Service?" Jones replied that he did not realize that and he thought the Peace Churches were free to administer CPS as they chose. Kosch laughed and said, "My dear man, the draft is under the United States Government operation. Conscientious objectors are draftees just as soldiers are. Their activities are responsible to the Government. The peace churches are only camp managers. Do you understand that?"[61] Though Hershey, too, believed that CPS was under Selective Service jurisdiction, he likely would have been much more diplomatic in his language. Unfortunately, misunderstandings such as these led to more heated negotiations later in the war.

By the late fall of 1941, Hershey was growing increasingly unhappy with Kosch as the director of Camp Operations. He did not think the program was working as well as it could be, and he toyed with the idea of making some changes in the Camp Operations division of Selective Service. Hershey sought input from French on replacing Kosch and another officer with French himself. French thought it might be better to have a military man like Kosch in the position because he could be "our best defense when emotionalism and hysteria develop." Though no changes were made (Kosch remained director of Camp Operations for the rest of the war), Hershey had made it clear to French that he was willing to replace Kosch if it would help the administration of CPS.[62] Though Hershey sometimes succumbed to cronyism, he was not above making a change if it became necessary. This incident also illustrates Hershey's respect for the Peace Churches, since he was willing to appoint a Quaker to a post directly by his side as the director of Camp Operations.

In September, the Peace Churches decided to extend the experimental CPS program to January 1, 1942, as long as Selective Service agreed to take over payment for the improvement of camps. The churches were also willing to extend the program even longer, possibly to 1943 or 1944, if the government extended funding further and permitted more options for alternative service, such as work in mental hospitals, on farms, and at overseas relief and rehabilitation efforts in Mexico, South America, Great Britain, and China.[63]

In late November, the Peace Churches decided to officially extend the program to at least 1943. Clarence Pickett of the Society of Friends, M. R. Zigler of the Brethren, Orie Miller of the Mennonites, and French met with Hershey on November 26, informing him of the Peace Churches' decision.[64] Hershey accepted the suggestions of the Peace Churches for extending the program and agreed to pay for "maintenance and repair of camps with the exception of camps owned or leased by church organizations." He also said the government would pay for shipping and handling of CPS camp orders and that the Selective Service was willing to examine new projects. Hershey was adamant, though, that this was not a "blanket approval to any projects other than those established."[65]

The final few months of 1940 and all of 1941 were a crucial period in the development and direction of conscientious objection under the Selective Service and Training Act of 1940. Those months saw the creation of the National Service Board for Religious Objectors, Civilian Public Service, and the Camp Operations Division in the Selective Service—all of which came about with the personal involvement of General Lewis B. Hershey. He was the most public government figure on the issue and was a staunch supporter of CPS both publicly and privately. Though there were a few months with Clarence Dykstra serving as director of Selective Service, Hershey was still the most important individual in the institution. He was the expert and had infinitely more experience and knowledge than Dykstra could ever hope to have. Clearly, Hershey, serving as the acting director, deputy director, then director of Selective Service, did much during the crucial years of 1940 and 1941 in helping to develop, administer, and shape the direction of conscientious objection and alternative service during World War II. Guided by his belief in religious liberty and the duty of service, he began to build a program that reflected those values.

Chapter 6

★ ★ ★ ★

Hershey and Conscientious Objection in the Time of War, 1941–1944

The Japanese Navy's surprise attack at Pearl Harbor on December 7 shocked millions in the United States and thrust the nation into the war as a combatant. It shifted the focus of Hershey and the Selective Service from drafting men for training to drafting them for fighting. Little about the handling of conscientious objection changed in practical terms beyond a minor modification in Hershey's attitude toward overseas service and an increase in the number of men assigned to CPS camps. But in a larger sense Civilian Public Service was now the alternative service program for a nation at war, rather than for one enacting peacetime conscription. In the years that followed, COs served in mental hospitals, worked on farms, labored on sanitation projects in the American South, and volunteered as scientific test subjects. Once again, Hershey's role in the program was pivotal. He made the most obvious impact with his power of approval for any change or special project desired by the NSBRO. During the war years, Hershey's beliefs, attitudes, and actions again came to light when shaping alternative service, particularly concerning major policy changes and his relationship with the Peace Churches. Furthermore, it was during this time that certain Peace Church representatives expressed their gratitude to Hershey. There was, however, resistance to Civilian Public Service, particularly from some of the assignees and radical pacifist groups such as the War Resisters League. Though tensions emerged later in the war, a genuine appreciation of Hershey's efforts from many quarters marked the early days.

This chapter details Hershey's role in securing farm labor projects, mental hospital units, and the overall relationship of Hershey to the Historic Peace Churches and NSBRO. CPS encompassed more than work on forestry, soil conservation, farming, and mental health. That said, Hershey's role in the daily administration and development of some smaller projects was minimal. For example, the Guinea Pig Units, in which men volunteered as test subjects for scientific experiments, were well known. While Hershey gave them final approval, little evidence suggests that he helped to shape the specifics of the program. In comparison, Hershey's actions played a significant role in shaping the direction of the farm labor projects. Therefore, the agricultural efforts of COs and Hershey's role in shaping the program are pertinent while the Guinea Pig Units are not. A different dynamic holds true for the CPS Training Corps, a proposed effort by the Peace Churches to implement training for assignees hoping to engage in relief and rehabilitation of the war-ravaged areas. Hershey played a significant role in developing the CPS Training Corps, but much of the story of that particular program involves Congress, so it will appear in the next chapter.

Pearl Harbor had only a limited effect on Hershey's work. If anything, Hershey seemed to become even more supportive of COs. Now with wartime conscription, Hershey remained adamant that both he and Kosch would continue to defend the rights of COs, even if it brought criticism. Hershey would remain on their side in the grand scheme of things, though he foresaw there might be pressures exerted on him by others. For instance, the patriotic fervor that arose in response to Pearl Harbor created an environment where retributions upon conscientious objectors could occur. If anything, Pearl Harbor made Hershey more accommodating toward COs, at least in the early stages of the war.[1]

One result of Pearl Harbor was that Hershey became more supportive of the idea of sending COs overseas to aid relief efforts in Britain and China. Hershey seemed to like the idea of overseas relief efforts from conscientious objectors, but he had hesitated to fully support it because of the uncertainties over the legality of sending men under government supervision to nations embroiled in war when the United States was officially neutral. Now his reservations left him; however, he left it to the state agencies to determine whether to allow assignees to go overseas. But Hershey was agreeable to the idea and made it known to the Peace Churches.[2]

The greatest change for Hershey and the Selective Service was the increase in draft calls and inductions. The United States' active participation in the war meant that the military, and CPS, was going to expand. Hershey told the Peace Churches that they could expect an increase of one thousand to twelve hundred men in camps by June 1942, a direct result of the anticipated increase in draft calls.[3] Hershey instructed all of the draft boards that war meant that deferments for industry, agriculture, or any other vital trade must be reexamined and men might need to be reclassified.[4]

Another change for Hershey and the Selective Service was heightened concern about public opinion toward conscientious objection and Civilian Public Service. One of Hershey's goals was to make the experience and sacrifice as equitable as possible between the CPS assignees and men drafted into the armed services. By late January 1942, there was some vexation within Selective Service over some of the privileges the men in CPS camps enjoyed. Kosch, speaking to the Peace Churches at a meeting in which Hershey was present, told French and the executive camp directors that Pearl Harbor had definitely changed public opinion. There were negative feelings toward COs and CPS because the assignees had more weekend furloughs and were allowed personal vehicles in camp. Kosch suggested that the churches needed to limit these practices so as not to arouse public ire. Kosch made it clear to the Peace Churches that the two sides (the Peace Churches and the Selective Service) approached the situation from different positions. In French's words, "At one point [Kosch] said we were seeking to preserve a philosophy of life, and he was attempting to do a difficult job which has been assigned to him." However, Kosch was adamant that although there was pressure on Hershey from certain quarters to change things, Hershey's commitment to protect conscientious objectors would not waver.[5]

The CPS experience in World War II was a tale of expansion. What began as an alternative service model based on the Civilian Conservation Corps in soil conservation and forestry units expanded to include a vast array of projects, ranging from COs laboring in agriculture to serving as scientific test subjects. As with other issues involving conscientious objection and alternative service, Hershey's importance to the development of new projects was undeniable. While Lewis Kosch handled most of the day-to-day activities and negotiations between the Peace Churches and the Selective Service, Hershey's vision was the ultimate trump card. If something was not up to Hershey's standard, it did not get approved. Kosch's role is significant in this part of the story as well. Because Hershey had appointed Kosch, anything done by Kosch ultimately reflected on Hershey. In their early negotiations, members of the Peace Churches, particularly Paul French, had admired Kosch, though that admiration paled in comparison to their appreciation of Hershey.

The prospect of CPS branching into other areas of service began to be discussed at least as early as September 1941, well before the attack on Pearl Harbor. On November 18, 1941, at a CPS meeting of executive camp directors in Hershey, Pennsylvania, the executives decided that any special projects should fall under the jurisdiction of NSBRO in terms of administration, selecting assignees, and seeking project approval from the Selective Service. They also determined that French was to be responsible for appointing the directors of the projects. The next day, French met with Kosch to discuss service outside the realm of the camps, and Kosch liked the idea so long as the nearest CPS camp served as the central base of operations. Kosch talked of this plan as though he was the driving force behind it, though French had brought the matter to his attention about two months prior to their meeting.[6]

There were numerous programs set up under the auspices of Civilian Public Service. A number of authors have recently cited the significance of conscientious objectors in changing the way American mental hospitals operated and how the Guinea Pig Units provided scientists and doctors with knowledge for improving the quality of life in the United States.[7] The purpose of this work is not to go into exact detail of each program and its creation but to focus on the projects that best illustrate the influence of General Hershey.

For example, Hershey played a distinct role in creating the farm labor project. There were a number of reasons that the Selective Service and Hershey considered farm labor a legitimate means of satisfying the "national importance" clause for alternative service. In terms of the legality and feasibility of the programs, there was minor precedent for farm labor. During World War I, some COs had received furloughs to work on farms. The Selective Service also believed that the rural background of many of the COs provided an opportunity for experienced men to work in a project for which they already possessed the proper training. Furthermore, there was a distinct desire among the COs in the camps to do something more meaningful than digging irrigation ditches or maintaining the timber in national parks.[8]

Beyond a desire to look for other projects than just the forestry or soil conservation camps, the major impetus in creating a farm labor program was the distinct agricultural labor shortage that had emerged by the fall of 1941. One of the earliest remedies tried by the Department of Agriculture for the shortage was CO labor.[9] Hershey was fully cognizant of the labor shortage in agriculture. His first response was to tell local draft boards that they needed to be careful in drafting farm laborers into the armed forces. He argued that modern agriculture required much more specialization and mechanical knowledge than in the past, which could only be gained through years of experience on the farm. Another reason for the shortage, Hershey reasoned, was that industrial jobs in the cities paid better and offered shorter hours than life on the farm.[10] The farm labor shortage created a window for more work of national importance for the conscientious objector.

Hershey discussed farm labor as a form of alternative service with French about one month after French's initial meeting with Kosch on the subject of detached programs. Delegating some of his authority, Hershey told French that NSBRO should discuss the matter with the United States Department of Agriculture (USDA), making sure to keep Kosch informed. On January 3, 1942, French proposed to Kosch the creation of fully separate agricultural units of COs, though small, for maintaining dairy cattle to aid in European relief after the war. For the interim, the milk produced from these dairy units would instead go to underprivileged schoolchildren so the units would not directly compete with local dairy farmers. Kosch was lukewarm to the idea. He preferred an individual furlough for each CO, keeping the men tied to their camp administration. He did agree with French, though, that farm labor might present a public relations problem if COs gained a monetary profit from their work.[11]

The meetings that followed involved the Selective Service, NSBRO, the United States Employment Service (USES), and the USDA. Points of discussion included prioritizing the areas that suffered from the most distinct labor shortages, outlining how men in CPS would be chosen for service in farm labor, the mechanics of supervision, and method of payment or if COs were to be paid at all.[12] From these discussions, four distinct plans emerged. First, if a shortage became severe enough in a particular area within fifteen miles of a CPS camp, men could work on that farm, but they would remain under the control of their particular camp. This was to be done only as a last resort to solve local labor shortages. Second, men could be sent to work on dairy farms approved by the USDA and the Employment Service. Third, men could also conduct dairy testing (testing and recording the quality of milk at dairies) in areas where the labor shortages directly caused the cessation of testing programs. Finally, men could also work at agricultural experiment stations and agricultural colleges where labor shortages disrupted food production.[13]

A few days later, French and Kosch met with executives from Agriculture Defense Relations, a part of USES. An agreement emerged from this meeting for an experimental farm service program for COs, with the USDA and the USES identifying the counties most in need of agricultural labor. The next day, the executives of NSBRO agreed to conduct the farm labor program as a service detached from the forestry and soil conservation camps. The men were to receive no pay beyond their basic expenses, and the leftover money was to go into a separate fund. The other executives also instructed French to draw up a memo for Hershey that outlined their plans. Kosch liked this idea, but the money issue made him uneasy, so he wanted to wait to discuss the matter privately with Hershey. On January 27, Kosch told French to move forward on the farm labor program unless significant public relations problems emerged.[14]

Throughout the negotiations, though, there were bureaucratic problems with the USDA and the USES. French thought both agencies seemed more concerned with finding reasons the program would not work rather than looking for solutions to use COs on American farms. On February 6, a meeting between the USDA, USES, French, and Kosch deteriorated into a stalemate. French finally had enough and suggested that they take the matter directly to Hershey. The meeting moved to Hershey's office, where the USDA and USES representatives laid out their objections to the NSBRO and Selective Service proposal, including the contentious issue of pay for the COs. French complained that if "we forget the lawyers for a few minutes...we would probably be underway in a week." Hershey simply asked Kosch if he wanted to cut through the red tape. When Kosch answered in the affirmative, Hershey approved the plan, completely sidestepping the roadblocks of the USES and USDA. Hershey also made it clear that he wanted the leftover funds to be administered by NSBRO, rather than another private agency such as the Red Cross. French later wrote in his diary, "The more I see of Hershey, the more I am convinced that he is really a big man."[15]

The various entities involved reached an agreement in June for the first agricultural units in CPS, when the U.S. Department of Agriculture, the U.S. Employment Service, the Selective Service System, and NSBRO produced a memo outlining their plan for CO work in agriculture. They explained, "Dairy farms have been selected because of the importance of dairy production for national welfare and the shortage of labor for these farms."[16] Hershey's approval of the memorandum placed him at the forefront of CPS development. This was the first step in taking COs out of the camps and placing them on farms, further defining "work of national importance" and, in turn, further defining what wartime service to the nation meant. Now men objecting to military service could serve their nation in a time of war beyond laboring in conservation or forestry camps.

This memorandum firmly established the farm program, the first of an important series of programs that grew extensively in 1943–1944. The areas that saw the most growth were dairy testing, experiment stations, and dairy farm labor. After three months serving in a CPS camp, men could volunteer to serve in one of these detached units.[17]

One of the most divisive issues to emerge from the farm labor programs in CPS concerned wages. COs received no pay for their labor. Instead, farmers paid the average rural wage of the county per CO to NSBRO, who used the money to administer the farm labor program and provide a small subsistence stipend to the COs. NSBRO then forwarded the remaining balance to the U.S. Treasury, which set the money aside in a special account not to be used for war programs. As a further guard against war spending, the money, known as the CPS Frozen Fund, could not be touched until after the war.[18] A Memorandum of Understanding between the Peace Churches and the Selective Service specified that the money would be used for postwar relief efforts.

In July 1942, Hershey wrote to the comptroller general of the United States, Lindsay Warren, outlining plans for the CPS agriculture projects. Warren noted that Hershey had the authority to approve these programs, but Warren did not support the plans for CO wages going to war rehabilitation. Hershey then asked Warren if NSBRO could use the money for general CPS administration, but Warren replied that he believed the entire payment structure for farm labor had no legal basis. The issue was never resolved. Decades later, NSBRO still had not seen any of the money from the Frozen Fund, the total value of which was about 1.4 million dollars in 1945.[19]

Another project area for CPS was in mental hospitals. During the early part of 1942, a number of requests from hospitals for CO labor arrived at the Selective Service. The requests came from general care hospitals, hospitals for the care of tuberculosis, and mental institutions. Because of the wartime labor drain, the mental hospitals were severely short of labor. The labor shortage was so acute that many institutions dropped the level of patient care "to a custodial level," and there were even reductions in care beyond that point. Thus began one of the most successful programs within Civilian Public Service–detached units in mental hospitals. Like the agricultural programs, there was a small precedent from the First World War, with COs working at a mental hospital in Virginia. This was why the first mental hospital unit in World War II was in Virginia, according to Hershey's 1943 report. By 1943, seventeen mental hospitals in ten states had begun using CO labor. The men working in the hospitals assisted in the general care of patients or helped to maintain the facility or hospital grounds. The COs provided a much-needed solution to a severe labor shortage in these institutions. As Hershey's second Selective Service report stated, "While the number of assignees available cannot begin to solve the problem of labor supply, they can be of considerable assistance."[20]

The hospital program was largely created in meetings between Paul French and Lewis Kosch, the idea having originated with CPS assignees in two forestry camps in Massachusetts. However, as was the case in most other instances, Hershey's influence is undeniable. Hershey approved this program, but public opinion again turned to a thorn in the side of Hershey, Kosch, and the Peace Churches. Furthermore, there were instances of COs in hospitals refusing to work. In early 1942, as plans were emerging to set the program in motion, interference from the American Legion threatened to prevent its implementation. Kosch came away from meetings with veterans groups feeling that the hospital program might provoke a visceral public relations backlash. In Elgin, Illinois (the Church of the Brethren headquarters, no less), the American Legion publicly decried the use of conscientious objectors in mental hospitals. Their interference prevented COs from using the state hospital at Elgin, but fortunately, it did not subvert the entire program. The American Legion also opposed CPS mental hospital units in Massachusetts, which ultimately led to that state being the only in New England without "a mental hospital or training school unit," according to hospital unit chronicler Steven Taylor.[21] This would not be the last time the Selective Service had to deal with the American Legion's anti-CO stance.

Hershey appears to have been less involved in the mental hospital program than the agricultural program, but he did play a part nonetheless. One reason for his reduced role was that the mental hospital units did not operate in conjunction with federal agencies the way that agricultural programs did. The Selective Service and NSBRO worked with state mental hospitals on a case-by-case basis to find places in need of CO labor. Hershey fielded letters on the subject from hospital directors, city mayors, and other various officials. There were definitely many opportunities to work in hospitals across the nation, but Hershey and his subordinates believed that the need in mental hospitals was the most acute. As Hershey said to New York City Mayor Fiorello LaGuardia,"It will thus be seen that the number of conscientious objectors required for such hospitals [state mental institutions] will preclude the consideration of other type institutions. We have had hundreds of requests from various municipal, county and state hospitals, as well as those privately operated, but we have given all of them the same answer, namely, we feel that the need for labor in state mental institutions over-shadows their needs, serious as we admit them to be."[22] In Hershey's mind, the need for labor in mental hospitals was more pressing than that in other areas of health care. Hershey also made it clear to others that there was also a limited supply of conscientious objectors, providing another reason for limiting their service to mental hospitals.[23]

Hershey wanted to avoid public relations problems, such as the Elgin hospital debacle, and this continued throughout the war. Such was the case in New York when Governor Thomas Dewey inquired about conscientious objector labor in New York state mental hospitals, Hershey answered that Selective Service did set up experimental mental hospital units, but the public reaction in Utica caused them to ultimately reexamine the situation. Hershey wrote, "After approval of the project at Utica... and upon publication in the New York papers, opposition was registered by the Utica Post of the American Legion, by the Ogdensburg Post of the Veterans of Foreign Wars, by the Hospital employees and by the Association of the State Civil Service Employees. In view of these protests, we did not think it advisable to proceed further with the project and so advised all concerned. At the same time, however, we did inform them we would reconsider at any time that it appeared the objections could be overcome."[24]

Hershey was a strong-willed man with a thick skin, but even he was not immune to public opinion, and he understood that a potential hot button issue like conscientious objection needed to be out of the public eye as much as possible. His response to negative publicity was to move the men away from the problem.

As with many bureaucracies, the Civilian Public Service had a habit of taking too much time to get the administrative machinery in place to get COs out of the camps and into the detached services. By mid-October 1942 that slowness was evident to Hershey, and he made it clear to the parties involved that things needed to move at a faster pace. After avoiding some of the problems with the veterans groups, Hershey was finally able to fight through many of the administrative roadblocks and approve the hospital units. However, the problems did not cease. The slowness in assigning men to the hospitals and finding suitable locations irritated him, and he believed it was due to inefficient administration on the part of NSBRO. The slowness in assigning men to positions began to disillusion many of the assignees, who threatened to quit CPS. During a meeting with French in mid-October 1942, when told of men wanting to leave CPS over this issue, Hershey lost his temper. He told French he was fine with letting them walk, apparently wanting to let the Department of Justice deal with insubordinate assignees. Hershey had simply had enough of insubordinate men in CPS camps. According to French, Hershey said,

> That we were not talking in terms of alternate service now but of special privilege for c.o.s. Said he had sent four million men to the army during the past two years and that none of them had any choice about where they went or what they did. He expressed the opinion in rather strong language that it was about time that we stop babying the men and let them take their own raps.
>
> Said he was sick and tired of the idea they should be permitted to do just about what they please and that he did not expect to continue that way much longer.[25]

Hershey's attitude toward the mental hospital situation and the discipline problems among CPS men reveal a number of themes in his thought toward COs. First, this is further proof of Hershey's desire to make alternative service an equitable sacrifice for assignees, just as men in the armed services were making sacrifices. Second, Hershey emphasized service above all else. As he told French, the emphasis in CPS was on service, not "special privilege." He firmly believed in the value of service to one's country, and to his mind Civilian Public Service was no different. Third, Hershey's stance here also highlights his career as a military officer. Though he was more than accommodating to COs, he was first and foremost a military officer charged with raising an army for wartime. That he believed in bureaucratic control and firm discipline was no fluke. It was a part of his professional training and work ethic.

While Hershey was clearly at the center of creating and administering alternative service during World War II, another fascinating dynamic during the war was Hershey's strong working relationship with the Peace Churches. No single man could ever be entirely responsible for a program as complicated and difficult to manage as Civilian Public Service, so it was imperative that Hershey and the representatives of the Historic Peace Churches, particularly NSBRO, had a strong, productive, and respectful working relationship, which they did.

Early in the war, the Peace Churches went out of their way to let Hershey know that they truly appreciated his efforts. After Hershey's promotion to major general in 1942, Paul Furnas, secretary of the AFSC Civilian Public Service administration, congratulated him on his new rank. Furnas wrote, "I want to express to you my hearty congratulations for the recognition which is represented in the title of Major General which I understand has come to you." He continued, "That a Quaker of my conviction should feel so pleased about the conferring of a military title, possibly indicates how deep is our appreciation for the wise, efficient, and humane administration which you have given to a large and difficult task." Furnas enclosed a draft of a memo to the AFSC's CPS Executive Committee that summarized Hershey's beliefs about religious training and conviction. Furnas had written in the memo, "We feel that it is an occasion for profound thankfulness on our part that the Director of Selective Service should be a man of such spiritual discernment."[26]

M. R. Zigler, chairman of the United Staff of the Church of the Brethren, executive secretary of the Church of the Brethren's General Ministerial Board, and chairman of NSBRO, wrote on behalf of the Brethren expressing their thanks as well: "The ministers of the Church of the Brethren, at our General Conference ... wish hereby to assure you of our very great appreciation for your service to us. Words cannot adequately express our thanks to you. We feel that you have had a sympathetic understanding of our faith; and you have untiringly striven that we should have our rights under the law of the land. You have given most valuable insight and advice."[27] A large number of Church of the Brethren ministers signed their names in an attachment, expressing their gratitude.[28] Signifying his appreciation of a stable relationship, Hershey replied, "I wish that I could somehow or other tell you and all of the others whose names I now read the satisfaction that I experience when I realize what your group has done to make my task easier."[29]

Apparently, the Selective Service wanted to make it known how much the Peace Churches appreciated the efforts of Hershey. In a letter sent little more than a week before Pearl Harbor and published in Hershey's first report, Zigler, Clarence Pickett of the AFSC, and Orie Miller of the Mennonite Central Committee wrote, "We wish you to know that we appreciate the sympathy and understanding with which your have faced this problem during the past year of more and assure you that we are hopeful that the same relationships can continue during the coming year so that jointly we can demonstrate the ability of a democracy to respect minority religious groups."[30] By placing this letter in Hershey's first report, Hershey and the Selective Service made an attempt to produce evidence for posterity of the Peace Churches' appreciation of Hershey and the Selective Service's efforts to implement alternative service in a tolerant and sympathetic manner.

Perhaps no better example than Paul French and his negotiations on behalf of NSBRO illustrates the working relationship between Hershey and the Peace Churches in the early days of the war. During the creation of CPS and through the first full year of the war, the meetings between Hershey and French were usually cordial and respectful, and a true understanding between the two men began to develop. French's comments at the end of his countless meetings with Hershey contained a number of illuminating observations. He expressed how lucky the Peace Churches were to have a man like Hershey, with his sympathy for men of conscience, holding the position of director of Selective Service. He also mentioned how friendly Hershey was, how many times Hershey seemed glad to see French, and his amazement that a man with the duties of Hershey could find the time to meet frequently with men representing such a small portion of the population. In his diary from the first full year of the war, French often describes Hershey as "a big man," meaning that he did not resort to petty squabbles or become vindictive in dealing with conscientious objectors. Instead, he remained open to discussion and sought to fight for their rights when necessary, whether it be in public or behind closed doors in Washington.[31]

That the Peace Churches were grateful to Hershey for his efforts in securing projects for conscientious objectors and supporting them in their efforts to practice their ideology was not unsubstantiated political hyperbole. Objectors had learned during the First World War just how bad things could be. To have a person in charge with the sympathetic stance of Hershey, a military man no less, was of great help to the Peace Churches, and its significance was not lost on them. Their comments to Hershey were not exaggeration, but heartfelt gratitude.

Still, that sentiment was not universal. Other pacifists, pacifist organizations, and CPS assignees either did not agree with Hershey or were extremely critical of him, the Selective Service, and CPS as a whole. One particular group that took issue with the entire structure of CPS was the radical and secular War Resisters League (WRL). As peace historian Scott Bennett has pointed out, "Most WRL leaders took a caustic view of CPS." The WRL did not support CPS from the outset and only became angrier as time went on. A number of its institutional reasons for denouncing CPS and Selective Service control were held by other groups and CPS assignees. This included the lack of pay, government-run camps, meaningful work, and the militarized control of the program. The WRL was also critical of Hershey's support for either Peace Church or government administration, believing this dynamic did not adequately provide for objectors outside of the Historic Peace Churches or those of differing political persuasions. Additionally, members believed that NSBRO did not adequately represent and lobby for the concerns of the WRL.[32]

The relationship between Hershey and the Historic Peace Churches was not always friendly and jovial, either. Indeed, their relationship deteriorated somewhat during the war. It was clear during 1942 that some strain on the relationship existed, and it had worsened by 1943 (concomitant to the rising anger within the WRL from 1940 to 1943). A big issue was camp discipline. Both Hershey and Kosch pointed this out to French and other representatives during the latter part of 1941, but the problems continued into 1942. Kosch believed that the Quakers were dragging their feet in trying to solve to the discipline problems in their camps, which consisted of men refusing to work or keep the camp in good working order. Kosch believed that the government should take over the camps if things did not improve. Hershey's annoyance over what he perceived to be lax discipline in the Quaker camps is definitely apparent in some of French's writings. According to French, Hershey told him that "our philosophy undoubtedly worked well in a summer volunteer work camp but that we must recognize that this was a different situation and that men were there because of a conscription law."[33]

While Hershey and Kosch both labeled the Quaker camps as having a problem with "discipline," what was really happening was resistance to CPS on the part of radical COs who rejected alternative service or the structure of the program. The Quaker camps did tend to have the most tension and resistance, but CPS as a whole was seen as problematic by some, and camps administered by the other churches also had some issues. According to peace historian Lawrence Wittner, radical COs saw the Peace Churches' willingness to cooperate with the government on CPS as a betrayal of pacifist principles.[34] The result in a number of CPS camps was resistance to the program in the form of nonviolent protest. Assignees who chafed under the militarized control of the Selective Service, the lack of pay or dependent support, what they saw as the lack of meaningful work, and other issues that violated their principles expressed their displeasure through noncooperation, petition writing, deliberate work slowdowns, strikes, and inefficiency. Some went so far as to stage hunger strikes or walkouts, knowing that a walkout almost certainly meant imprisonment for the refusal to submit to the authority of the government. The resistance to CPS was there from an early stage, and the walkouts began in 1942. Different forms of nonviolent protest in the camps toward CPS continued throughout the war.[35]

Though the problems with discipline and resistance in the camps continued, little more about the matter came up in the meetings between NSBRO and Hershey during 1942. The relationship between Hershey and NSBRO remained good, but some other groups became annoyed with him over his reluctance to approve government-administered camps. This tension over government camps came to the forefront in 1942 as some of the camp "discipline" problems were becoming more pronounced. Many of the CPS men, particularly those not of the Historic Peace Church tradition, did not like serving under a denominational agency different from their own faith. The Fellowship of Reconciliation, the War Resisters League, and the Federal Council of Churches supported the objections of some of the CPS men. Hershey's reasoning for his reluctance to institute government-run camps was legitimate. First, he thought it could become too convoluted and complicated for the Selective Service to run alternative service camps. Second, he feared that Congressional disapproval could threaten the entire structure of Civilian Public Service, bringing it to a halt. Government-administered camps needed Congressional approval to receive additional funding for administration, something not in the existing budget for Selective Service.[36]

On June 8, 1942, Hershey met with representatives of the Federal Council of Churches and the Lutherans to discuss the matter of government camps. At this point Hershey agreed to look into the matter by surveying the CPS assignees to attempt to glean their position on government-administered camps. In a questionnaire sent to the men, the Selective Service outlined their position and the government's rules for camp administration. It also made it clear that "no distinction would be made between defense and non defense work assigned."[37] This lack of delineation meant that assignees in the government camps were required to work in the jobs assigned to them, regardless of their personal convictions. French also attached a two-page letter, stating his own personal views, which echoed Hershey's stance, and noting that it would be tough to get out of a government camp once assigned and that refusal to work could incur prosecution by the Department of Justice.[38]

This survey, which appeared to be biased against the use of government camps, provoked a three-way fight among the Selective Service, NSBRO, and other denominations with interests in the CO question. Only upon NSBRO's recommendation did Hershey finally approve the government camps on April 16, 1943. NSBRO's recommendation was to pay the men, stay away from defense projects, and try to limit what the men viewed as mind-numbing manual labor. Hershey agreed, except for paying the COs. Once Hershey agreed, the first government-administered camp (without CO pay) began on July 1 at Mancos, Colorado, with three other camps to follow at Lapine, Oregon (established in January 1944), Germfask, Michigan (May 1944), and Minersville, California (June 1945).[39]

The negotiations for CPS camps administered by the Selective Service reveal two important tenets of Hershey's position on alternative service.

The first is that Hershey wanted to deal solely with NSBRO on matters of CPS. Recall that it was his recommendation that led directly to the formation of NSBRO in 1940, when he expressed his desire to deal with one organization covering all of the different groups. Doing so made his job much easier and streamlined the process considerably. The government camp issue revealed, through the disagreements among the groups, that if more people and agencies got involved, the entire program could become gridlocked. Second, Hershey continuously rejected proposals to pay COs. This was not out of malice, but out of an apprehension about public opinion. Ever concerned about the possibility of Congress taking away CO provisions or public opinion raising trouble, Hershey's motive here was to avoid problems before they began. Though the men of CPS were doubtlessly unhappy about it, Hershey's stance remained constant throughout the war.

In 1943 the friendly relationship between Hershey and the Peace Churches disintegrated further. Much of the tension came from the Chicago Conference on Social Action, called by a committee of CPS assignees to discuss some of the COs' complaints. According to Mulford Sibley and Philip Jacob, "The conference…was an attempt to initiate direct negotiations between the assignees and those who exercised authority over them." Included in their invitations were Hershey and other government and religious officials. Hershey, however, balked at attending the Chicago Conference and decreed that no CPS assignee was to attend either. Hershey believed that the meeting could elicit pressure on CPS from Congress or other government agencies, something he definitely wanted to avoid. He thought those attending a conference might try to garner publicity for their situation, which could be political poison for a program already unpopular in some sectors of the federal government. He felt that the Peace Church agencies rather than the men in the camps should organize any meetings needed. Kosch echoed this sentiment.[40] Recall both Hershey and Kosch's distaste for lax discipline and insubordination in the camps. To them, this was another example of such behavior. Kosch told French that both he and Hershey believed that the biggest problem was the men's organizing without the approval of the Selective Service. To Kosch and Hershey, there was a massive difference between organizing among the men and promoting a conference organized by the church administrative agencies.[41]

Many groups, including the Fellowship of Reconciliation and the War Resisters League, denounced Hershey's action. They argued that Hershey was violating the men's civil rights.[42] Although Hershey cancelled furloughs for those hoping attend the conference, it went on as planned, though few attended. The Selective Service refused to allow men who attended conference to go into the detached services, prompting a showdown between NSBRO and the Selective Service. Because the assignment of men into these programs was the job of NSBRO, leaders there believed that the Selective Service overstepped its bounds. Both the Peace Church agencies and NSBRO were quite unhappy with the situation.[43] Paul Furnas believed that if a compromise on the relationship between the Selective Service and the Peace Churches could not be reached, then the AFSC should withdraw from the program. French felt that Hershey and the Selective Service were now ordering around NSBRO rather than negotiating with it.[44]

Hershey began to believe even more firmly that NSBRO and the Peace Churches were failing in their administration of CPS. When French asked Hershey if NSBRO could receive more administrative control, particularly in the area of mental hospital assignments, Hershey refused on the grounds that they had not been successful in what he had already granted them. Hershey was particularly upset with Clarence Pickett, who wrote a letter directly to President Roosevelt expressing his displeasure over the CPS arrangement. Hershey preferred to keep the problems in-house and not display any internal misgivings or problems in view of others in the government. [45] With his letter to Roosevelt, Pickett had put those disagreements on display. His letter of May 18, 1943, was, in part, a response to critical statements about CPS made by Roane Waring, the national commander of the American Legion, to President Roosevelt. Pickett sought to outline the specifics concerning CPS but went on to air his grievances concerning the dual administrative structure. Pickett's statements reflect both the confusion regarding the initial intent of dual administration and some of the misgivings of the Peace Churches. He wrote, "When Civilian Public Service was first established, it was with the understanding that the program was under the direction of the historic peace church agencies, except for the work program which was to be directs by a federal, state, or private agency doing 'work of national importance.' Increasingly Selective Service though its connection with the work director has tended to dominate the administration of the camps. The double-headed administration is no longer workable." What Pickett wanted instead was for most of the administration to revert to the Peace Church service organizations and for there to be a liaison officer between the camps and the Selective Service.[46]

Hershey and Kosch were clearly unhappy about this development. At the behest of Stephen Early, one of Roosevelt's secretaries, Hershey outlined his views on the matter and included a memorandum from Kosch on the state of the administration and the possibility of government-run camps. On the matter of administration, Hershey stated that he was open to the possibility of granting more independence to the Peace Churches after the establishment of a government camp. However, Hershey argued in no uncertain terms for maintaining the current means of administration. He wrote, "I shall be so bold as to suggest that for the good of country, for the good of conscientious objectors in general, and even for the good of the Friends who are conscientious objectors in particular, we should proceed on the course we are now following."[47]

On October 14, 1943, Hershey and Kosch met the NSBRO executive board for dinner in an attempt to repair the relationship between the Peace Churches and the Selective Service. NSBRO presented a memorandum to Hershey outlining their grievances. Some of the issues they presented included pay for the men (which included the dependents of the assignees), establishment of "reception centers" for the assignees so they could best determine where and under which agency they wanted to serve, and the approval of projects more in line with the individual desires of the assignees.[48] Hershey and Kosch listened to their grievances but did not alter their position. The AFSC wanted more socially relevant programs, but Hershey did not see the need. The Quakers argued that they were not the type to run a program that forced men into certain programs or made them work. French recalled that Hershey testily responded "that he thought one of our troubles was that many of the men had not found their souls and that he felt it was possible that they might find them on the end of a shovel handle."[49]

The Peace Churches again asked for pay for COs, and Hershey and Kosch again rejected the idea, citing the need for Congressional approval and the risk of the churches losing CPS over the matter. On the matter of assignees' dependents, Hershey appeared deeply concerned and promised to look into it. Pickett brought to Hershey's attention the AFSC's threat to withdraw from administration of the CPS camps if the Peace Churches' pleas for better camp governance went unheeded.[50]

Though this meeting illustrates the evolving relationship between Hershey and the Peace Churches, few tangible changes came from it immediately. For example, Hershey denied the churches' request for additional projects in education and juvenile delinquency, but an important facet of Hershey's belief structure emerged on this point–his rejection of the doctrine of pacifism. When the churches asked for a program helping juvenile delinquents, Hershey struck down their proposal, saying their pacifist stance was counterproductive. He argued that lack of preparation in the United States prior to World War II could be blamed in part on the pacifists' activities in the 1920s and 1930s making the United States complacent in world affairs. He claimed to have seen this complacency coming when he was at Ohio State.[51] One matter that particularly bothered him was teaching pacifism to American youths. In a letter to Eleanor Roosevelt, he expressed his reservations. He wrote, "While the nation is engaged in an 'all out' war effort it would appear inconsistent for a Government agency to assign [a] man to a position where he is given every opportunity to spread the doctrine of pacifism to our youth in its formative period." He continued, "It is felt that a man holding such convictions cannot help but impress them to a certain extent on his charges who are composed of youths in their formative period."[52] This letter makes it clear that while Hershey sympathized with COs, he did not believe that pacifism or nonresistance was a positive course of action for American society. His emphasis was on service, and that emphasis played into his conception of CPS. In his mind, CPS was an alternative service program, not a vehicle for COs to use to proselytize.

The October meeting was the last of Hershey had with representatives of the Peace Churches and NSBRO for more than a year. He delegated even more authority to Kosch, and there were almost no changes in major policy until the end of the war. As always, it was his prerogative to approve any major changes in policy, but after the October meeting, he seldom met personally with French, other NSBRO members, or Peace Church representatives. Most of the ongoing negotiations and program development stayed in Camp Operations under Kosch and his administrative staff.

Hershey continued to be the face of the Selective Service and discussed conscientious objection in Congress on occasion, but his workings with CPS lessened during 1944. Though 1944 was a much slower year for Hershey and CPS, his influence remained intact. By this time the administrative framework was already established, and no major changes were required. The vision put forth by Hershey during the early part of the war continued through to the end of Civilian Public Service. Some tension and unhappiness still existed between the Peace Churches and the Selective Service, particularly over pay and dependency, but little of substance actually changed. The biggest shift came in 1945, when it became clear that the time to end CPS was approaching.

The wartime experience of Lewis Hershey and the Historic Peace Churches in Civilian Public Service reveals a relationship that began on friendly terms but eventually became strained and frustrating for both sides. Early on, certain members of the Peace Churches expressed their heartfelt gratitude for his efforts. Hershey's commitment to alternative service never faltered, but the Peace Churches and the CPS camps definitely tested his patience from time to time. Throughout the war, Hershey fought for CO rights and approved various projects for the COs. Many times, the negotiations for setting up the new programs dragged on for months, even years. Hershey did not approve all proposals set before him, nor was he central to every single program development in CPS. That said, all programs required final approval from Hershey, as Roosevelt's executive order giving Hershey the authority to define work of national importance had lasting influence. During the war years, Hershey played a significant role in the direction of alternative service. Even when he was not fully involved in a discussion on a specific matter, one can see his philosophy and desires in the final product.

There are a number of specific instances that illustrate the points made above. Hershey's actions in securing farm labor definitely helped push the program though to implementation. However the problems in setting up mental hospital units and the Chicago Conference irritated him a great deal. A military officer foremost, he had no tolerance for lax discipline and poor administration in the CPS camps. He was not hostile to CPS and truly wanted it to succeed, but he believed that work stoppages and unapproved social action conferences threatened the program and aroused negativity from certain quarters. Throughout the war, he worried about public opinion and sought to avoid troubles in this arena wherever he could, particularly when it came to veterans groups such as the American Legion or the Veterans of Foreign Wars. By 1944, his direct influence had lessened when he handed more authority to Lewis Kosch, but the wheels he had set in motion continued to turn. His belief in the duty of service continued to shape alternative service as CPS evolved. Because of the authority granted to him and the structure of his institution, the specter of General Hershey continued to loom over alternative service and conscientious objection throughout World War II.

Chapter 7

★ ★ ★ ★

Hershey and Congress Examine Conscientious Objection

Though the Historic Peace Churches and the Selective Service handled most aspects of Civilian Public Service, Congress sometimes became involved and imposed its will on CPS. During the war, Hershey appeared before Congress on numerous occasions to testify about manpower, labor, and conscription. A few times he went to Capitol Hill to discuss conscientious objection. These occasions were linked with attempts to gain aid for COs' dependents, workmen's compensation, and a foreign relief and rehabilitation program, none of which were successful. The Senate fleetingly tried to eliminate section 5(g) of the Selective Service Act (the section that provided for conscientious objection) in 1943, but nothing became of the bill. Though some of Congress's actions did have a direct impact on COs, the most significant reason for examining Hershey's wartime relationship with Congress is that it further reveals his complex and nuanced views of conscientious objection. During these hearings, Hershey went into detail on his views concerning pay for COs, public opinion, the nature of CO service, and his role as a military director of a civilian institution. Furthermore, he supported an attempt by the Peace Churches to establish a program for overseas relief and rehabilitation, but Congress disallowed their efforts. Hershey's experience with Congress during World War II provides a number of insights into his attitudes toward conscientious objection and alternative service.

He truly believed in the concepts behind alternative service and sought to protect the assignees from some of the problems in CPS. He felt that negative public reactions would threaten the existence of CPS and made it clear that he sought to avoid controversy in that regard. Overall, he displayed a deft political touch in avoiding Congressional limitations on his authority over conscientious objection. Though not always successful, Hershey's dealing with Congress revealed both the limits of his power and his sympathy for the CO.

Most historical analyses suggest that the CO had few, if any, friends in Congress. Mulford Sibley and Philip Jacob, in *Conscription for Conscience,* state, "Congress did nothing during the war to liberate the c.o.; instead, it imposed additional restraints. It excluded foreign service for CPS men, denied financial assistance to their dependents, and stalled their final release from service." Sibley and Jacob are overwhelmingly sympathetic to conscientious objectors, and they paint Hershey, the Selective Service, and Congress in a negative light. They highlight three main areas of Congressional action concerning COs: the lack of aid to CO dependents, the absence of general workmen's compensation to COs, and the lack of CO pay. Sibley and Jacob place the responsibility for the lack of CO pay squarely on the Hershey's shoulders. As illustrated below, his reluctance to pay CPS assignees stemmed from his desire to avoid public relations problems. Sibley and Jacob note this motivation yet claim, "Later, both Hershey and his staff outspokenly argued that the c.o.'s did not deserve pay." Sibley and Jacob offer no evidence to support their assertion.[1] Moreover, in 1946 Hershey told Sibley and Jacob that he believed COs should be paid in the future, a far cry from stating that they "did not deserve pay."[2]

Other interpretations of Congress and conscientious objection are scant. Melvin Gingerich and Leslie Eisan do not discuss much in *Service for Peace* and *Pathways of Peace,* respectively, but Albert Keim gives the matter some attention. He and Grant Stolzfus contend, "Civilian Public Service had almost no friends in Congress during World War II. In fact, it had many enemies. Given the president's thinly veiled hostility to the program, opening the matter for further examination might well have led to disaster."[3] Keim later revised his thinking and labeled Congress no help whatsoever. In "Mennonites and Selective Service in World War II: An Ambiguous Relationship," he writes, "Given the total lack of support in Congress for conscientious objectors—there was not even one member who could be counted on for help … the options available to the peace churches were very limited."[4]

Most congressmen were, in fact, ignorant about conscientious objection and Civilian Public Service. In numerous hearings, Hershey explained the situation to senators and representatives by equating their work in the camps with the Civilian Conservation Corps and praising their efforts in programs such as assistance in mental hospitals. He emphasized that the work was not an invitation for "slackers" to avoid the draft.[5]

The full picture of Congress and the conscientious objector cannot be painted in broad brushstrokes because such an approach does not account for the individual efforts of senators or representatives, efforts overshadowed by congressional inaction or restriction. To say the CO had no friends in Congress is a distortion of the truth, similar to saying that Hershey believed COs did not deserve pay. Men like Jerry Voorhis, who supported COs during the hearings on the Selective Service Act in 1940, and John Sparkman, who worked behind the scenes for them in 1943, were sympathetic. But Voorhis and Sparkman represented an almost invisible minority. An examination of the Congressional experience with the conscientious objector does provide us, however, with deeper insights into the beliefs of Lewis Hershey.

Some matters that came before Congress during World War II included COs' wages, payments to their dependents, and compensation for COs killed or injured during service. While Hershey did not personally testify on all of these matters, the Selective Service men who did testify either represented his views or spoke for him personally. One of the earliest issues pertaining to conscientious objection to come before Congress was workmen's compensation. Representatives of the Selective Service discussed this Senate bill before the Military Affairs' Subcommittee on August 19, 1942. The bill, S. 2708, intended to amend the Selective Service Act by extending the provisions of the Employee's Compensation Act of 1934 to men in CPS. The bill called for forty-two dollars per month to be paid to the dependents of an assignee in the event of his death or disablement.[6] The public reasoning for the bill was that it was a preemptive attempt to avoid claims on the federal government for COs injured or killed while in CPS. Hershey supported this measure, but he could not attend the hearing in August.[7] In a letter written to the president of the Senate, he pointed out that the men in CPS camps exposed themselves to the same types of dangers that confronted the men in the Civilian Conservation Corps. It was perfectly within the realm of reason to predict that some injuries or deaths might occur in the course of camp operations. He also stated that the figure of forty-two dollars came from the amount provided as compensation by the Civilian Conservation Corps.[8]

Because Hershey could not attend the hearing, Kosch and Major J. T. Coatsworth represented his views. Kosch discussed the rights of the conscientious objector and the nature of the CPS camps. He stated that the Selective Service supported the bill because it "protect[ed] the government in future claims that might come up." He also outlined the duty of national service that Hershey had made clear countless times, both publicly and privately. Kosch said, "It is not combat service, it is not service in the Army, but it is a service that is set up by the law of the country; so, we feel that the Government is responsible for them, as long as this law is in effect."[9]

Hershey and Kosch's point of view on workmen's compensation was not the only significant testimony given during this particular hearing. Kosch and Coatsworth also discussed public opinion and COs, further revealing the views of their director. Hershey's views on public opinion were a major factor in his actions concerning COs, and they are analyzed later in this chapter.

At this hearing, Kosch also discussed pay for the CO (beyond compensation for death or disability). Though Kosch's statements echoed those of his friend and superior officer Hershey, they also reveal that Kosch was brusquer and did not have the political savvy of his boss. Rather than discuss public opinion and the avoidance of negative publicity, Kosch called lack of pay a central feature of what defined conscientious objection. He asserted, "We have been against payment due to the fact that we feel that the very fact that a man does not get paid is one means of sorting the conscientious objector from the slacker or the fellow who is just trying to hide behind the skirts of the religious objectors."[10]

In one of the few times that a chamber of Congress supported conscientious objectors through legislation, the Senate passed this bill, but the congressional session ended before the House acted on it, delaying the bill until 1943, when the Senate Committee on Military Affairs heard testimony again in conjunction with a bill to end conscientious objection entirely.[11] It was then that Hershey took a strong stand in support of extending compensation to CPS assignees and rejected wholesale the idea of eliminating the provisions for conscience in the Selective Service Act.

Another contentious issue that Hershey discussed before Congress involved CO wages. He repeatedly told the Peace Churches that Congress would not support pay for COs and that they risked losing the entire program over the issue, especially if it came to the public's attention. However, Hershey's testimony before Congress suggests that he was more concerned about public opinion than he let on to the churches. He even went so far as to suggest to Congress that a large percentage of the

COs would not accept pay, which, while not a lie, was not the complete truth. Hershey argued that the lack of pay actually deterred men from declaring as a conscientious objector, because if paid, some might consider themselves noncombatants rather than civilian servants.[12]

When Hershey testified against eliminating the provisions for conscientious objection in 1943, he discussed his personal views on the matter of pay. In arguing that he did not believe the men in the camps would accept pay, he claimed that they, much like him, did not want to incite public animosity. He explained that COs paid their way or the religious agencies covered their expenses. The cost for each man was 35 dollars per month, out of which each man received $2.50 for personal items such as toothpaste, shaving cream, and other toiletries. However, there was no money in the system for labor wages. The men who worked in the forestry camps, soil conservation camps, and mental hospitals did so for free. The men working on the farms had their wages placed in the frozen fund.[13]

When Senator Monrad Wallgren (D-WA), heard that COs were working for no pay, he told Hershey, "You are treating these fellows worse than the Japs," referring to the Japanese Americans placed in concentration camps under Franklin Roosevelt's Executive Order 9066. Hershey replied, "Maybe so, but we have, in your State [*sic*], groups in two of your hospitals for insane, and there the food and so forth is furnished by the State of Washington in return for their services, and as to the $2.50, the State of Washington pays them for taking care of these various matters." In this case, Hershey implied that the public good from their work was more important than the lack of pay. Wallgren later pressed Hershey further, asking him outright, "Do you feel that they [COs in mental hospitals] should be paid?" This time, Hershey answered fully,

> Definitely not. It would destroy the best public relations. The thing we have to consider is they have not received any pay so far, and I think I would be supported by 60 or 70 percent of these people, who consider that that is one of the contributions they are making to show that they are really conscientious objectors and conscientiously believe what they came to believe, and I know some that will not accept, under any circumstances, Government money. I do not believe any of the Mennonite Church members, by and large, would accept any money.[14]

On the surface, Hershey's contradictions here are puzzling. Since the earliest negotiations in 1940, the Peace Churches had been trying gain fair pay for men assigned to Civilian Public Service. Hershey and Kosch were both major roadblocks to those attempts. Hershey repeatedly stated that he did not support pay for COs. He also told the Peace Churches that the federal government, particularly Congress, did not support paying COs, and they risked losing all of CPS over the matter (something Dykstra also pointed out to them when negotiations with President Roosevelt stalled in late-1940). While Wallgren's line of questioning suggests otherwise (though he was only one man), Hershey's reasoning to the Peace Churches may well have been an accurate assessment, but hard evidence is scarce.

Hershey supported a stipend to be paid to the dependents of COs, yet, as with workmen's compensation, he was unable to attend a hearing on the matter. In the fall of 1943, Paul French appeared before the House Committee on Military Affairs, hoping to gain an expansion of the federal government's dependency allotment program for servicemen to cover CPS assignees. This was an important measure for conscientious objectors as serving in CPS created significant financial burdens on everyone involved: the COs, their families, their churches, and NSBRO. The efforts by French were part of a larger effort to revise some of the provisions for family allowances for men in the armed services. French made it clear that there were no provisions for the families of COs. His idea was to take money from the CPS Frozen Fund in the U.S. Treasury and use that to help ease the financial burden on the families of CPS assignees. French also told the committee that this idea found favor in the Selective Service, particularly from Kosch. His proposed legislation provided for the money to go to NSBRO, where it would be properly redistributed to the CPS men.[15] French's measure, however, did not have enough support to pass.

The issue of CO dependents would reappear before Congress. The House Committee on Military Affairs recommended in May 1944 that a bill be passed to provide for the dependents of CPS assignees. The plan called for the money set aside in the U.S. Treasury's Frozen Fund to be released to the Selective Service for the purpose of providing for CO dependents. The families were to receive the money based on need, but the amount could not exceed the funding for the family of a man in the armed services. According to the wording of the bill, the person responsible for determining need would be Hershey.[16] Though supported by NSBRO, Hershey, and the House Committee on Military Affairs, three congressmen objected on the House floor, and Congress adjourned with no vote being taken, allowing the bill to die. The issue would never be resurrected.[17] Hershey's support for dependency reveals both his sympathy for the CO and the limits of his influence.

The most illuminating facet of Hershey's testimony before Congress was his concern about public opinion. Nowhere else was Hershey as frank about how he believed COs should best be handled to avoid negative public reaction. Hershey believed that the best course of action for the CO was to stay out of the public eye. This is a sentiment echoed by Albert Keim and draft historian John O'Sullivan.[18] Hershey stated this bluntly to the Senate Committee on Military Affairs in 1943:"We have about 1,500 to 2,000 [CPS assignees] that are now acting as attendants in State [*sic*] hospitals for the insane. We have got quite a few of them that are in different zones of forestry work. Some of them are putting out fires up in the west coast of the country, but they must not be allowed to get too much credit for it. It isn't good for them. I wouldn't want the press to report this."[19] Though Hershey does not appear to be terribly enlightened in this instance, he was not speaking duplicitously to Congress and the Historic Peace Churches. If anything, Hershey was a master at the game of politics. He knew that speaking in a celebratory manner before Congress might have dire consequences for Civilian Public Service and conscientious objection as a whole. Furthermore, he sympathized with the COs, understood their position, and sought to protect and help them, but he did not agree with their nonresistant stance. As a part of the military establishment, he was a true advocate for the importance of military service and preparedness. He believed that it was in the best interest of the CO to stay out of the public eye, and he did not heap hyperbolic praise on CPS or the assignees. Instead, he took a pragmatic approach, seeking to keep negative reactions to a minimum.

During the August 19, 1942, hearing that Hershey could not attend, Kosch presented some testimony that might as well have come directly from Hershey. Kosch pointed out that Hershey and the Selective Service did not approve some of the larger social programs suggested by the Peace Churches because they did not want them to be publicized. In his blunt manner, Kosch stated,

> We try to discourage that ["missionary work"]. In other words, we are not setting up projects that puts [*sic*] them in a position where they can do, it [*sic*] like social-welfare work, teaching in schools, and so forth. We have had pressure put on us to put them in to teaching schools where they are short of funds, and so forth, but we have refused to do it, because we do not believe that the Government should be a party to helping these men spread their pacifist propaganda. Around these camps you find there is a certain amount of it done due to the fact that if the churches invite the people in to talk we can't say "no" to it. However, if the churches do not ask them in, there is no particular way they have of spreading their propaganda on these jobs, because they are work jobs; and, as I say, we are opposed to setting up any type of project which would lend itself to the spreading of their propaganda.[20]

Major Coatsworth also appeared before the committee, personally representing Hershey. Mostly, his statements echoed those of Kosch, particularly in regards to support for the measure coming from a desire to protect the government. Coatsworth also pointed out that the men were not "slackers," but their choice was a result of an "isolated" lifestyle in which they came of age "under the influence of their church and elders."[21]

The line of reasoning from Kosch and Coatsworth appears insensitive on the surface, but an examination of the larger dynamics at work helps account for their assertions. Granted, Hershey did not believe in the message of the conscientious objector, but he did believe in the privilege to object, provided that the objector performed some sort of national service. For Kosch and Coatsworth to say that the measure was simply for government protection was probably a political tactic to keep Congress from becoming overly hostile to CPS. If Kosch, Coatsworth, or Hershey were to stand in front of the subcommittee and say, "I believe they should be compensated because it is the right thing to do and COs should be protected," they would have opened Selective Service to the possibility of having all of the conscientious objector provisions called into question.

In terms of his views on public opinion, Hershey's most insightful and illuminating testimony before Congress during the war came in February 1943. In a hearing before the Senate Committee on Military Affairs, Hershey made official statements and answered questions concerning two bills. One bill (S. 675) considered the extension of the aforementioned Employee's Compensation Act to conscientious objectors. The second bill, however, threatened to undermine the entire structure of conscientious objection in the United States. Senator Elmer Thomas (D-OK) proposed a bill (S.315) that would likely eliminate both Civilian Public Service and noncombatant guarantees. Thomas's impetus for the legislation was a resolution drafted by the Oklahoma American Legion. It read, "*Be it further resolved, and we petition,* That the national legislative committee of the American Legion petition the Congress of the United States of America, for a change in the Selective Service Act, so as to eliminate the classification of 'conscientious objectors,' and amend the law, so as to provide that all men subject to the draft shall do service in the armed forces of the United States."[22] Thomas's legislation was simple and straightforward. He proposed, "That section 5 of the Selective Training and Service Act of 1940, as amended, is amended by striking out subsection (g) thereof.[23] Besides the threat to the Selective Service for the entire structure of conscientious objection, the possible elimination of noncombatant guarantees was deeply troubling.

On February 14, Hershey appeared before the Senate Committee on Military Affairs to discuss both S.315 and S.675, speaking broadly on the controversial topics concerning COs. In addition to his comments on the CO and public opinion, Hershey also mused on the relationship of the CO to the army, his concept of alternative service, and his own unique status. He stated that he did not support S.315 because he believed it placed an undue burden on the army. He said that striking out the option for noncombatant service was problematical. Those who were noncombatants did not mind serving in the Medical Corps, but extending noncombatancy to other areas might cause dissension among those serving or planning on serving as medics. He truly believed in the mission of CPS, and he did not view it as an invitation to "slackers," as Senator Joseph O'Mahoney (D-NY) called them. Hershey assured the senators that he truly believed COs were completely sincere, reaffirming his earlier statements of 1940, in which he called for the protection of sincere objectors. [24] In sum, he said, "The Selective Service System believes that the Selective Training and Service Act of 1940, as amended, has, as a practical matter, reasonably solved a distressing situation, as in all wars, that of what to do with those whose conscience prevents them from participating in full measure in the Army."[25]

Second, Hershey did not support Thomas's bill because he feared it would hurt army camp morale.

> as a soldier—I should say former soldier—I may say that [the COs'] presence in those [army] camps is very unfortunate, because they will go to prison or anything, except that they will not serve, and some of them have the martyr complex, some are a little psychopathic, and as a rule, sometimes if they are left completely alone, they will come around, whereas, if you arouse opposition, you develop a martyr complex, and they would do anything rather than fight. I would like to deprive the Army of having that problem to deal with.[26]

Thus, if the government left the COs alone rather than coercing them into military service, some of the CPS assignees could be "salvaged" and might eventually join the army.[27] Again, this is an example of his nuanced and complex view of conscientious objection. He did not believe in the message of the CO, but he respected the privilege of conscience in a democratic society, as long as the objector performed some form of national service.

Hershey testified that he wanted to make the CO's sacrifice equitable to that of a conscript in the armed forces. He said, "I think by and large, the great majority agree that the thing, itself, [CPS] is a fine thing, and we have tried to parallel the army in the privileges and the withholding of privileges, and the granting of passes. We have pretty much applied to them about what the Army does. We do ship them away from their homes, we do not let them stay in their home territories." Keesling interjected that the Selective Service did not allow the assignees to stay on the land of relatives either, to which Hershey added, "That is a very bad public-relations problem right there." He pointed out that the Selective Service shipped inductees to entirely new locations, such as men from the East Coast serving on the West Coast, despite the high transportation costs.[28]

Hershey again outlined his preferred method of dealing with conscientious objectors and the American public—invisibility. Austin S. Imirie of Lewis Kosch's Camp Operations Division informed the senators of the Guinea Pig Units, in which COs served as test subjects for the Office of Scientific Research and Development and the Surgeon General's Office of the United States Army. Imirie noted that about seventy-five men were currently in the Guinea Pig Units. Hershey explained that they constituted about 1 percent of the CPS assignees at that time. Hershey said, "That is almost 1 percent, not a very large figure, but I have opposed publicizing that sort of things because the conscientious objector, by my theory, is best handled if no one hears of him."[29]

Hershey also described to the Senate Committee on Military Affairs how he rationalized his appointment as director of alternative service when the law called for a civilian director. On that exact point, Senator John Chandler "Chan" Gurney (R-SD), said to Hershey, "You are not a civilian, as I see it." Many during and after the war have criticized the federal government on this point. Hershey's response was skillful, if not a bit inaccurate, as one of the major critiques from some CPS assignees was the militarized nature of CPS. "[The Selective Service Act of 1940] did not say, 'under a civilian;' it said 'under civil direction.' No one has ever challenged it and I truly believe I would say, with a little satisfaction to me that the groups mostly involved agree that I am a civilian, at least when I deal with them." Imirie noted that the individual camps all possessed civilian administrators, and Hershey added one final statement on the matter: "The directors of these camps are hired, also, by the religious groups. The Government does not pay them." Neither Gurney nor any other member of the committee pressed Hershey further on the matter.[30] Beyond answering to some of the criticism, this exchange illustrates how Hershey viewed himself. He believed he was neither solely an army officer nor solely a civilian director, but a unique amalgam of the two.

He recognized that he dealt mainly with civilians and often appeared in public wearing civilian clothes.

What one sees from Hershey's testimony before Congress on public opinion and the nature of the CO is that Hershey thought the best course of action for IV-E COs was to keep them away from situations that could reflect poorly on the Selective Service and threaten CPS. While he may or may not have been entirely correct, he firmly believed that keeping a tight lid on publicity was the best course of action. In doing so, his belief structure regarding public opinion shaped the direction of CPS by keeping the camps and other projects out of the limelight.

Workmen's compensation and dependency benefits were not the only measures supported by Hershey that failed to pass through Congress. Congress also rejected the CPS Training Corps. Ernest Miller, president of Goshen College (a Mennonite School in Indiana), conceived of the Training Corps in late 1942 to prepare CPS men in the Peace Church colleges for overseas relief efforts. He wanted to establish a program that could provide a college education for those already enrolled when drafted and train them in relief efforts, in the same way that military draftees could remain in college to take classes to prepare them to be officers in the armed forces.[31]

Orie Miller of the Mennonites and French met with Hershey on September 3 to discuss the Training Corps. Hershey initial reaction to the proposal was supportive but guarded. He told Miller and French that he would consider relief training, but he wanted some time to contemplate the program. He had few reservations about sending men overseas as long as the Peace Churches obtained clearance from the State Department. On September 7 during a follow-up meeting with French and Kosch, Hershey decided to approve the Corps once NSBRO submitted the specifics of the program.[32] Tentative approval for the plan came in November 1942.[33]

Though the churches had Hershey's support, many NSBRO board members and representatives of the Peace Churches were apprehensive about Congress's reaction to the program. Miller was fearful of problems with the draft boards, which tended to be inconsistent with some hostile to conscientious objectors and the concept of alternative service. For that reason, the Selective Service did not issue any memoranda to the boards concerning the Training Corps, and the churches instructed draftees not to mention the program to the local boards, reflecting Hershey's desire for CPS to keep a low profile. Men would be chosen for the program after receiving their IV-E classification.[34]

There were disagreements within NSBRO over the number of men to be inducted; initial estimates of six hundred men became a point of contention. Some NSBRO members wanted to induct as many as one thousand men. French presented these numbers to Hershey, who listened to the suggestions but was willing to approve only 2 percent of the total number of men already in the camps, or about 160 men, for service in the Training Corps. According to French, Hershey believed that he could not justify placing a large number of men in college when there was already a nationwide shortage of labor. While some executive board members believed otherwise, they wanted this program badly enough to compromise even beyond the reduction in manpower.[35]

Although the Training Corps had Hershey's support and approval, it never came to fruition. On July 1, 1943, Congress passed the Military Appropriations Act (H.R. 2996) with a clause added by Alabama Representative Joe Starnes, chair of the House Subcommittee for Appropriations. The amendment ended the possibility of relief training in the colleges and relief aid overseas sponsored by CPS. It read as follows:

> [N]o appropriation contained in this Act shall be used for any expense pertaining to (1) the instruction, education, or training of *class IV-E conscientious objectors* in colleges, (2) the service of such conscientious objectors outside the United States, its territories, and possessions, (3) the transportation of such conscientious objectors to or from any college or any such service, or (4) the compensation of military or civilian personnel performing any services with respect to the matters set forth in (1), (2), or (3) above after the enactment of this Act, except any services which may be necessary promptly to terminate any such class IV-E conscientious objector college or foreign-service projects existing on the date of the enactment of this Act....[36]

This legislation killed any possibility for CPS to train its men in Peace Church colleges or to send them overseas under the auspices of CPS during the war.

Starnes previously had made clear his disapproval of the Training Corps. He stated in a hearing on June 10, "The country would not approve such a policy in my judgment—these people should be kept at home at constructive work." Furthermore, he particularly did not support the use of army transportation to move the men to the areas where they would be providing relief. "The space used by these men should be used in transporting food, supplies and fighting men to China and our other allies." [37] At least in a public sense, Starnes clearly saw the priorities of the United States as winning the war and everything that entailed, rather than undertaking attempts to rebuild while the war raged. Starnes chaired the House Committee on Appropriations, and the committee considered it "incongruous ... to use such funds upon persons possessing convictions or beliefs that relieve them from the foremost obligation of every citizen to his country."[38]

There were other, less public reasons for Starnes's rejection of the Training Corps. These reasons included, most notably, a general aversion to the role of the first lady, Eleanor Roosevelt, in the federal government. Mrs. Roosevelt did play a role in approving of the concept of the Training Corps, working with Clarence Pickett of the American Friends Service Committee. Her role in government irritated many members of Congress, and her efforts on the part of the Training Corps were no exception. Knowledge of this came from various meetings by Paul French with Kosch, John Sparkman (another Alabama Representative), and Starnes himself.[39]

The various executive board members of NSBRO still held out some hope that portions of the Training Corps could be salvaged. French and M. R. Zigler met with Hershey on July 1 to discuss alternatives. As French recalled, Hershey was "sorry to see it go out." Congress's action dismayed Hershey, but he realized he could do little about it. French wrote, "[Hershey] was not inclined to evade a direct mandate of Congress through some administrative device. He said that he believed in a government of laws and not of men and that one of his major criticisms of the administration was that administrators ignored Congress and made their own laws." French then asked Hershey if appointing a civilian to Camp Operations in place of Kosch would help their cause. Hershey replied that were it not for the clear desire of Congress to disallow the Training Corps, he might consider replacing Kosch for that purpose. Hershey said he would think about drawing his own salary as a civilian director, ending some of the ambiguities about military money and a civilian program. However, as with Kosch and his Camp Operations position, Hershey knew that doing so would not circumvent the intent of Congress in this particular instance.[40]

In August, Hershey wrote French, reiterating his stance toward the Training Corps and his desire to let congressional action stand. "Since Congress has definitely expressed itself on this Project [*sic*], I do not feel that I can take any action contrary to their expressed wish nor any action that would circumvent it. Since this action was taken by the Congress as a whole, it is not felt that any one member can nullify it."[41] Hershey may have been dismayed at the churches' loss of the Training Corps, but he was adamant that he was not going to personally undermine the intent of Congress.

The interaction of Hershey and Congress over the CPS Training Corps reveals a number of things. First, Hershey believed in the value of CPS and thought this plan was a noble endeavor, as evidenced by his initial support and his disappointment over Starnes's amendment. Second, Hershey's meeting with French and Zigler to discuss alternatives provides further evidence that he was indeed sympathetic to conscientious objectors and the desires of NSBRO to improve CPS. He was not a man who actively sought to restrict COs or place hardships on them. He wanted the Training Corps to go through, and when it did not, he felt sorry for the men who had invested much time and personal desire in the possibility of overseas relief, hoping to bring CPS closer to the "work of national importance" the legislation of 1940 called for. Finally, and most significantly, Congress's rejection of the Training Corps again revealed the limits of Hershey's power. Just because Hershey wanted a program to succeed or be passed, members of the federal government who disagreed could either set up roadblocks or overrule him. Hershey was not all-powerful. He was a military director of a civilian institution who wielded enormous power and influence and was sympathetic to the CO, but he respected the balance of power in the federal government.

Throughout his career, Lewis Hershey was a frequent visitor to the United States Congress, providing testimony on the multitude of subjects that were a part of national military manpower policy. World War II was no different for him, and alternative service for COs was one of the many subjects he discussed during his time on Capitol Hill. Congress's relationship with the conscientious objector was not a friendly one, though some congressmen could be counted on to at least listen with a sympathetic ear to what the Historic Peace Churches had to say. Congress was not supportive of COs during the war, and it neglected to adopt any legislation that provided workmen's compensation for COs or dependent stipends to CO families. It also struck down the CPS Training Corps and the attempt to train COs for overseas relief and rehabilitation efforts. During the hearings or negotiations into these matters, Hershey's attitudes showed clearly in his testimony. Though the actions of Congress are of importance to conscientious objection, the most important information to emerge from the various hearings and negotiations are the complex and nuanced views held by Lewis Hershey. He openly and frankly discussed why he did not support pay for COs, relating to his beliefs that conscientious objection was an entity best kept out of the public eye and that providing COs with a wage could arouse a negative public reaction. Hershey supported a workmen's compensation plan for CPS and payments to the dependents of CO families. However, his support for those possibilities, much like his support for the CPS Training Corps, revealed that his power as the director of Selective Service was not all-encompassing. He also mused on the relationship of the CO to the federal government and his own status as a military man in a civilian agency. Additionally, his support for the various failed suggestions and programs, though futile, further demonstrates that he was sympathetic to the COs' desires and the hardships they faced during World War II.

Overall, Hershey's willingness to defend before Congress both COs and his efforts in administering alternative service illustrates that he truly believed in the concepts he put forth. Had Hershey been indifferent to CPS, he would not have made an effort to protect COs from congressional action or inaction. Though sometimes futile, his actions suggest that he believed he was doing what was best for COs and their relation to the American state and society.

Chapter 8

Hershey and the End of Civilian Public Service, 1945–1946

As 1944 turned to 1945, much had changed for the U.S. forces fighting in Europe and the Pacific. Having staved off a last-ditch effort by the German Army in the Ardennes Forest, Allied forces advanced across the Rhine into Germany. In the Pacific theater, the Allies recaptured the Philippines and prepared to invade Iwo Jima. However, gains overseas meant little for conscientious objectors except the possibility of a quicker end to the war and the demobilization of Civilian Public Service. Though General Hershey dealt with other issues surrounding conscientious objection, ending CPS in a streamlined fashion occupied much of his time for CO matters. Demobilizing CPS turned out to be a thankless task. On one hand, COs and their Peace Church representatives wanted the quick and timely discharge of CPS assignees. On the other hand, Congress, veterans groups, and the War Department wanted to make sure that COs did not receive an "easy way out" of their national service obligations before the fighting men returned home from their overseas mission. Hershey once again led negotiations for matters concerning conscientious objection, and as always, his beliefs and ideals shaped his actions. In keeping with his vision of alternative service as comparable to service in the armed forces, his plans for demobilizing CPS initially mirrored plans for military demobilization, including a point system. However, resistance from Congress, veterans groups, and the War Department and Hershey's fears of negative public reaction led him to compromise on plans for discharging CPS assignees. Though wrought with controversy and frustration, the actual demobilization process worked, and it stood as yet another example of Lewis Hershey's importance to conscientious objection in World War II, demonstrating his deft touch with political negotiation and his dedicated attempts to protect his vision for alternative service.

The discussions for demobilizing CPS did not begin until the European phase of the war ended with Germany's unconditional surrender on May 7–8, 1945. Hershey, Kosch, and the Historic Peace Churches worked together on a plan to end CPS and discharge the assignees in a timely fashion. Hershey had tried to implement alternative service and CPS in a way that mirrored the armed forces in terms of an individual's duty to serve. This ending phase was no different, as he wanted to implement a point system for CO discharges similar to the army's. His initial plan involved one point earned for each month of service, twelve points for each child, and three points for a spouse. Men who had served less than one year could not be released, and an assignee lost one point for each day's absence or refusal to work. Furthermore, no assignee could be released if he was subject to legal prosecution.[1] Though this plan seemed perfectly reasonable to Hershey, it inspired strong opposition almost immediately. Thus, he had revised his plans considerably by the time the Selective Service began to send men home from CPS.

Most of the initial discontent came from Congress, veterans groups, and servicemen. The main point of concern was the use of points in determining the discharge of CPS assignees. Many believed this system made it easier for COs to go home sooner than those who fought overseas. The process proved to be a source of frustration and disgruntlement for everyone--the Selective Service, Congress, the Peace Churches, and various veterans groups--throughout 1945. Hershey found himself caught between two groups with which he dealt on a regular basis. On one side were the veterans groups, such as the American Legion and the Veterans of Foreign Wars, who called for the CPS men to remain in camp until every draftee in the armed forces came home. On the other side were the Peace Churches, who wanted the men to be discharged as soon as possible.[2] Though Hershey dealt with many other matters concerning conscientious objection, the demobilization of CPS was the most pressing and most important CO issue he administered during the final years of the war and immediately thereafter.

Some early portions of Hershey's plan quickly fell by the wayside, such as how CPS men received their points. Hershey initially thought that men involved in the firefighting (smoke-jumping) and the Guinea Pig Units should receive extra points due to their individual sacrifices and the dangers they faced, but he did not pursue it beyond his initial musings on the subject. On May 15, 1945, the likely plans for discharging CPS men based on a point system, age, and dependency appeared in *The Reporter,* the biweekly publication from NSBRO on matters concerning conscientious objection. This plan did not include extra points for the smoke jumpers or the men in the Guinea Pig Units, but the possibility existed for men receive one point for each month of service and twelve points for each dependent child, with a maximum of three children allowed. Hershey and Kosch (and the Society of Friends) also made it clear in late May that they wanted CPS to end six months after the end of the war with Japan.[3] This turned out to be wishful thinking.

In June, the plan for the end of CPS became more explicit. The Selective Service lowered the age limit from forty-two to forty. CPS assignees now earned three points for a wife in addition to the aforementioned credits for time served and children. June also marked the time when lost points for men who refused to work or were absent without leave at any point in their CPS service became publicly reported to the COs. The Legal Section of Selective Service also announced that CPS would cease six months after the end of the war.[4] However, as Hershey, Kosch, and the Peace Churches formulated plans for demobilization that summer, members of Congress and the veterans groups began to criticize Hershey for what they viewed as unfair advantages being given to those who, to their minds, had not shared in the sacrifices required by duty to the nation.

The veterans groups in particular were vehement in their opposition to the CPS demobilization plan. They directed some of their critiques toward the spousal credit, because there were no points for spouses in the military's plan for postwar demobilization. The American Legion and the Veterans of Foreign Wars made it quite clear to Hershey and the Selective Service that they did not support discharging COs before the men in the armed forces came home. The stock response from Hershey and the Selective Service was that they merely followed the legal dictates of Congress. Because the Selective Service Act of 1940 provided for conscientious objection and the Selective Service held administrative power over COs, they were entirely within their legal rights to provide for and administer demobilization proceedings for COs as they saw fit.[5] Their line of reasoning, though, did not quell the growing opposition to CPS demobilization.

The actions of the veterans groups brought Hershey to the boiling point. His task was to raise an army for combat without extensively disturbing the industrial and agricultural production of the nation, all the while setting and approving policies for conscientious objection. In all, it was a thankless job that brought criticism from many quarters. By 1945, Hershey's patience was wearing thin. By simply examining the matter of conscientious objection, one can see how Hershey's friendly demeanor with the Peace Churches during the first couple of years of the war began to change as he became more frustrated with a lack of camp discipline, administrative problems, and the ever-looming public opinion issue. Being told by veterans groups how to do his job (which was how he viewed the situation) was simply too much. Kosch relayed Hershey's attitude to French during a meeting between the two on June 15. Hershey's staff drafted a number of letters to the various veterans groups responding to their critiques and outlining the stance of the Selective Service, but Hershey rejected them because the language in them was not forceful enough. Cooler heads prevailed when Kosch reasoned with Hershey. In the words of French, "The General felt that they should tell the Legion and the VFW that the matter was none of their business–with the usual Army profanity–and Kosch agreed with him, but felt it unwise to write such a forthright communication."[6] The public response from the Selective Service was that it only followed the law as set forth by Congress.[7]

The veterans groups were not alone in thinking the initial plans for CPS demobilization provided COs an unearned advantage. Hershey and the Selective Service faced criticism from Congress as well. Many of the grumblings in the legislature focused on the point system. The initial response from the Selective Service was that the point system simply determined the order of a person's discharge, not the percentage of men sent home from CPS. Another source of criticism was that the CPS men had more opportunities to accumulate points because the Selective Service decided not to limit the number of children that could be counted toward a point total.[8] Congressman Arthur Winstead (D-MS) introduced legislation that strictly limited the demobilization proceedings for CPS. Winstead felt that it was "unfair" for COs to receive a wife credit and points for children beyond the three received by those in the army. In the army, the maximum number of children for which a soldier could receive points was three, while there was no limit on children for men in CPS. As an alternative, Winstead offered a bill that created a point system for CPS *exactly* like the army's. However, under Winstead's plan, no assignee would have qualified for a discharge from CPS based on points: the highest number of points possible was eighty-four (in most cases). A man needed eighty-five points to be discharged. Winstead pointed to armed service morale as one of his major reasons for introducing the bill. He stated, "If the Selective

Service follows this plan, it will be one of the most demoralizing blows to this country and to the men in service we have had during the entire war. If the conscientious objectors are conscientious, they will not want advantages over the fighting man."[9]

Privately, Winstead expressed a more tolerant viewpoint, but his words rang hollow with Kosch and French. Winstead told French in a personal conversation that he did not wish to end demobilization completely, but Kosch thought Winstead's motivations were more nefarious than he let on. Later, French came to agree with Kosch, believing Winstead had lied to his face. In order to keep demobilization going at an acceptable rate and avoid any impediments, Kosch was willing to drop the wife credit and limit the children for points to three, thereby mirroring the plan for the army, something Hershey clearly would have supported if only for avoiding more negative reactions.[10] It was quickly becoming clear that Hershey needed to compromise if he wanted to send COs home in a timely fashion.

Winstead eventually became even more restrictive, calling for complete removal of the point system for CPS. In an informal hearing before the House Committee on Military Affairs on July 9, the committee rejected Hershey and the Selective Service's plan for the end of Civilian Public Service and instead backed Winstead's proposal. Responding to the charge that the Selective Service's plan was much too lenient, Kosch argued that the points system might seem more liberal than that of the armed services until one considered that the CPS men received no dependents' benefits. Hershey's legislative liaison Frank Keesling maintained that CPS was a form of government or national service, comparable to serving in the military, and implored the committee to consider the CO in government service as having status similar to that of a soldier. However, it was all to no avail. Only July 11, the committee approved Winstead's plan, but at the behest of Congressman John Sparkman, one of the few legislators on whom the Peace Churches could count for support, it agreed to allow for hardship cases to be discharged. In its report, the committee described its motivation: "It is the opinion of the committee that conscientious objectors performing assigned civilian work should not be permitted release to resume normal life while the armed forces are still engaged in combat with the enemy and members of such forces are denied release. To provide for release of such conscientious objectors under the point system would adversely affect morale in the armed forces."[11] That did not prove to be the final word in the demobilization of Civilian Public Service, as the bill never came up for a vote in the House. However, the possibility it would pass provided a significant roadblock for Hershey for some time. With that hanging over their heads, Hershey, the Selective Service, and the Peace Churches sought ways to discharge conscientious objectors in a systematic fashion.

With the dropping of the atomic bombs on Hiroshima and Nagasaki on August 6 and 9, respectively, it appeared as though the war with Japan would be over soon. This fact was not lost on Hershey, as he appeared to be in an excellent mood during an August 8 meeting with Kosch and representatives of the Peace Churches. French claimed it was "one of the most friendly meetings we have had with the General in a year or two."[12] By the end of August, with Winstead's bill languishing in the legislative process, Hershey and Kosch decided it was in their best interests to implement their own plans for demobilization if the House of Representatives did not act on the bill by October 1. They had stopped pressing for the point system on July 19, waiting to see what Congress was going to do, but they held out hope they could still implement such a system. Hershey and Kosch hoped to have a representative at the American Legion convention in September to soothe some of the resistance to the Selective Service's CPS discharge policy and prevent the passing of a resolution denouncing the demobilization plans for CPS.[13] This is further evidence of Hershey's desire to have public opinion reflect positively on the provisions for conscientious objection and to have all matters remain within the walls of national headquarters. Hershey definitely did not like outsiders telling him how to manage the responsibilities placed on him. Though he became frustrated with certain issues at times, he believed, and rightly so, that he alone held the power to decide exactly how CPS should end and how the men should be discharged from their national service.

Hershey's desire for the Selective Service to maintain its autonomy also manifested itself in his correspondence with the War Department, yet another entity that pressured Hershey on the CPS demobilization issue. Early on, Hershey had made a mistake by not consulting the White House on his plans to end the CPS, and that led to some of the problems. In June, Undersecretary of War Robert Patterson informed Hershey that he was not happy about Hershey's plans to demobilize quickly based on a point system. Patterson told Hershey that he understood COs were outside of the War Department's jurisdiction, but he was concerned about the effect on morale in the armed forces "if men who refuse to fight are relieved prior to the relief of men who do the actual fighting." Patterson concluded, "From the viewpoint of the War Department it would appear that an individual who has been classified as a conscientious objector and assigned to a civilian public service camp for work of national importance should not be released until the major demobilization is completed after the defeat of Japan."[14]

Hershey made it clear to Patterson that as the director of Selective Service he was the chief administrator of Civilian Public Service. He wanted to demobilize CPS as quickly as possible because the men in the camps received no benefits, yet many expected COs to remain in the camps for the same amount of time as the men in the armed forces. He argued that his system favored men with dependents to a greater degree than those in the army because there were no benefits for dependents in CPS. Even so, Hershey was aware of the possibility of negative morale consequences if men in CPS went home more quickly and in greater percentages than did those in the military overseas. He told Patterson, as he had told many others before, that the discontent from certain quarters, mainly veterans groups, seemed to be more with the laws established in 1940 than with the present Selective Service administration of CPS. Hershey said that if Congress thought the Selective Service was violating the original intent of the law, then he was willing to change his approach. He firmly supported his stance and the work performed by the COs. He wrote, "Inasmuch as these men have complied with the law and performed the duty required of them, I can see no reason why they should be discriminated against. It would appear just as logical for the Navy to complain that the discharge of men from the Army was detrimental to their morale at this time."[15] However, the War Department disagreed, and Patterson told Hershey that they wanted him to wait until Congress took final action on the Winstead Bill.[16]

Hershey formulated another line of argument beyond the "congressional will" justification. He intended to argue to the Budget Bureau that continuing CPS and keeping men in the camps for a prolonged period was a waste of taxpayer money. Hershey understood the effectiveness of financial arguments with an agency that was fiscal in nature. When the war officially ended with Japan's surrender in September 1945, Hershey still held on to his treasured point system for CPS (though he and Kosch suspended public advocacy of it), hoping to make the CO discharges as equitable as possible as compared to those in the military. He and Kosch also suggested that CPS needed to end in three months. To facilitate this, Hershey met with a subcommittee of the House Committee on Military Affairs consisting of Sparkman, Paul Kilday (D-TX), Andrew May (D-KY), Dewey Short (R-MO), and Leslie Arends (R-IL). French believed that these particular committee members wanted to see CPS demobilize as quickly and painlessly as possible.[17]

After the meeting with the members of the House, Hershey was ready for demobilization to commence but without one of his favored elements: there was to be no point system. The subcommittee members told Hershey that if the Selective Service instituted a point system, the Winstead Bill would be revived. The reasoning for this was the ever-present worry about public opinion. It concerned everyone on the subcommittee as well as Hershey and Kosch. The representatives supported Hershey's plan, but they ordered that the Selective Service should in no way call it a point system and stated that they were not willing to go on record as supporting the plan. Public opinion and its potential affect on their reelection apparently trumped their concern for conscientious objectors. Even Winstead had no vested concern about conscientious objection. During a September 12 meeting, Kosch informed French "that Congressman Winstead told him that he had little personal interest in the bill he had proposed, but that he had introduced it at the request of veterans groups and would push it if the veterans demanded such action." Hershey and Kosch concluded that a rational approach to the situation would not work, and they needed to get men out of CPS as quickly as they could. They believed that a no-win situation was on the horizon with public opinion, especially with the veterans groups.[18] That meant dropping the point system entirely and discharging the oldest men in CPS quickly.

At a meeting on September 21, Kilday and Winstead agreed to allow CPS demobilization, and Winstead agreed to withdraw his bill. By mid-October, NSBRO thought the ending of CPS was proceeding smoothly. The plan for discharging CPS assignees was "on a basis of age, length of service, dependency, and hardship;" however, as had been made clear in previous meetings with congressmen, there was no point system. French wanted to get 3,500 to 4,000 men out of CPS by the end of 1945. Kilday and Winstead had no objection to those numbers, but Kosch doubted the administrative apparatus was up to the task. Soon after the meeting, Kosch and French agreed on a goal of 2,500 to 3,000 men out by the end of the year and assignees with more than two years of CPS service out by May 15, 1946.[19]

Hershey and Kosch also attempted to placate veterans groups, particularly the Veterans of Foreign Wars. The VFW agreed to stop pressuring Congress on CPS demobilization in mid-September. Hershey decided to attend the VFW convention in early October to put forth the position of the Selective Service and, hopefully, to mollify the more obstinate chapters.[20] However, over the next few days, Hershey began to change his mind concerning CPS demobilization. He informed Kosch that he wanted discharges to wait until the beginning of 1946, allowing the various veterans groups' conventions to occur first. Beforehand he intended to release only over the age of thirty-eight. Hershey's decision bitterly disappointed French.[21] French had worked hard to achieve timely discharges for the men in CPS, but he also knew the overwhelming power of Hershey in the Selective Service. If Hershey said no, then that was the end of the discussion.

Hershey's abrupt change of heart is somewhat puzzling. Throughout the summer of 1945, he supported the efforts to demobilize CPS and discharge the assignees. Recall, though, that Hershey was always conscious of public opinion and the sometimes tenuous regard Congress held toward conscientious objection. Hershey sensed that it was best to wait until after the national VFW convention and allow some of the most vicious attacks on conscientious objection to die down.

French traveled to the VFW convention in Chicago to convince Hershey to change his mind. Hershey demurred, saying the VFW lobby simply had too much pull in Congress and that pressing for immediate demobilization while military personnel were still overseas risked making matters even worse for COs. French reminded Hershey that some of the men in the camps believed that they were being singled out and refused equal treatment because they had taken an unpopular stance during the war. Hershey sincerely sympathized with them and wanted to see them discharged in a timely fashion, but he held firm, believing that waiting until early 1946 was the best way to avoid a public relations or legislative problem. French continued to press Hershey on this issue, and Hershey listened, but he refused to relent. He even cited the American Legion's national convention in November as a further reason to avoid large-scale CPS discharges in 1945.[22]

This was simply not acceptable to the representatives of the Peace Churches. On October 10, French and Paul Furnas, now the director of Friends CPS; Albert Gaeddert, director of Mennonite CPS; and Harold Row, director of Brethren CPS, met with Hershey and Kosch to voice their displeasure. They called for more immediate demobilization of Civilian Public Service, saying that it "should continue on a systematic basis," regardless of the position of the veterans groups. Unlike Hershey, they did not give credence to the reaction of the veterans groups. Hershey reaffirmed his stance, again citing public opinion. After three hours of deliberation with the Peace Church contingent, he was more receptive to a limited demobilization in 1945. He believed that by November 30 he could discharge men over thirty-eight and those over thirty-five with two or more years of service. He thought that men with four years of CPS service could be out by December 30 and that proceedings for the discharge of men with three years of service could begin on January 1, 1946, and finish May 30. The next day, though, he made it clear that while their agreement stood, he was not going to issue a public declaration or a formal decree, because he still felt that it could cause a negative public reaction.[23]

At this time, Hershey believed that much of the discontent toward him and his organization over the demobilization of CPS would soon pass now that the fighting in the Pacific theater was over. He expressed that view often in his official correspondence, particularly with senators and representatives. As the opposition died down, Hershey believed that it would become much easier to release men from their alternative service.[24] He also believed that his new plan would not rouse the public's ire. However, remaining cautious, he did not announce the CPS demobilization plan publicly until February 1946.[25]

Hershey and Kosch were still concerned with public opinion, though, from the end of 1945 into early 1946. In early 1946, Kosch publicly responded to an editorial in the *Washington Daily News* that actually supported the COs. Now Hershey and Kosch faced criticism on both sides of the equation. The editorial criticized the Selective Service for its slowness in discharging men from CPS. Kosch wrote, "Inasmuch as conscientious objectors did not start their program until approximately six months later than the armed forces, it is felt that in fairness to everybody concerned their demobilization should fall somewhat behind that of the armed forces."[26]

During the latter part of 1945 and into early 1946, Hershey also dealt with the end of the draft itself. Because Hershey's primary role was to administer the draft through the Selective Service, the possibilities of ending the draft commanded much of his attention. Hershey saw conscription in the United States after the war as a means of ensuring global security, but the armed forces disagreed with his emphasis on an army of draftees. Congress, too, wanted to end the draft. But President Truman wanted to replace the draft with Universal Military Training. Under his plan, all eligible men would receive military training for six months instead of military service for a specified duration, though his plan did not come to pass. From the military came the argument that while the draft was not the ultimate answer, the army of occupation required conscripts to fill its ranks. Then, in early 1946 manpower problems emerged.

Low draft calls coupled with a low volunteer rate meant that demobilization became more deliberate. Hershey, along with others such as General Dwight Eisenhower, Robert Patterson, and Secretary of State James Byrnes, called for the draft to be lengthened. Furthering the intensity of the argument was the emerging tension with the Soviet Union over foreign policy and fears of Soviet aggression in Eastern and Central Europe. As a result, in June 1946, Congress extended the draft to March 31, 1947.[27]

By the spring of 1946, CPS demobilization was still crawling along too slowly for the taste of the Peace Church representatives. Though a plan was in place, they believed that not enough men were leaving the camps. On March 4, Hershey and Kosch met with French, Furnas, M. R. Zigler of the Brethren, and Orie Miller of the Mennonites. The Peace Church contingent expressed its desire for a faster rate of release. Kosch responded that over 50 percent of the men in CPS had been sent home, which was actually a higher rate than that of the army. Hershey told the men that plans were for all men with eighteen months of service to be discharged by October and after that, eighteen months' service would automatically merit release from CPS.[28]

The answers offered by Hershey and Kosch apparently were not good enough for Paul Furnas. Shortly after his meeting with Hershey and Kosch, Furnas brought the issue of demobilization to Truman in a letter in which Furnas claimed that CPS men were not being discharged at a rate comparable to that of the men serving in the armed forces. Furnas wrote, "In conversation with General Hershey, he has not denied the soundness of a policy of discharging men when the need for the man on an emergency basis has passed. However, he is not discharging men on that principle and he concedes that he is largely influenced by the attitude of some veterans' organizations toward men classified IV-E."[29] Hershey clearly took issue with the claims made by Furnas. In a requested reply to Truman's military aide Brigadier General Harry H. Vaughan, Hershey cited resolutions adopted by the VFW, which called for no CPS man to be discharged before all servicemen returned home, and the American Legion, which asked the Selective Service to discharge CPS men in a way that "no group of them is released before a like group from the armed forces and that under no circumstances will the rate of discharge exceed that from the military forces." Hershey's reaction was stern. He claimed that if the Selective Service had truly followed the dictates of the VFW, then "no conscientious objector would yet have been discharged." He also explained that the less harsh wording of the American Legion's resolution was a result of the Selective Service's careful explanation of the draft law and headquarters' policy concerning conscientious objectors.

He declared, "This is proof that veterans groups pressure has not dictated our program of release."[30]

For Hershey to say that the pressures from the VFW and the American Legion did not influence him is, at the very least, somewhat hyperbolic. Negative publicity concerning alternative service and conscientious objectors concerned him greatly and evidence reveals that Hershey sought to mollify the veterans groups without directly adopting their suggestions. Therefore, the reactions from those groups *did* affect his outlook. However, what is also clear is that during the spring of 1946, CPS demobilization was a contentious issue, and Hershey found himself in a position where it was going to be extraordinarily difficult to please everybody.

By the end of January 1946, the Selective Service had demobilized about 45 percent of the men in CPS, compared to about 61 percent of men in the military. Although the Peace Churches might have been unhappy with the rate of discharge for CPS, the Selective Service sent men home at a fairly steady rate from late 1945 until early 1947. To be fair, the steadiness of the rate was less an issue than the quantity of men being sent home. Though the Selective Service continuously sent men home throughout 1946, the last man did not leave CPS until the end of March 1947, the same time the Selective Training and Service Act of 1940 expired.[31]

All told, about twelve thousand men performed their national service in an alternative fashion by serving in CPS. This was out of the seventy to seventy-five thousand men who initially claimed to be conscientious objectors. An estimated twenty-five thousand men served as noncombatants in the military; fourteen thousand were reclassified after first receiving a I-A-O or IV-E classification; the Justice Department convicted sixteen hundred for failure to report; and roughly twenty thousand men who claimed CO status never received that classification from their local draft boards.[32]

During World War II, the United States had 34.5 million men register for the draft. The fifty-two thousand men who received either the I-A-O or IV-E classification made up about .15 percent of the total draft population. The largest percentage of COs came from the states of Kansas, Indiana, and Washington. Not surprisingly, the largest denominational representation in the CPS camps came from the Mennonites (4,610 men), the Brethren (1,468), and the Society of Friends (902). However, the Methodists (845) and the Jehovah's Witnesses (532) also had a strong representation compared to other denominations in CPS.[33]

Though Hershey was an immensely powerful person within his own bureaucratic institution, he was not above the political process, and he was not able to inflict his will wantonly on any organization or group he chose. Hershey was adept at the political game, as evidenced by his dealings with Congress throughout the war and during the negotiations for demobilizing Civilian Public Service. Were it not for Hershey's efforts in discharging CPS assignees, Congress or the War Department might have required COs to remain in camps even longer. Granted, the men remained in camps for longer than the Historic Peace Churches wished, but Hershey walked a fine line throughout 1945 and 1946. Trying to make two opposing groups happy was a thankless task, but it was one that Hershey performed adeptly. He put forth the best plan possible given the situation. He needed to prevent Congress or the veterans groups from becoming too agitated while maintaining some form of demobilization that was fair to conscientious objectors. While his solution may not have been the result for which COs had hoped, the likelihood of any person doing better than Hershey was low. Indeed, this was yet another example of how Hershey shaped alternative service and in many ways protected COs from entities that did not have their best interests at heart.

Chapter 9

★ ★ ★ ★

Hershey and the Legacy of Alternative Service

As CPS demobilized, Hershey began to muse on the successes and failures of the alternative service program. In the final days of CPS, Hershey and Kosch discussed with the Peace Churches what they believed had worked and what should be changed in the future. Many people involved in those evaluations concluded that had someone other than Hershey been in charge of conscientious objectors during World War II, the tale of COs probably would have been much different and perhaps even tragic. However, not everyone took a celebratory view of Hershey's role. Throughout Hershey's term as director, the concept of alternative service for conscientious objectors remained intact, though there was a brief period of deferment for COs during the early years of the Cold War. There were changes, such as when the Supreme Court fundamentally altered what defined a conscientious objector in the case *United States v. Seeger* (1965), but alternative service remained firmly entrenched. By firmly outlining the service duty of *all* eligible men, Hershey's administration of conscientious objection during World War II established the principle that even if a man objected to military service, his national obligations must be fulfilled. That tenet remained firmly in place until President Richard Nixon removed Hershey as director in 1970.

After a long and sometimes tenuous six years of CPS, Selective Service Director of Camp Operations Lewis Kosch pondered the question of the best alternative service policy for the future. Kosch felt that the church administration made things entirely too difficult. He and Hershey wanted the COs to work directly for the government rather than the Peace Church service agencies. They both believed that COs should receive pay, dependency benefits, and workmen's compensation. Furthermore, alternative service should not be seen as inferior to service in the armed forces. In their eyes, the government should sponsor a civil service program equal to the armed services but less confusing and convoluted than the numerous administrative groups and projects sponsored by various government agencies.[1]

About the same time as Kosch met with French in July 1946, Philip Jacob and Mulford Sibley, interviewed Hershey for their book, *Conscription of Conscience,* which would become the standard history of conscientious objection during World War II. In the interview, Hershey echoed some of Kosch's views, but Hershey had more to say on other topics as well. Hershey believed that COs should be paid and the funds should come from the government, though a CO receiving higher pay than an army private could cause a public relations problem. He also believed that the most efficient way to ensure CO compensation was probably a government-controlled camp system rather than the cumbersome dual administrative roles of CPS. However, he also supported "private agencies and individuals" developing and supporting CO programs without pay, if men chose to work in those endeavors. Hershey also commented "in vigorous language" that he supported dependency and compensation payments to CPS assignees, reaffirming the position he had put forth to Congress.[2] However, Hershey eventually changed his mind about the camps. For the remaining years of conscription in the United States, the Selective Service did not use work camps as a means of alternative service. It did, however, retain control over conscientious objectors.

In his evaluation of CPS and the Selective Service's handling of conscientious objectors, Hershey was cognizant of his own responsibility for both CPS and the assignees. He noted that President Roosevelt's executive order had placed the responsibility for the conscientious objector on him. Although he delegated some of his authority to men like Lewis Kosch, any problems that emerged landed on Hershey's desk no matter the circumstances, and his was the final decision. He was grateful to the Peace Churches for their help in developing CPS because he believed that they knew better than anybody else the nature of the objectors.[3]

Hershey was the federal government's authority on conscientious objection and became the architect of alternative service. Though he had to compromise at times and delegate his authority, his voice rang above all others on the matter, whether in public or behind closed doors.

Hershey also evaluated the role of the Peace Churches in administering CPS. He had glowing remarks for the Mennonites. He believed that they had the best and smoothest administrative system because the local Mennonite ministers and fathers provided an authoritarian tradition; he put the Brethren in the middle, and he felt the Friends caused considerable trouble. As Sibley and Jacob relate, "Hershey said the Friends believed no one should give orders to anyone else."[4] Recall that most of the discipline problems in the camps came from those operated by the AFSC. Furthermore, the AFSC was frequently at odds with Hershey and the Selective Service over the administration and direction of CPS. There appeared to be no love lost between the AFSC and Hershey.

Hershey was willing to admit that CPS definitely had its problems and failed at some of its objectives. He said that the introduction of the government-run camps was a result of those failures. Hershey claimed that there were three reasons for men to be assigned to government camps: "they were *persona non grata* in church camps," they "didn't want to be on church charity," or they "did not want to be subjected to religious rites—to be 'prayed over' at meals, as [Hershey] put it."[5] Therefore, in Hershey's mind, the government camps existed to solve some of the problems in CPS by providing a place for the recalcitrant COs, some of whom likely did not fit the "religious training and belief" definition of the Selective Service Act.

Hershey and his staff were constantly concerned about public opinion. They made sure to select projects and locate camps in areas where they believed there would be less resistance to conscientious objectors. They put few camps in the South and none in Oklahoma, where, according to Sibley and Jacob, "greater intolerance was expressed toward c.o.'s than anywhere else in the country." Hershey maintained that though there was greater public acceptance of conscientious objectors during World War II than there had been during the First World War, people of older generations and veterans groups were still likely to harbor ill feeling toward COs. He mentioned that in confronting the veterans groups, Kosch could be particularly persuasive, appearing in his military uniform with a "Prussian" bearing (Hershey's words), and telling them "I don't like the damn thing, but it's the law."[6]

Finally, Hershey reiterated his belief in the role of local draft boards and the importance of a decentralized system of conscription. For him, true democratic government was decentralized. He believed that the draft boards, overall, had done an adequate job in the classification of COs, though there were some instances of discrimination.[7] Hershey's belief in the importance of the draft board was central to his concept of conscription in the United States. Conscientious objection was also handled in a decentralized fashion, true to Hershey's wishes. For example, in a 1955 interview, Hershey, speaking specifically about the Jehovah's Witnesses, decried national centralized definitions of classification as denying certain Americans the freedom of worship. He said, "If we decide in Washington that a certain man is not a minister of the Gospel, when he says he is, then we are denying to a segment of the population the right to worship as they choose." Using some of his trademark humor, he observed, "Jesus himself couldn't have gotten deferment as a minister under some standards. He was engaged in secular employment—he was a carpenter." Finally, he brought his comments full circle when he said, "I know many persons have taken advantage of this loophole, but I'm willing to get away with it in order to protect freedom of worship in America. You can't have conformity and liberty at the same time."[8] Where Hershey drew the line was the insincere objector.

Although there were other men involved in the creation of alternative service during World War II, none were more instrumental than General Lewis B. Hershey. This was not lost on those who clamored for greater recognition for conscientious objection. Without delving too deeply into a dangerous game of counterfactual history, a military man other than Hershey in charge of the draft and conscientious objectors made possible a nightmare scenario similar to that of World War I. Numerous men who worked for the benefit of conscientious objectors said as much during or after World War II. One example was the executive secretary of NSBRO, Paul French. Though their relationship was strained at times, particularly during the latter years of the war, Hershey and French felt mutual respect. French spoke quite highly of Hershey, noting many times that Hershey was a "big man," above petty bureaucratic squabbles and biases, concerned with what was best for the conscientious objector.[9] Likewise, Joseph Weaver, a Mennonite NSBRO staff member, commented that without Hershey, "we would have never gone through the war as intact as we were as a peace organization."[10] Weaver's statement illustrates that Hershey's efforts created an atmosphere that allowed for the Historic Peace Churches to maintain their peace witness while still serving their nation, per Hershey's concept of conscientious objection and alternative service.

The best evaluation of Hershey's importance to conscientious objection came from M. R. Zigler, a major leader in the Church of the Brethren throughout the twentieth century. Zigler's efforts in peacemaking garnered him much attention both in the Church of the Brethren and in other Protestant denominations. Though French had more frequent contact with Hershey throughout the war, Zigler was the chief executive of NSBRO and developed both a personal and a professional relationship with Hershey. Over the years, Hershey and Zigler became good friends. At Zigler's behest, Hershey attended the Church of the Brethren Annual Conference in 1944 and Zigler's On Earth Peace meeting in 1974. Hershey viewed Zigler with "respect" and "affection." In an interview not published until 1996 (many years after the deaths of Hershey and Zigler), Zigler said that Hershey was "very sympathetic" to the COs and stated,

> My own judgment, he's [Hershey] a good man. Very good man. He had been a head of Boy Scouts along with his military, which explains some things to me, and I feel personally that Mr. Hershey had a religious background, even though he didn't belong to any church, at least he claimed he didn't. He always said he was never washed [baptized]. But on the question of religious liberty he was very strong. And I would say that perhaps he was the finest exponent of religious liberty that I've ever met, and certainly the best as far as any officials in American government are concerned. He had a deep respect for opposition and even wished that that could be the position of everybody. I mean, he didn't like war.[11]

Zigler had a long and storied career within the Church of Brethren and had the opportunity to meet thousands of people and develop a sense of their stance toward religious liberty. To call Hershey "the finest exponent of religious liberty I've ever met" bordered on hyperbole, but the statement was grounded in truth. Zigler's remarks reflect his deep appreciation for Hershey and the rare traits Hershey possessed, something many members of the Historic Peace Churches often found lacking in the American government. Zigler, in the same interview, also pointed out just how important Hershey was in steering conscientious objection in a new direction during World War II, not only shaping a working relationship between the churches and the federal government, but also establishing alternative service as the means of providing for conscientious objection. When asked whether the Peace Churches' relationship with the government "worked fairly well," Zigler responded, "Yes, but if we had a different man than General Hershey, ... I don't know what might have happened. I think that ought to be said."[12]

However, not everyone celebrated Hershey as a great promoter of tolerance within the government and the military establishment. A. J. Muste, executive secretary of the Fellowship of Reconciliation (FOR) and a major figure in twentieth-century American pacifism, defended CPS as a means to provide a pacifist witness in the face of war and conscription, but as the war evolved, he expressed his discontent at many of the dynamics that emerged. He claimed that working without pay made CPS a form of involuntary servitude. He was also wary of the Peace Churches' complicity in conscription as they worked closely with the Selective Service. By 1943, Muste no longer believed that FOR should be a part of NSBRO (it was a partner and helped to support NSBRO financially). He believed, as did members of the War Resisters League, that CPS was overly militarized and did not reflect pacifist values to their fullest extent or provide meaningful work. Muste wavered somewhat on his stance concerning the withdrawal from NSBRO, but in 1944, FOR's membership voted to end the organization's role as a voting member of NSBRO yet remain as a consulting pacifist body.[13] While Muste did not express his ire directly at Hershey, he clearly did not support conscription and should not be counted as a supporter of Hershey's actions during World War II.

As evidenced by some of the aforementioned walkouts, strikes and slowdowns, and general distaste for CPS from some of the assignees, the IV-E draftees by no means universally revered Hershey, either. This is particularly true of the radical pacifists and members of the War Resisters League. The WRL could never be counted as a supporter of CPS or Hershey, and it denounced the compromise between the Historic Peace Churches and the Selective Service in creating the program. As the war continued, the anger in the WRL over CPS and the entire arrangement only intensified. Much like Muste, they pointed to the militarized control of the camps, the lack of pay, and the seemingly unimportant nature of many of the work details. Evan Thomas and Frank Olmstead, WRL chairmen during World War II, were both critical of CPS by the war's end. Thomas had been against CPS from the beginning, and Olmstead came to denounce the program at its end. Neither supported the relationship between the churches and Hershey's Selective Service.[14]

No one was more sharply critical of Hershey and Civilian Public Service than sociologist Gordon Zahn, a Catholic conscientious objector during the war. Zahn believed that conscientious objection was a right not a privilege. He was particularly critical of Hershey's and the Selective Service's policies and actions toward COs during World War II. He stated that Hershey was wrong to seclude COs in remote camp locations. Most of his criticisms about CPS were about perceived inequities in the program. If Hershey had been truly concerned about the equality of sacrifice between COs and servicemen, there would have been pay and benefits for COs just as there were for soldiers. He also believed that "Men were routinely inducted into Civilian Public Service who never would have been accepted by the military."[15]

Zahn was also critical of Hershey's ability to compromise in difficult situations and protect COs and alternative service from opponents. He wrote,

> To give him his due, General Hershey did try to protect CPS from the more vindictive attacks and demands of Congressmen, veterans organizations, jingo-journalists, and the like. The protection, however, took the form of cushioning and compromising—in almost every case at the expense of those he was protecting. Indeed, there are perfectly good sociological reasons to assume that he and the officials around him shared the general disapproval of conscientious objectors. Given the circumstances, it is likely that concern for bureaucratic convenience and defence of "turf" may offer a better explanation for those efforts to forestall adverse public reaction than concern for the men themselves or respect for their rights.[16]

Zahn clearly objected to both the fundamental concept of CPS and Hershey's methods of incorporating alternative service. He was certainly entitled his opinion; however, Zahn's assessment that Hershey possessed a "disapproval of conscientious objectors" misses the mark entirely. Hershey may have disagreed with their stance toward military service and pacifism in general, but his actions did not reflect a disdain for COs.

As it turned out, Hershey's insights into public opinion and his desires to protect COs from negative publicity were more on target than Zahn gave him credit for. During the war, Princeton psychologist Leo Crespi undertook a study to discern the attitudes of some Princeton students toward conscientious objection. The purpose of his study was to test the 1923 findings of Clarence Case, a sociologist who argued in *Non-Violent Coercion* that there was a general, negative view of COs throughout society. Crespi administered a test to one hundred sixty-three Princeton students from sixteen to twenty-three years of age. Crespi found that rather than being overwhelmingly hostile, the students were more neutral in their attitudes. He also discovered that the students were more accepting of religious-based objection than of the secular variety. Furthermore, if an objector fulfilled his service duty, the students were more tolerant. In other words, the more work an objector did, the more he became accepted in the eyes of nonobjectors.[17] These findings reveal attitudes very much in line with Hershey's thinking.

However, Crespi did not find overwhelming sympathy for the CO. Most of the students (78 percent) were against COs proselytizing or convincing other people of their conviction. Furthermore, 83 percent approved of keeping the names of conscientious objectors out of print in newspapers "in order to protect them from intolerance."[18] This suggests that while the students at Princeton may have been tolerant, there were bound to be sectors of American society that were not. Students believed most COs were sincere in their beliefs, but that was not necessarily the view among all Americans. In the final line of his article, Crespi concluded, "[A]ttitudes towards CO's are as diverse as the individuals who hold them, and related significantly to their frames of reference."[19] All of this underscores the wisdom of Hershey's attempts to keep the COs and alternative service out of the public eye.

The fact that a number of people involved in conscientious objection appreciated Hershey's administration of alternative service (particularly from Peace Church quarters) speaks volumes about his importance. As evidenced by their actions during the interwar period, the Peace Churches wanted to avoid the poor treatment and confusing policies of World War I. There were bound to be disagreements and tensions between Hershey and the churches because they approached the matter from two separate viewpoints, but many of those involved understood the difficulties Hershey faced, and they appreciated his efforts. Hershey's cooperation with the Peace Churches was significant not just because it helped to shape conscientious objection, but also because many of the leaders in the Historic Peace Churches found this high-ranking army officer to be a person whom they could respect and with whom they could work, something unseen in the years prior to World War II.

CPS formally ended in 1947. Though this "experiment in democracy" did not last beyond the World War II-era draft, the fundamental concept behind it, alternative service, remained firmly entrenched.

The initial concern of the Historic Peace Churches in the postwar era was President Harry Truman's call for universal military training (UMT) rather than conscription and military service. Truman's plan did not ultimately pass; but an escalation of tension between the United States and the Soviet Union led to the reinstatement of the draft in 1948. The Selective Service Act of 1948 was quite similar to that of 1940 concerning conscientious objectors, but with explicit language that only religious objectors qualified for CO classification and civilian service. The impetus behind this was to avoid the ambiguities about political, ethical, and moral objectors that had bedeviled Hershey during World War II.[20]

The provisions for conscientious objection, found in section 6 (j) of the 1948 Act, were much more explicit than they had been in the previous acts: "Nothing contained in this title shall be construed to require any person to be subject to combatant training and service in the armed forces of the United States who, by reason of religious training and belief, is conscientiously opposed to participation in war in any form. Religious training and belief in this connection means an individual's belief in a relation to a Supreme Being involving duties superior to those arising from any human relation, but does not include essentially political, sociological, or philosophical views or a merely personal moral code."[21]

Whereas the Selective Service Act of 1917 limited conscientious objection to members of the Historic Peace Churches, and the Selective Service Act of 1940 was ambiguous in what constituted "religious training and belief," the 1948 version was much clearer on these points.

During the earliest years of the Cold War, conscientious objectors found themselves in a situation different from that of 1940–1947. Rather than requiring induction and alternative service, the 1948 Act granted a deferment to any CO who did not accept noncombatant military service.[22] Deferments did not last long, though. Part of the reason for the total deferment was that Hershey did not want to be directly responsible for administering a program of alternative service for COs. Because the United States was not at war, people were more tolerant of complete deferments. That point of view eventually changed. The 1948 draft law was to last for five years, but an amendment cut the length of the draft to two years. President Truman and Congress then extended the draft only a matter of days after the invasion of South Korea by North Korean forces, with the intent of conscription lasting for one year. For a time, deferment continued for conscientious objectors, but the higher number of draft calls and increasing casualty lists incited criticism of officials over the perceived lack of sacrifice by conscientious objectors. Ray Wilson, a Quaker in the Friends Committee on National Legislation, believed that Hershey did not want to reinstitute CPS because of the difficulties incurred during World War II, but Wilson envisaged the return of the program due to the new war. The wording of the new draft legislation in 1951 called for COs to engage in "work of national importance," just as they had during World War II.[23] The total deferment of COs ended, and some form of national service was once again required of all drafted men.

Although Congress determined that alternative service should return to the United States, there was no consensus on what form that service was going to take. What did seem clear was that work camps were not ideal, and very few supported a model of service based on CPS. Furthermore, nobody else in the federal government wanted to handle conscientious objectors and alternative service, so the task once again fell to Selective Service.

The Selective Service began by instituting new classifications for the CO. The Selective Service replaced the old IV-E classification with two new classifications: I-O, which meant the CO was "available for civilian work," and I-W, which meant the CO was "performing civilian work." With an executive order on February 20, 1952, President Truman officially sanctioned the Selective Service's new alternative service program. Unlike CPS, there was no work camp structure, but the concept of service remained the same. The Peace Churches avoided the cumbersome administrative responsibility they had assumed during World War II, and the government lifted some old restrictions on the type of work, such as overseas assignments.[24]

The men were freer to choose the service they performed. Once classified, the individual CO proposed three possible means of fulfilling his service obligation from which the Selective Service accepted one. Men could serve in either paid or volunteer jobs administered by the government or nonprofit entities. They held jobs in health, education, science, and charity, though they could not work in their local areas. Furthermore, men could volunteer for alternative service before being drafted. Specifically, some men worked stateside on farms, while others labored overseas in relief efforts, agriculture, or construction. Some served as test subjects for the National Institute of Health in Bethesda, Maryland, recalling images of the Guinea Pig Units from World War II. However, most of the men worked in hospitals. In the words of Keim and Stolzfus, "I-W became nearly synonymous with hospital work, since so many conscientious objectors engaged in such jobs. By 1954, more than 80 percent of all I-Ws held hospital jobs."[25]

The I-W program marked a considerable improvement over the CPS model of World War II for COs, Hershey, and the Selective Service. COs could now receive pay, something for which they had been clamoring since 1940. As he stated during the final days of CPS, Hershey desired pay for COs as well. COs also had a more meaningful form of service, and the cumbersome dual-administrative structure, with its ambiguities and tensions, was gone. Furthermore, the men had a set limit for the duration of their service, much like their military counterparts. They did not serve for the entirety of the war, as they had during World War II, but for two years, as did the military servicemen.

The I-W program was by no means perfect, however. Congress did not provide the funding requested by the Selective Service, so much of the money had to come from elsewhere in the Selective Service's budget. Finding jobs for the COs was still difficult, and COs still received no benefits for dependents, despite Hershey's support for this measure.

Furthermore, the Peace Churches remained uneasy about the control of the Selective Service over the individual CO, despite changes in the relationship. This caused the AFSC to remain out of the I-W program, while the Mennonites and the Brethren conceded overall control to the Selective Service. This was definitely the desire of General Hershey, as he informed the Peace Churches in no uncertain terms that this time the Selective Service had the ultimate authority over placement, transfers, and the like. If the Peace Churches helped coordinate activities and service opportunities, that was fine, but they were completely subordinate to the Selective Service. Hershey was perfectly clear on that point.[26]

The Vietnam era saw a seismic shift in the classification of conscientious objectors, but as it had during the Korean conflict, the concept of alternative service remained based on the precedents set by Hershey during World War II. In fact, the specific alternative service plans refined in 1951 remained in place throughout the remaining years of conscription in the United States. What changed during Vietnam was the definition of a conscientious objector. This momentous shift came from *United States v. Seeger* in 1965, which established the right of individuals to claim moral or ethical reasons for conscientiously objecting to military service, a distinct shift from the overtly religious definitions of conscientious objection required earlier. Five years later, the Supreme Court upheld the *Seeger* decision in *Welsh v. United States,* stating that an established belief in atheism or "characterization of his beliefs as 'nonreligious'" was permissible, as long as the person's objection to war was still "moral, ethical, or philosophical."[27]

United States v. Seeger was the most important Supreme Court case in the history of conscientious objection because it fundamentally changed the basic requirements for a man to be a conscientious objector. *United States v. Seeger* was actually one of three cases argued together before the Supreme Court in 1965, along with *United States v. Jakobson* and *Peter v. United States.* During the 1950s, Seeger, Jakobson, and Peter claimed CO status when called before their local draft boards. However, they did not cite traditional religious beliefs as their reason for objecting to military service. All of the men based their objections on a more secular interpretation of personal religion, invoking moral, ethical, or secular spiritual reasoning. The Selective Service Act, as passed in 1948, exempted men who objected to war based on "religious training and belief," just as in the 1940 Act. [28]

In the majority opinion, Justice Thomas Clark argued that the central issue in the arguments was the axiom "religious training and belief." The Supreme Court decided that "religious training and belief" could be extended to much broader moral and ethical connotations. In the words of Clark, "A sincere and meaningful belief which occupies in the life of its possessor a place parallel to that filled by the God of those admittedly qualifying for the exemption comes within the statutory definition."[29] In other words, an ethical or moral objection to war that stood in place of a mainstream religious belief was an acceptable basis for conscientious objection to military service. In *Welsh v. United States,* the Court upheld its 1965 *Seeger* ruling, finding in 1970 that Elliott Welsh should have his conviction for draft evasion overturned because his reasoning for objecting to military service fell under the findings of the Court in *United States v. Seeger.* The particulars of the case were similar to those in *Seeger,* and the Court found that Welsh's beliefs constituted a personal form of religion for him.[30]

Therefore, the only real change for COs after World War II (beyond the elimination of work camps and the introduction of individualized service) was the addition of secular reasoning to the established religious basis for the legal definition of conscientious objection. With the *Seeger* ruling, a man could object to war if his personal convictions constituted a form of religion for him. However, the principles of service established during World War II remained firmly in place throughout the years of conscription in the United States, and that is why Hershey's efforts during World War II in administering and shaping alternative service were so pivotal. All subsequent efforts either built upon his actions or sought to rectify some of the problems coming out of CPS.

One of Americans' most enduring memories of the Vietnam War era was the antiwar movement and its large national and local protests. Hershey was not immune to the unrest on the home front. As the war in Vietnam became more unpopular and protests grew, Hershey became a focal point. The protestors pointed to him as a key figure of the establishment responsible for sending young men to die in Vietnam.[31] By the late 1960s, Hershey had become a political liability, a fact not lost on Richard Nixon, the Republican nominee for president in 1968.

Nixon announced during his campaign that he wished to end the draft after achieving victory in Vietnam. He argued that it was not the proper instrument to use in a guerrilla war like the one in Vietnam. While his sincerity is debatable, Nixon certainly gained political capital by calling for the end of the draft. Once Nixon assumed office in 1969, he began the shift toward an all-volunteer force with some reforms. His advisers recommended a number of changes to quell the growing antiwar protests and alleviate some of the resentment among America's youth. Their two most visible and viable recommendations were shifting to a lottery system and replacing Hershey as the head of the Selective Service. Hershey was now seventy-five years old, and though he was still in good health, his unpopularity was costing Nixon. As George Flynn adeptly explains, "Hershey was like an embarrassing corpse in a murder mystery, which kept falling out of closets or appearing in bathtubs, to the general consternation of the host." Hershey refused calls for him to resign, saying he would respond only to a direct order from President Nixon.[32]

That order came on October 10, 1969. Nixon informed Hershey that he was going to be reassigned as a manpower adviser to the president, effective February 1970. He also recommended Hershey's promotion to a full, four-star general.[33] So ended an era in the history of American conscription. Hershey had been in charge of the Selective Service for twenty-nine years, served in six administrations, and provided the manpower management for three major wars.[34]

Hershey's new job in the Nixon White House was largely ceremonial, though he tried his best to convince Nixon to preserve the decentralized draft system built over the past three decades. When Nixon's advisers recommended an all-volunteer force in 1970, Nixon wholeheartedly agreed. Hershey tried to persuade him to wait until 1971 for any major changes because that was the year the draft was up for renewal. The draft did not end as quickly as Nixon wanted, as Congress extended it for two more years. Inductions, and the era of conscription, finally ended in 1973.[35] This also meant the end of conscientious objection and alternative service under the auspices of a draft.

With the draft gone and Hershey's health beginning to decline, Nixon terminated Hershey's position. No longer fit for duty because of his age and health, his expertise in manpower seemingly obsolete, Hershey retired as a four-star general on April 10, 1973, the highest-ranking officer in American military history to have never directly participated in combat. Hershey spent his retirement caring for his wife, Ellen, whose own health was poor. In February 1977, Hershey suffered a stroke. He recovered, but the stress of this episode contributed to Ellen's death in April. On May 19, on a trip home to Angola with his son Gilbert alongside, Hershey died in a hotel room near his boyhood homestead, where the many hours of farm labor and the values of the Midwest had helped to shape his entire outlook on life and national service. He was buried next to Ellen in Arlington National Cemetery under a rather large headstone.[36]

Hershey, one of the most important American general officers of the twentieth century, is often overlooked because of his unusual dual role as army general and civilian bureaucrat. Furthermore, he was not a field general in a society that celebrates its battlefield leaders as heroes. In his role as director of the Selective Service through three major wars of conscription, Hershey was responsible for providing troops for better-known or celebrated generals such as George Marshall, Dwight Eisenhower, Douglas MacArthur, Matthew Ridgway, and William Westmoreland. Hershey affected the individual soldier's (and CO's) life far more than any other general in the twentieth century. Mentioning Hershey's name to the average American born after Vietnam elicits a questioning glance, but any American male of draft age during World War II, Korea, or Vietnam knows *exactly* who General Lewis B. Hershey was. In addition, as has been presented here, his conception and administration of conscientious objection and alternative service had far-reaching effects that further defined the citizen soldier tradition in American history. Those beliefs and actions mostly remained in place throughout the remaining years of conscription in the United States, emphasizing the duty of all eligible men to perform some sort of national service when called by the nation.

Conclusion

As an examination of General Lewis Blaine Hershey's record and the CPS experience during World War II makes clear, Hershey's personal belief in a duty of service for all eligible males, plus a tolerance for religious liberty, shaped alternative service during that conflict and beyond. Alternative service thus became the central precedent for conscientious objection to emerge from World War II, lasting until the end of the draft in 1973. Furthermore, through Hershey's efforts, the American military's citizen soldier tradition became further defined as the duty of all eligible Americans extended even to those who conscientiously objected.

Hershey's efforts in creating, administering, and justifying alternative service were the engine driving the CPS experience during World War II. By expressing his desire for a cooperative body with which to negotiate, Hershey was instrumental in the creation of NSBRO. As the final authority on what constituted "work of national importance" Hershey ultimately decided what the CPS assignees would actually do. His approval or denial shaped the character of alternative service and provided its tangible projects, as he authorized programs for farm labor, forestry work, and the Guinea Pig Units, but he rejected some urban social work and other programs suggested by the Peace Churches.[1] Through shrewd political negotiation during the war and at the end of CPS, he kept alternative service under Selective Service control. His desire to avoid negative publicity meant that many camps were located in remote locations; moreover, he sought to limit press coverage so as not to attract unwanted attention. Though CPS was a cooperative endeavor, the efforts and desires of Lewis Hershey permeated everything.

While some reacted negatively to Selective Service control, many others recognized just how important Hershey was to the peace witness of the Historic Peace Churches. Some members of the Historic Peace Churches later recounted how Hershey's directorship was of vital importance in protecting the CO during World War II. Given the inconsistent treatment of conscientious objectors throughout American history, the precedent set by Hershey and the protections he enacted were no small feat. There was no standardized policy during the colonial era, and the alternatives available during the Civil War violated many of the COs' beliefs concerning participation in war. The most glaring example of what could go wrong in providing for conscience in wartime occurred during World War I, when the federal government placed COs into military camps and imprisoned them when they refused to cooperate.

The World War II experience of Lewis Hershey in matters of conscientious objection and alternative service provides a fascinating insight into one of the great paradoxes of modern military history. Here was a man who rose to the rank of lieutenant colonel prior to the outbreak of World War II, which was no small feat in the interwar period. He was a military professional when that career path was only beginning to be accepted in American society. As one might expect of a career military professional, Hershey possessed a strongly held conviction that it was the foremost duty of all eligible men to serve their nation in times of national emergency. During World War II, he oversaw a massive bureaucracy dedicated to providing men for the military while maximizing industrial and agricultural production. Fundamentally, the role of the Selective Service was to administer the manpower of the society so the state could advance its national and international interests. Yet, in the face of that mission, Hershey was the most ardent champion of the rights of conscientious objectors within the federal government. While championing service, he also protected conscience.

That duality in Hershey's character regarding service and the CO helps to explain further who Hershey *really* was. Using broad brushstrokes to describe him usually results in an inaccurate portrayal. He viewed himself as both soldier and civilian, hence his frequent public appearances in civilian clothing. He was a classic bureaucrat, fully aware of his place in the federal government, yet he wielded significant power, and he was able to use his considerable influence to bend certain projects, mandates, or legislation to his desires. He did not merely assume the role of a bureaucrat and administer CPS with no say in its direction. He had a vision for alternative service and sought to make that a reality. He was a complex man full of seeming contradictions, yet his reasoning made those contradictions disappear. Singularly representing apparently antithetical viewpoints—the obligation to serve and the right to object—fits perfectly with an overall description of Hershey. How an individual could simultaneously believe in both is complicated, but it can be explained.

Of considerable importance in Hershey's attitude about conscientious objection was his belief in minority rights. As he said at the opening of the CPS camp at Patapsco, Maryland, in May 1940, CPS was an "experiment in democracy." The idea behind it was to protect the individual rights of a small minority in the United States and prevent their being trampled. In his mind, it was important for a democracy to tolerate dissenting viewpoints and provide for individual liberties. However, that did not exempt objectors from the duties of service. The rights of minorities when it came to national service did have limits.

Hershey's belief in the rights of sincere religious objectors was in place even before his ascendancy to the director's office. Before the establishment of the Selective Service and Roosevelt's order granting him the authority to define work of national importance, Hershey made clear his support of the rights of sincere religious objectors during the tense discussions in Congress over peacetime conscription in 1940. This stance stood in contrast to that of some of his army colleagues, who called for strict limitations for conscientious objectors. For the chief expert on manpower in the United States to advocate CO protection demonstrated an enlightened viewpoint, indeed.

Hershey's insistence on decentralization of the draft was also of major importance for conscientious objectors during World War II. Throughout his years as director, Hershey staunchly defended the decentralized draft. This held significance for conscientious objectors as well as for men in the armed services. Local draft boards performed an essential job in raising an army of conscripts: classification. For the CO, this meant that the local draft board determined his initial fate. Granted, Hershey centralized the policies of induction at the national headquarters, but he left the operation of classification to the local boards. This emphasis on decentralization further shaped conscientious objection during World War II, as draft boards were inconsistent. Some COs had no problem gaining their IV-E or I-A-O classifications, while others faced blatant hostility.[2] This was a part of the story of conscientious objection during World War II, and Hershey's belief in decentralization played a significant role in shaping that.

Though pivotal and central to conscientious objection and alternative service, Hershey's power was not limitless. Most of his obstacles arose in Congress. He ran into trouble in situations where government funding or transportation was to be used for COs, such was with the CPS Training Corps. Recall that the majority of CPS funding came from the Peace Churches, not the federal government. Though he decided what constituted work of national importance, he opened himself to interference if funding from outside the Peace Churches was involved. He approved of the overseas relief training and activities in the CPS Training Corps, but the efforts of Congressman Joe Starnes killed any chances for the COs to help rebuild the war-torn areas of Europe and Asia during the conflict. He was unable to secure workman's compensation or dependency benefits for CPS assignees, even though he pushed strongly for them before Congress. He also wanted to implement a point system to end CPS and send assignees home but found himself rebuffed by a reluctant Congress. Even though Congress limited his power at times, he proved an adept negotiator with a keen understanding of the political process, as evidenced by his success in developing the means to discharge COs from CPS after the war.

Hershey carefully considered the role of public opinion and the publicity that could focus attention on a controversial program. Hershey was wary of any negative public reaction against CPS or the institution of conscientious objection. Accordingly, he tried to keep conscientious objectors out of the limelight. This approach was not limited to his dealings with the press. Hershey seldom discussed conscientious objection publicly. If interviewed on a specific subject, such as conscientious objection, Hershey would put forth his thoughts on the matter, but he would not voluntarily elaborate. An examination of Hershey's speeches reveals that when he addressed manpower and service, he did not mention conscientious objection. He discussed the matter openly only when speaking to the COs themselves or to representatives of their religious denominations.[3]

Though all of the aforementioned beliefs and actions of Hershey were significant in his shaping of CPS, they revolved around his concept of a duty of service for eligible males. While he did not personally agree with the stance taken by the conscientious objector, he respected it; however, that did not translate into a complete deferment for religious objectors. Instead, the federal government required them to perform some type of national service, the so-called work of national importance. It was that point that made many COs unhappy, as they viewed the work as menial and unimportant. Hershey, however, remained steadfastly committed to the idea that conscientious objection was a privilege in a democratic society, not a guaranteed right, and that national service was a duty.

Hershey's views on service and the CO further defined the tradition of the citizen soldier in the United States. With the introduction of alternative service in the form of CPS, the central ideas behind the citizen soldier became intertwined with individual liberty. Under Hershey's perception of civic responsibility, if a person objected to service in the military based on sincere religious beliefs, he could perform alternate service to fulfill his duty to his state, but he would not be entirely exempt from his national responsibility. World War II and Hershey's efforts in shaping alternative service set the pattern for alternate means of fulfilling national commitments, which continued throughout the years of conscription in the United States. After the Second World War, even when the definition of conscientious objection changed, the obligations of the objector did not. He was required to serve in some capacity. Therefore, the concept of the citizen soldier no longer pertained only to armed service. As a result, some form of service, whether it was as a soldier, noncombatant, or alternative service assignee, was required when the state called upon its citizens in times of crisis.

The central dynamic driving the citizen soldier concept is the idea of service, just as service was at the heart of CPS. Since Americans have traditionally viewed professional armies as separate from the state and a threat to its very existence, the best defenders of the nation are those with the strongest interest in its survival: its citizens. The American citizen soldier tradition blurs the line between military and civilian society, rendering the interests of the two coincident.[4] To be sure, there are flaws in the concept of the citizen soldier, particularly when one considers that many young male citizens had no choice once drafted, but it was a concept in which Hershey fervently believed.

Hence, an examination of Lewis Hershey's pivotal role in conscientious objection and alternative service during World War II provides illuminating insights into not only the religious history of the United States, but its military history as well. Examining conscientious objection and alternative service through the lens of the federal government and the military, or more specifically, Hershey and the Selective Service, provides a view of how the government sets the parameters for national obligation during a time of threats both real and perceived. During World War II, alternative service became a possible means of fulfilling one's service duty. This continued after World War II. Only for a very brief time after the war did conscientious objection result in deferment. General Hershey's actions during World War II in the establishment, administration, and protection of conscientious objectors and alternative service placed the concept of service ever more firmly in the American military tradition.

Notes

★ ★ ★ ★

Introduction

1. George Q. Flynn, *The Draft: 1940–1973,* 175–76, 182, 215–18; George Q. Flynn, *Lewis B. Hershey, Mr. Selective Service,* 307; and Melvin Small, *Antiwarriors: The Vietnam War and the Battle for America's Hearts and Minds,* 1, 109.

2. During the draft just prior to the Korean War, COs received a complete deferment, and no alternative service was required of them. However, that deferment did not last long and was an anomaly in a discussion of conscription and conscientious objection during the twentieth century. The issue of CO deferment prior to the Korean War is discussed in greater detail in the conclusion.

3. The standard works for the Historic Peace Churches' experience during World War II are Leslie Eisan, *Pathways of Peace: A History of the Civilian Public Service Program as Directed by the Brethren Service Committee;* and Melvin Gingerich, *Service for Peace: A History of Mennonite Civilian Public Service.* Eisan offers little discussion of Hershey, while Gingerich mentions that COs might have experienced "unbearable conditions" were it not for Hershey. See Gingerich, *Service for Peace,* 368. It is also worth mentioning that there are studies of conscientious objection and pacifism that do not focus on the Historic Peace Church experience but instead discuss the World War II experience as part of the larger peace movement during the twentieth century. The best examples are Scott H. Bennett, *Radical Pacifism: The War Resisters League and Gandhian Nonviolence, 1915–1963;* Charles Chatfield, *For Peace and Justice: Pacifism in America, 1914–1941;* and Lawrence S. Wittner, *Rebels against War: The American Peace Movement, 1941–1960,* which Wittner later updated to cover the peace movement to 1983.

4. The gold standard for the history of conscientious objection during World War II is Mulford Quickert Sibley and Philip Jacob, *Conscription of Conscience: The American State and the Conscientious Objector, 1940–1947.* The authors are overly critical of the government, the Selective Service, and in some cases, General Hershey, describing the Selective Service as "sharply restrictive" and calling it "the chief agent of restraint upon the conscientious objector in CPS." In separately

authored sections within their work, Sibley and Jacob disagree on whether the churches should have refused to work with the government concerning CPS administration. Jacob gives proper credit to the Selective Service for allowing the churches to practice religious liberty separate from military interest. However, taken together, Sibley and Jacob are among the most critical of Hershey and the Selective Service. See Sibley and Jacob, *Conscription of Conscience,* 201, 200, 308, 471–75. Also of importance are the works of Albert Keim. His studies of CPS are well done and a bit more evenhanded than that of Sibley and Jacob, but they lack the depth of *Conscription of Conscience.* The best example is Albert Keim *The CPS Story: An Illustrated History of Civilian Public Service.* However, Keim does compare the camps to the Soviet gulags because the men were not paid for their work. See Keim, *The CPS Story,* 100. Interestingly, one of the most evenhanded, albeit brief, overviews of General Hershey comes from Steven J. Taylor, *Acts of Conscience: World War II, Mental Institutions, and Religious Objectors,* 43–45.

5. Most of the work done on Hershey comes from George Q. Flynn. Two books, *Lewis B. Hershey: Mr. Selective Service,* and *The Draft: 1940–1973,* represent the most extensive studies done by Flynn. His book on Hershey is the only scholarly biography in existence, and Hershey is featured extensively in his history of the draft. Flynn adeptly describes Hershey as the ultimate federal bureaucrat with a keen understanding of both civil and military matters. He paints him as liberal in his dealings with conscientious objectors in both his books and his article "Lewis Hershey and the Conscientious Objector: The World War II Experience." Other authors that examine conscription in the twentieth century but offer scant attention to either Hershey or conscientious objection during World War II are John Whiteclay Chambers II, *To Raise an Army: The Draft Comes to Modern America;* and J. Garry Clifford and Samuel R. Spencer, Jr., *The First Peacetime Draft.*

6. Samuel J. Huntington, *The Soldier and the State: The Theory and Politics of Civil-Military Relations,* 315–16; and Arthur A. Ekirch, Jr., *The Civilian and the Military: A History of the American Antimilitarist Tradition,* 270.

7. The extension of the privilege of conscientious objection to secular objectors came in 1965 with the Supreme Court's decision on *United States v. Seeger.* See conclusion.

Chapter 1

1. The draft provisions for conscientious objection in World War I are discussed in detail in chapter 3. Please refer to that chapter for specific citations.

2. For a more in-depth discussion of the interwar efforts of the Historic Peace Churches and JANSSC, see chapter 4.

3. *Selective Service Act, Statutes at Large* 54 Part 1, 889 (1940).

4. U.S. President, Executive Order 8675. (Document printed in *Conscientious Objection: Special Monograph No. 11,* 7.) See chapter 5 on the creation of Civilian Public Service for a broader discussion of Roosevelt's executive order conferring the authority over work of national importance to the director of Selective Service.

5. Sibley and Jacob, *Conscription of Conscience,* 56–57.

6. Eisan, *Pathways of Peace,* 88–92; Gingerich, *Service for Peace,* 108–24; Keim, *The CPS Story,* 41–43, 49–55; Sibley and Jacob, *Conscription of Conscience,* 130–32;

Bennett, *Radical Pacifism,* 81; Uriah Mast, "Historic Peace Church Members Encounter CPS: Uriah Mast," 44, 48; Robert Doak, "Historic Peace Church Members Encounter CPS: Robert Doak," 61; Ivan Amstutz, "Historic Peace Church Members Encounter CPS: Ivan Amstutz," 77; Benjamin L. Reid, "CPS Men from Outside the Historic Peace Tradition: Benjamin L. Reid," 96; Gordon Zahn, "CPS Men from Outside the Historic Peace Tradition: Gordon Zahn," 109; Hoosag Gregory, "Reflections on the CPS Experience: Hoosag Gregory," 203; and J. Benjamin Stavely, "Reflections on the CPS Experience: J. Benjamin Stavely," 218, 223. All of the citations in this note, beginning with Uriah Mast, are interviews from Heather T. Frazer and John O'Sullivan, *We Have Just Begun to Not Fight: An Oral History of Conscientious Objectors in Civilian Public Service during World War II.*

7. Robert C. Cottrell, *Smokejumpers of the Civilian Public Service in World War II: Conscientious Objectors as Firefighters for the National Forest Service,* passim; Eisan, *Pathways of Peace,* 74–88; Gingerich, *Service for Peace,* 125–47; Keim, *The CPS Story,* 43–48; and Sibley and Jacob, *Conscription of Conscience,* 126–30.

8. Eisan, *Pathways of Peace,* 92–97; Gingerich, *Service for Peace,* 177–212; Keim, *The CPS Story,* 55–57; Sibley and Jacob, *Conscription of Conscience,*132–34.

9. Eisan, *Pathways of Peace,* 290–312; Gingerich, *Service for Peace,* 270–73; Keim, *The CPS Story,* 75–79; Nicholas A. Krehbiel, "'We Felt Like We Were Serving Humanity:' McPherson County, Kansas Conscientious Objectors during World War II," 58–59; Sibley and Jacob, *Conscription of Conscience,* 143–49; and Todd Tucker, *The Great Starvation Experiment: The Heroic Men Who Starved So That Others May Live,* passim.

10. *The Good War and Those Who Refused to Fight It,* Paradigm Productions, Independent Television Services Script, Bullfrog Films, 2000, 10; and Taylor, *Acts of Conscience,* 85. Koop's quote is from the film transcript.

11. Ibid.

12. Eisan, *Pathways of Peace,* 207–15; Gingerich, *Service for Peace,* 213–51; Keim, *The CPS Story,* 59–72; Alex Sareyan, *The Turning Point: How Men of Conscience Brought About Major Change in the Care of America's Mentally Ill,* xii; and Sibley and Jacob, *Conscription of Conscience,* 134–40.

13. Taylor, *Acts of Conscience,* 1.

14. Eisan, *Pathways of Peace,* 273–95; Gingerich, *Service for Peace,* 252–70; Keim, *The CPS Story,* 73–75; Scott H. Bennett, ed., *Army GI, Pacifist CO: The World War II Letters of Frank and Albert Dietrich,* 41–42; and Sibley and Jacob, *Conscription of Conscience,* 140–43.

15. *Conscientious Objection,* 313–15, 318.

16. Allan R. Millett and Peter Maslowski, *For the Common Defense: A Military History of the United States,* xii.

17. Eliot Cohen, *Citizens and Soldiers: The Dilemmas of Military Service,* 121–25.

18. Ibid., 123–24.

19. Ibid., 124–25.

20. Hershey quoted in ibid., 125. Hershey used the word ancestor when comparing the militia and the Selective Service.

21. Lewis B. Hershey to Brig. Gen. John McA. Palmer, May 27, 1941, General Hershey's Staybacks, Planning Office Staybacks, Lewis B. Hershey Collection, Army Heritage and Education Center, Carlisle, PA.

Chapter 2

1. George Q. Flynn, Lewis Hershey and the Conscientious Objector: The World War II Experience," 1.
2. Anabaptism traces its origins to Switzerland.
3. Flynn, "Lewis Hershey and the Conscientious Objector," 4.
4. Keim, *The CPS Story,* 24; and Tucker, *The Great Starvation Experiment,* 45.
5. Flynn, "Lewis Hershey and the Conscientious Objector," 2–3.
6. Lewis B. Hershey Diary, September 7–8, 1916, Lewis B. Hershey Collection, Trine University, Angola, IN; and Flynn, *Lewis B. Hershey,* 18.
7. Hershey Diary, September 14, 1916.
8. Hershey Diary, April 17, 1917.
9. Hershey Diary, November 15, 1917.
10. *Selective Service,* February 1, 1941.
11. Ibid.
12. Flynn, "Lewis Hershey and the Conscientious Objector," 2; and Sibley and Jacob, *Conscription of Conscience,* 57–64.
13. *Selective Service,* May 1, 1941.
14. Ibid.
15. Robert Elder and James Hattersley, *Report of Interviews with Lewis B. Hershey, General, USA (Retired),* Part IV, 31–32.
16. Lewis Hershey to L. Taylor Krawczyk, October 1, 1941, Center for Conscience and War, Series A, Correspondence with General Lewis B. Hershey, Swarthmore College Peace Collection, Swarthmore, PA. Hereafter cited as SCPC. Taylor later became one of the more famous conscientious objectors during World War II for a hunger strike he undertook while imprisoned along with Stanley Murphy. See Bennett, *Radical Pacifism,* 88–94. I am indebted to Bennett for his help in identifying Hershey's letter as indeed corresponding with Taylor. According to Bennett, Taylor was born Louis Krawczyk.
17. Ibid.
18. *Selective Service in Peacetime: First Report of the Director of Selective Service, 1940–1941,* 188.
19. Ibid.
20. *Conscientious Objection,* 1.
21. Flynn, *Lewis B. Hershey,* 3–5.
22. Quoted in Richard Seiverling, *Lewis B. Hershey: A Pictorial and Documentary Biography,* 14.
23. Flynn, *Lewis B. Hershey,* 6–7, 10–12.
24. Ibid., 13.
25. Ibid., 14–15. Kosch served as Chief of Camp Operations during World War II; his was the division that dealt with the administration of Civilian Public Service.
26. Hershey Diary, September 7–8, 1916; and Flynn, *Lewis B. Hershey,* 16–20.
27. Flynn, *Lewis B. Hershey,* 20–24, 26.
28. Hershey Diary, November 16, 1917.
29. Hershey Diary, September 25, 1918.
30. Flynn, *Lewis B. Hershey,* 27–29; and Hershey Diary, December 4, 1918.
31. Flynn, *Lewis B. Hershey,* 32–42.
32. Ibid., 42–45, 45 (quote).
33. Ibid., 45.

Chapter 3

1. Millett and Maslowski, *For the Common Defense,* 2.

2. John O'Sullivan and Alan Meckler, eds., *The Draft and Its Enemies: A Documentary History,* 3; John K. Mahon, *History of the Militia and the National Guard,* 7–10; and Michael D. Doubler, *Civilian in War, Soldier in Peace: The Army National Guard, 1636–2000,* 8–9.

3. Millett and Maslowski, *For the Common Defense,* 2–3.

4. Doubler, *Civilian in Peace, Soldier in War,* 7; and Millett and Maslowski, *For the Common Defense,* 3.

5. Doubler, *Civilian in Peace, Soldier in War,* 10–26; Millett and Maslowski, *For the Common Defense,* 5–6; and O'Sullivan and Meckler, *The Draft and Its Enemies,* 4–5.

6. Doubler, *Civilian in Peace, Soldier in War,* 10–26; and Millett and Maslowski, *For the Common Defense,* 13–19, 27–43.

7. The term conscientious objector did not come into use until the twentieth century. Before that, people referred to objectors as "nonresisters." Because of the possibility for confusion and the focus on the twentieth century in this work, the term "conscientious objector" will be used in all discussions throughout this book unless otherwise noted. See John Whiteclay Chambers II, "Conscientious Objectors and the American State from Colonial Times to the Present," 23.

8. Peter Brock, *Pacifism in the United States: From the Colonial Era to the First World War,* 21–66; and Peter Brock, ed., *Liberty and Conscience: A Documentary History of the Experiences of Conscientious Objectors in America through the Civil War,* 3–4.

9. Brock, *Pacifism in the United States,* 28–29; Brock, *Liberty and Conscience,* 4; and Stephen Kohn, *Jailed for Peace: A History of American Draft Law Violators, 1658–1985,* 6.

10. Chambers, "Conscientious Objectors and the American State from Colonial Times to the Present," 25.

11. Brock, *Liberty and Conscience,* 5; Chambers, "Conscientious Objectors and the American State from Colonial Times to the Present," 25–26; and Kohn, *Jailed for Peace,* 8.

12. Hugh Barbour and J. William Frost, *The Quakers,* 74–79; and Kohn, *Jailed for Peace,* 8–9.

13. Barbour and Frost, *The Quakers,* 123–26; and Brock, *Liberty and Conscience,* 6.

14. Chambers, "Conscientious Objectors and the American State from Colonial Times to the Present," 27.

15. Brock, *Pacifism in the United States,* 61–62; and Brock, *Liberty and Conscience,* 6.

16. Brock, *Pacifism in the United States,* 159–82; and Brock, *Liberty and Conscience,* 5–7.

17. O'Sullivan and Meckler, *The Draft and Its Enemies,* 5–6.

18. E. Wayne Carp, *To Starve the Army at Pleasure: Continental Army Administration and American Political Culture,* 5, 14–15; and O'Sullivan and Meckler, *The Draft and Its Enemies,* 6–7.

19. O'Sullivan and Meckler, *The Draft and Its Enemies,* 8–9.

20. Chambers, "Conscientious Objectors and the American State from Colonial Times to the Present," 27.

21. Kohn, *Jailed for Peace,* 9–10.

22. Brock, *Pacifism in the United States,* 183–258; and Brock, *Liberty and Conscience,* 48.

23. Brock, *Liberty and Conscience,* 48.
24. Kohn, *Jailed for Peace,* 10–11.
25. Quoted in John Whiteclay Chambers II, ed., *Draftees or Volunteers: A Documentary History of the Debate over Military Conscription in the United States, 1787–1973,* 63–65.
26. Ibid., 80–83.
27. Brock, *Liberty and Conscience,* 77.
28. Chambers, "Conscientious Objectors and the American State from Colonial Times to the Present," 29; Kohn, *Jailed for Peace,* 17–19; Charles Debenedetti, *The Peace Reform in American History,* 41, 54–56; Charles F. Howlett and Robbie Lieberman, *A History of the American Peace Movement from Colonial Times to the Present,* 66, 71–72. For a history of the Peace Movement during this era, see Valarie H. Ziegler, *The Advocates of Peace in Antebellum America.*
29. Brock, *Liberty and Conscience,* 78; and Chambers, "Conscientious Objectors and the American State from Colonial Times to the Present," 29.
30. Brock, *Liberty and Conscience,* 78–80.
31. James W. Geary, *We Need Men: The Union Draft in the Civil War,* 3–5; James M. McPherson, *The Battle Cry of Freedom: The Civil War Era,* 430–31; and Albert B. Moore, *Conscription and Conflict in the Confederacy,* 13–14.
32. Geary, *We Need Men,* 3–5; McPherson, *The Battle Cry of Freedom,* 431–32; and Moore, *Conscription and Conflict in the Confederacy,* 15–16.
33. McPherson, *The Battle Cry of Freedom,* 431–32, 611–12.
34. Ibid., 492–94; and Eugene C. Murdock, *One Million Men: The Civil War Draft in the North,* 6.
35. McPherson, *The Battle Cry of Freedom.* 600–601; and Murdock, *One Million Men,* 4–7.
36. McPherson, *The Battle Cry of Freedom,* 600.
37. For studies on the New York City Draft Riots, see Iver Berstein, *The New York City Draft Riots: Their Significance for American Society and Politics in the Age of the Civil War;* and Adrian Cook, *The Armies of the Streets: The New York City Draft Riots of 1863.*
38. McPherson, *The Battle Cry of Freedom,* 603–6; Murdock, *One Million Men,* 199–201. The challenges differ for each author. McPherson states that the differences between class and service (at least in New York and Ohio) were not all that profound while Murdock asserts that the entire idea of commutation was to keep substitution prices low as a favor to poorer classes.
39. McPherson, *The Battle Cry of Freedom,* 432, 492, 605.
40. Murdock, *One Million Men,* x-xi.
41. Geary, *We Need Men,* 173–74.
42. *Ibid.,* 174.
43. Chambers, "Conscientious Objectors and the American State from Colonial Times to the Present," 30.
44. Edward Needles Wright, *Conscientious Objectors in the Civil War,* 4–5.
45. Brock, *Liberty and Conscience,* 113.
46. Chambers, "Conscientious Objectors and the American State from Colonial Times to the Present," 31.
47. Wright, *Conscientious Objectors in the Civil War,* 71–72, 121–29, 131–38.
48. Chambers, "Conscientious Objectors and the American State from Colonial Times to the Present," 31.

49. Brock, *Liberty and Conscience,* 114.

50. Wright, *Conscientious Objectors in the Civil War,* 138–39.

51. Davis was a graduate of West Point, served in the Mexican War, and was the secretary of war under President Franklin Pierce. Although Lincoln also had military experience, it was only briefly as an officer in the Illinois militia during the Black Hawk War, and he never saw combat.

52. Brock, *Liberty and Conscience,* 113–14.

53. Chambers, "Conscientious Objectors and the American State from Colonial Times to the Present," 31.

54. Chambers, *To Raise an Army,* 11.

55. Ibid.

56. Allan R. Millett, "Over Where? The AEF and the American Strategy for Victory, 1917–1918," 235.

57. Chambers, *To Raise an Army,* 1, 189–92, 200, 216.

58. Ibid., 215; and Chatfield, *For Peace and Justice,* 68.

59. *Army Emergency Increase, Statutes at Large* 40 Part 1, 78 (1917). This statute is collectively referred to as the Selective Service Act of 1917.

60. Albert Keim and Grant Stoltzfus, *The Politics of Conscience: The Historic Peace Churches and America at War, 1917–1955,* 36; and Howlett and Lieberman, *A History of the American Peace Movement,* 211–12.

61. Keim and Stolzfus, 36–38, 41; and Chambers, *To Raise an Army,* 159, 215.

62. Chambers, *To Raise an Army,* 215.

63. David Kennedy, *Over Here: The First World War and American Society,* 163.

64. Kennedy, *Over Here,* 163; Chatfield, *For Peace and Justice,* 71; and Norman Thomas, *The Conscientious Objector in America,* 144–51.

65. Chatfield, *For Peace and Justice,* 71; Howlett and Lieberman, *A History of the American Peace Movement,* 212–13; and Chambers, *To Raise an Army,* 216. Wood is quoted in Chambers. Chatfield places most of the blame for mistreatment in the camps on "petty officers whose main concern was to see that orders were obeyed and who often were unsuited to tasks involving diplomacy and understanding."

66. Quoted in Thomas, *The Conscientious Objector in America,* 154–55.

67. Chambers, *To Raise an Army,* 217.

68. Kennedy, *Over Here,* 164; Chatfield, *For Peace and Justice,* 70–72; and Keim and Stoltzfus, *The Politics of Conscience,* 49–54.

69. Kennedy, *Over Here,* 164–65, 165n; and Thomas, *The Conscientious Objector in America,* 197.

70. Chambers, *To Raise an Army,* 216–17.

71. Keim and Stoltzfus, *The Politics of Conscience,* 40–41.

72. Chambers, *To Raise an Army,* 249–50.

73. Millett and Maslowski, *For the Common Defense,* 416.

74. David Kennedy, *Freedom from Fear: The American People in Depression and War, 1929–1945,* 617–19.

75. Kennedy, *Freedom From Fear,* 631; and James L. Stokesbury, "The U.S. Army and Coalition Warfare, 1941–1945," 281.

76. Russell F. Weigley, *History of the United States Army,* 438–40. See also Maurice Matloff, "The 90-Division Gamble."

77. Allan R. Millett and Williamson Murray, *A War to Be Won: Fighting the Second World War,* 533–37.

78. Flynn, *The Draft*, 35–38.
79. Ibid., 80.

Chapter 4

1. William Robert Miller, *Nonviolence: A Christian Interpretation*, 49; and Herman Hoyt, "Nonresistance," 32–34.
2. Dale Stoffer, "Beliefs," 50–51.
3. Sibley and Jacob, *Conscription of Conscience*, 39, and for an excellent introductory overview of the different "Currents and Crosscurrents" of pacifism and conscientious objection during World War II beyond what is briefly presented on these pages, see pp. 38–43
4. Myron Augsburger, "Christian Pacifism," 86–91.
5. William Estep, *The Anabaptist Story: An Introduction to Sixteenth-Century Anabaptism*, 11–15.
6. Ibid., 30.
7. Ibid., 13–21, 30–43.
8. Harold S. Bender, "Mennonite Origins and the Mennonites of Europe," 25–30; and Estep, *The Anabaptist Story*, passim.
9. Kenneth Ronald Davis, *Anabaptism and Asceticism: A Study in Intellectual Origins*, 22–23; Estep, *The Anabaptist Story*, passim; and Walter Klaassen, ed., *Anabaptism in Outline: Selected Primary Sources*, 23–24.
10. Bender, "Mennonite Origins and the Mennonites of Europe," 20–21.
11. Estep, *The Anabaptist Story*, 201.
12. Bender, "Mennonite Origins and the Mennonites of Europe," 47–52; and Estep, *The Anabaptist Story*, 29, 47, 53, 72.
13. George H. Williams, *The Radical Reformation*, xxviii.
14. Bender, "Mennonite Origins and the Mennonites of Europe," 49.
15. Estep, *The Anabaptist Story*, 151–76; and John Hostetler, *Mennonite Life*, 9–10.
16. Bender, "Mennonite Origins and the Mennonites of Europe," 56–58; Hostetler, *Mennonite Life*, 10; John Hostetler, *Amish Society*, 41–45; and C. Henry Smith, "Mennonites in North America," 129–30.
17. James Juhnke, *A People of Two Kingdoms: The Political Acculturation of the Kansas Mennonites*, 10–11.
18. Bender, "Mennonite Origins and the Mennonites of Europe," 44–45.
19. Sydney Ahlstrom, *A Religious History of the American People*, 176.
20. Peter Brock, *The Quaker Peace Testimony, 1660–1914*, 10; Barbour and Frost, *The Quakers*, 5–8, 41–46.
21. Ahlstrom, *A Religious History of the American People*, 187–81, 111–13.
22. D. Elton Trueblood, *The People Called Quakers*, 65.
23. Ibid., 70; and John 1:9 KJV.
24. Trueblood, *The People Called Quakers*, 70.
25. Ibid., 247.
26. Barbour and Frost, *The Quakers*, 7–10.
27. Trueblood, *The People Called Quakers*, 257.
28. Brock, *The Quaker Peace Testimony*, 10–11, 23.
29. Quaker declaration quoted in Trueblood, *The People Called Quakers*, 195.
30. Ibid., 190.
31. Barbour and Frost, *The Quakers*, 247.

32. Donald Durnbaugh, "Early History," 1–9.

33. Dale Brown, *Understanding Pietism,* 11–12, 22–23; and F. Ernest Stoeffler, *German Pietism during the Eighteenth Century,* ix-xi.

34. Brown, *Understanding Pietism,* 24–25, 18–19.

35. Donald Durnbaugh, *Fruit of the Vine: A History of the Brethren, 1708–1995,* 90–102.

36. Ibid., 291–92.

37. Stoffer, *German Pietism During the Eighteenth Century,* 43, 52–53.

38. Ibid., 50–51.

39. Durnbaugh, *Fruit of the Vine,* 431–32. The quotation comes from Durnbaugh. These are the published words of the conference, not Durnbaugh's.

40. Ibid., 432.

41. *Ibid.,* 432–34.

42. Henry Krehbiel is a distant relative of mine, inasmuch as most, if not all, Krehbiels from central Kansas are related in one form or another.

43. Robert Kreider, "The Historic Peace Churches Meeting in 1935," 22–23.

44. Durnbaugh, *Fruit of the Vine,* 435–36.

45. "The Conference of Historic Peace Churches, October 31—November 2, 1935, Newton, Kansas," Vertical File—Conference of Historic Peace Churches (1935—Newton, KS), Mennonite Library and Archives, North Newton, KS.

46. "The Conference of Historic Peace Churches, October 31—November 2, 1935, Newton, Kansas."

47. The Historic Peace Churches to Franklin Roosevelt, January 10, 1940, Lewis B. Hershey Papers, Army Heritage and Education Center, Carlisle, PA.

48. Flynn, *The Draft,* 9–12.

49. Clifford and Spencer, *The First Peacetime Draft,* 14–16, 48–101; and Flynn, *The Draft,* 9–12. For more information on the Plattsburg Movement, see Chambers, *To Raise an Army,* 81–83

50. Clifford and Spencer, *The First Peacetime Draft,* 48–49.

51. Joint Army Navy Selective Service Committee, *American Selective Service: A Brief Account of Its Historical Background and Its Probable Future Form* (Washington: U.S. Government Printing Office, 1939), 1.

52. Flynn, *The Draft,* 12–13.

53. Clifford and Spencer, *The First Peacetime Draft,* 85–88; and *Conscientious Objection,* 67.

54. Congress, Senate, Committee on Military Affairs, *Compulsory Military Training and Service: Hearings before the Committee on Military Affairs,* 76th Cong., 3nd sess., July 3, 5, 10, 11, and 12, 1940, 3.

55. *Conscientious Objection,* 68–70.

56. Senate, *Compulsory Military Training and Service: Hearings before the Committee on Military Affairs,* 372–385; and Clifford and Spencer, *The First Peacetime Draft,* 128.

57. Congress, House, *Selective Compulsory Military Training and Service: Hearings before the Committee on Military Affairs,* 76th Congress, 3rd sess., July 10, 11, 24, 25, 26, 30, 31, and August 2, 12, 13, 14, 1940, 126. (Sparkman served as a voice of support for conscientious objectors throughout the war, particularly in trying to help the Peace Churches during the CPS Training Corps debates. See chapter 6.)

58. Senate, *Compulsory Military Training and Service: Hearings before the Committee on Military Affairs,* 55.

59. Ibid., 305
60. Ibid., 160.
61. Ibid., 160–65.
62. Ibid., 165.
63. Ibid.
64. Robert C. Cottrell, *Roger Nash Baldwin and the American Civil Liberties Union*, 279; Judy Kutulas, *The American Civil Liberties Union and the Making of Modern Liberalism, 1930–1960*, 90; Samuel Walker, *In Defense of American Liberties: A History of the ACLU*, 149–50; and Clifford and Spencer, *The First Peacetime Draft*, 124–25.
65. Clifford and Spencer, *The First Peacetime Draft*, 124.
66. Senate, *Compulsory Military Training and Service: Hearings before the Committee on Military Affairs*, 307–9.
67. Ibid., 309–10.
68. House, *Selective Compulsory Military Training and Service: Hearings before the Committee on Military Affairs*, 189–92.
69. Ibid., 201–2, 209.
70. Congress, Senate, Committee on Military Affairs, *Compulsory Military Training and Service*, 76th Cong., 3rd sess., S. Rep. 2002, 3.
71. Congress, House, Committee on Military Affairs, *Compulsory Military Training and Service*, 76th Congress, 3rd sess., H. Rep. 2903, 5.
72. Clifford and Spencer, *The First Peacetime Draft*, 221–22; *Conscientious Objection*, 84.
73. *Conscientious Objection*, 84.
74. French Diary, September 7, 1940.
75. French Diary, September 7–13, 1940.
76. Clifford and Spencer, *The First Peacetime Draft*, 221; and Walker, *In Defense of American Liberties*, 151. Walker also points out that because of the lack of a secular CO provision in the 1940 draft bill, many COs did, in fact, go to prison.
77. *Selective Training and Service Act, Statutes at Large* 54 Part 1, 889 (1940).
78. Ibid.

Chapter 5

1. *Conscientious Objection*, 157–58.
2. Sibley and Jacob, *Conscription of Conscience*, 4–5.
3. Bennett, *Radical Pacifism*, 81.
4. M. R. Zigler, "The Organization and Functioning of CPS: M. R. Zigler," 5.
5. U.S. President, Executive Order 8606. (Document printed in *Conscientious Objection*, 5.)
6. Ibid.
7. Eller, *Conscientious Objectors and the Second World War*, 28.
8. French Diary, September 23, 1940.
9. *Conscientious Objection*, 158–59.
10. Gingerich, *Service for Peace*, 56; and Sibley and Jacob, *Conscription of Conscience*, 116.
11. *Conscientious Objection*, 160.
12. French Diary, October 2, 1940. At this point, Hershey was the acting director of the Selective Service as President Roosevelt had not yet filled the position permanently.

13. French Diary, October 2, 1940.

14. Gingerich, *Service for Peace,* 54–55 (quote printed in Gingerich).

15. Ibid., 55. Quote is the wording of the Mennonite Central Peace Committee, appearing in Gingerich.

16. Ibid.

17. *Conscientious Objection,* 160; and Gingerich, 55.

18. *Conscientious Objection,* 160–61.

19. Henry Lewis Stimson Diary, XXX, 158 (microfilm edition, reel 6). Hereafter cited as Stimson Diary.

20. Stimson Diary, XXXI, 9, 26–27; Flynn, *Lewis B. Hershey,* 75; and Flynn, *The Draft,* 23.

21. French Diary, October 15, 1940.

22. French Diary, November 14, 1940; and Memorandum from National Council for Religious Conscientious Objectors to Selective Service. Printed in *Conscientious Objection,* 162.

23. *Conscientious Objection,*163.

24. Lewis B. Hershey to Paul French, November 28, 1940, Center for Conscience and War, Series A, Correspondence with Lewis B. Hershey, SCPC.

25. *Conscientious Objection,* 163.

26. Paul French to Clarence Pickett, December 3, 1940 (document printed in Philip Jacob, ed., *The Origins of Civilian Public Service: A Review of the Negotiations during the Fall of 1940 between Government Officials and Representatives of the Churches Most Immediately Affected by the Drafting of Conscientious Objectors*); *Conscientious Objection,* 164; and Albert Keim, "Service or Resistance? The Mennonite Response to Conscription in World War II," 153.

27. French Diary, December 10 and 16, 1940; and Jacob, *The Origins of Civilian Public Service,* 7–8.

28. Jean Edward Smith, *FDR,* 19–29, 47, 92–95, 99–116, 165–86, 191, 228–47, 287. Another excellent recent biography is H.W. Brands, *Traitor to His Class: The Privileged Life and Radical Presidency of Franklin Delano Roosevelt.*

29. Thomas H. Greer, *What Roosevelt Thought: The Social and Political Ideas of Franklin D. Roosevelt,* 4.

30. Ibid., 5.

31. Keim, "Service or Resistance?" 153.

32. French Diary, December 22 and 28, 1940.

33. *Selective Service in Peacetime,* 191–92.

34. U.S. President, Executive Order 8675 (document printed in *Conscientious Objection,* volume II, 7).

35. Hershey became acting director of Selective Service upon Dykstra's resignation in April.

36. French Diary, January 22, 1941.

37. Ibid.

38. French, Untitled Meeting with Lewis Hershey, March 28, 1941, Correspondence with Lewis B. Hershey, January-August, 1941, SCPC.

39. *Selective Service,* September 1, 1941; Stimson Diary, XXXIV, 48, 214, 216; and Flynn, *Lewis B. Hershey,* 75.

40. *Conscientious Objection,* 165.

41. Hershey Diary, 1916–1936, Trine University Lewis B. Hershey Papers, Angola, IN. There is no specific citation here, but after a reading of Hershey's diary

entries (there are only entries from 1916 to 1923, plus a book for 1936) it is clear that Hershey and Kosch were lifelong friends.

42. Paul French, Untitled Meeting with Lewis Hershey Notes, March 28, 1941, Center for Conscience and War, Series A, Correspondence with Lewis B. Hershey, SCPC. The text of Hershey's meeting with French is as follows: "[h]e [Hershey] planned to bring a personal friend into Selective Service to act in this capacity for him and that he hoped that he and his new appointee could personally get to know each of the camp directors and camp staffs so there would be a common understanding by Selective Service of the program and an understanding by our directors of what limitations Selective Service labored under. He expressed the hope that after he got to know the camp directors they would find out he didn't have a tail and horns."

43. Ibid.

44. Paul French to Lewis B. Hershey, April 10, 1941, Center for Conscience and War, Series A, Correspondence with Lewis B. Hershey, SCPC.

45. Lewis B. Hershey to Paul French, April 16, 1941, Center for Conscience and War, Series A, Correspondence with Lewis B. Hershey, SCPC.

46. Robert E. S. Thompson, "Onward, Christian Soldiers!: The Nation's Conscientious Objectors Work Out Their Convictions," *Saturday Evening Post,* August 16, 1941, 27; *Selective Service,* May 1, 1941, 4; and *Conscientious Objection,* 165.

47. *Conscientious Objection,* 166–67.

48. Lewis B. Hershey, "Testimony before the Subcommittee of the House Committee on Appropriations Considering H.R. 2935...," in National Service Board for Religious Objectors, ed. *Congress Looks at the Conscientious Objector,* 64; and Eisan, 74.

49. *Selective Service in Peacetime,* 194–95.

50. National Service Board for Religious Objectors, "Bulletin #118," December 2, 1941, SCPC; and French Diary, November 6, 1941; and Memorandum on Conversation with General Hershey–Sibley and Jacob, July 26, 1946, Center for Conscience and War, Series A, Correspondence with Lewis B. Hershey, SCPC, 5. This process was the "presidential appeal," which usually went to Hershey rather than to President Roosevelt. For a specific example of how this process worked for the individual CO, see Bennett, *Army GI, Pacifist CO,* 33–37. Albert Dietrich, a conscientious objector, had his requests and appeals for IV-E status rejected at every level until his case came before General Hershey, who granted his request.

51. *Selective Service in Peacetime,* 193–94.

52. Ibid., 200.

53. National Service Board for Religious Objectors, "Bulletin #114," October 17, 1941, SCPC.

54. French Diary, September 2, 1941.

55. Thompson, "Onward Christian Soldiers," 27; and French Diary, June 18, and October 3, 1941.

56. French Diary, August 1, 1941.

57. Ibid., September 2, 1941.

58. Ibid., November 5, 1941.

59. There was resistance to CPS from a number of assignees throughout the war. This was not limited to the Quaker camps, but Hershey and Kosch did express a fair amount of frustration toward the AFSC in this regard. Some behavior

that the Selective Service considered discipline problems were noncooperation, deliberate inefficiency, vandalism, sabotage, refusal to work, and refusal to follow camp rules. These were nonviolent methods undertaken by assignees who rejected the underlying foundation of CPS. This resistance in CPS was one of the major reasons for establishing the government-run camps later in the war, particularly for those objectors who chafed under Peace Church administration. Most of the resisters were secular COs, objectors of a religious affiliation other than the Peace Churches, or atheists. The resistance to CPS is discussed in more detail in chapter 6. Though Hershey (and the law) was clear about the religious dimensions of objection, some secular objectors slipped through the system, and many of them caused a fair amount of trouble in the camps. See Sibley and Jacob, *Conscription of Conscience,* 271–78; Bennett, *Radical Pacifism,* 99–104; Wittner, *Rebels against War,* 72–81; and *Conscientious Objection,* 233, 235.

60. French Diary, October 28, 29, November 1, 5, 1941.

61. Thomas E. Jones, *Light on the Horizon: The Quaker Pilgrimage of Tom Jones,* 141–42; Sibley and Jacob, *Conscription of Conscience,* 311. The conversation between Kosch and Jones is recounted in Jones' memoir, noted here.

62. French Diary, November 15, 1941.

63. Paul French to Lewis B. Hershey, September 10, 1941, Center for Conscience and War, Series A, Correspondence with Lewis B. Hershey, SCPC; and Paul French to Lewis B. Hershey, October 21, 1941, Center for Conscience and War, Series A, Correspondence with Lewis B. Hershey, SCPC; and M. R. Zigler, Clarence Pickett, and Orie Miller to Lewis B. Hershey, November 27, 1941, Center for Conscience and War, Series A, Correspondence with Lewis B. Hershey, SCPC.

64. French Diary, November 26, 1941.

65. Lewis B. Hershey to Paul French, December 19, 1941, Center for Conscience and War, Series A, Correspondence with Lewis B. Hershey, SCPC.

Chapter 6

1. French Diary, December 11, 1941; and NSBRO Minutes, December 12 and 13, 1941, Center for Conscience and War, Box 1100, SCPC.

2. French Diary, November 26 and December 11, 1941.

3. French Diary, December 11, 1941.

4. *Selective Service,* December 15, 1941.

5. French Diary, January 29 and February 4, 1942.

6. French Diary, November 18, 19, 1941.

7. For examples, see Sareyan, *The Turning Point;* Taylor, *Acts of Conscience;* and Tucker, *The Great Starvation Experiment.*

8. *Conscientious Objection,* 169; Keim and Stoltzfus, *The Politics of Conscience,* 48–49; and Sibley and Jacob, *Conscription of Conscience,* 132.

9. *Conscientious Objection,* 169.

10. *Selective Service,* September 1, 1941.

11. French Diary, January 3, 1942.

12. *Selective Service in Wartime: Second Report of the Director of Selective Service, 1941–1942,* 268–69.

13. *Conscientious Objection,* 169–70; and Sibley and Jacob, *Conscription of Conscience,* 132–34.

14. French Diary, January 7, 8, 9, 27, 1942.
15. French Diary, February 6, 1942.
16. "Memorandum of Understanding between the United States Department of Agriculture, the United States Employment Service, the Selective Service System, and the National Service Board for Religious Objectors Relative to the Assignment of Conscientious Objectors to Farm Engaged in Vital Agricultural Production, General Hershey's Staybacks, 1942, Box 3, Lewis B. Hershey Collection, Army Heritage and Education Center, Carlisle, PA.
17. *Selective Service as the Tide of War Turns: Third Report of the Director of Selective Service, 1943–1944,* 184–85.
18. *Conscientious Objection,* 170; *Selective Service in Wartime: Second Report of the Director of Selective Service, 1941–1942,* 269; and Sibley and Jacob, *Conscription of Conscience,* 132.
19. Steve Nolt, "The CPS Frozen Fund: The Beginning of Peace-Time Interaction between Historic Peace Churches and the United States Government," 203–5. As of the publication of Nolt's article in 1993, the issue of money from the World War II CO labor had not been resolved. Much of this article examines the efforts of the Historic Peace Churches and NSBRO (though the name changed a number of times) throughout the remainder of the twentieth century to rectify this problem.
20. *Conscientious Objection,* 169; *Selective Service in Wartime: Second Report of the Director of Selective Service, 1941–1942,* 269–70; and Sibley and Jacob, *Conscription of Conscience,* 134–35.
21. French Diary, January 21, 27, 1942 and Taylor, *Acts of Conscience,* 175–76.
22. Lewis B. Hershey to Fiorello LaGuardia, November 21, 1942, General Hershey's Staybacks, 1942, Box 1, Lewis B. Hershey Collection, Army Heritage and Education Center, Carlisle, PA.
23. Lewis B. Hershey to Dr. Raymond Waggoner, March 6, 1943, General Hershey's Staybacks, 1942–1943, Lewis B. Hershey Collection, Army Heritage and Education Center, Carlisle, PA.
24. Lewis B. Hershey to Thomas E. Dewey, February 22, 1943, General Hershey's Staybacks, 1942–1943, Lewis B. Hershey Collection, Army Heritage and Education Center, Carlisle, PA.
25. French Diary, October 13, 14, 1942.
26. Paul J. Furnas to Lewis B. Hershey, May 11, 1942, Letters to Hershey, 1940–1943, Trine University Lewis B. Hershey Collection, Angola, IN.
27. M. R. Zigler to Lewis B. Hershey, June 15, 1942, Letters to Hershey, 1940–1943, Trine University Lewis B. Hershey Collection, Angola, IN.
28. Ibid.
29. Lewis B. Hershey to M. R. Zigler, no date, Letters to Hershey, 1940–1943, Trine University Lewis B. Hershey Collection, Angola, IN.
30. *Selective Service in Peacetime,* 201.
31. There is no specific citation here beyond Paul French's diary. In representing conscientious objectors and the Historic Peace Churches, no man met with Hershey on a personal level more often than French. An overall examination of French's entries about his meetings with Hershey provides these descriptions of Hershey. To cite all of the meetings between the two men would create a citation of overwhelming specificity and little substance.

32. Bennett, *Radical Pacifism,* 79–81.
33. French Diary, February 16, 1942.
34. Wittner, *Rebels against War,* 83.
35. Bennett, *Radical Pacifism,* 80–81, 99–104; and Wittner, *Rebels against War,* 72–81.
36. French Diary, June 9, 1942; and Sibley and Jacob, *Conscription of Conscience,* 242–43.
37. Sibley and Jacob, *Conscription of Conscience,* 243.
38. Ibid., 244.
39. Ibid., 244–46; and Keim, *The CPS Story,* 110.
40. French Diary, March 30, 1943; and Sibley and Jacob, *Conscription of Conscience,* 264–265.
41. French Diary, April 3, 1943.
42. Henry Dyer to Lewis B. Hershey, April 9, 1943, Center for Conscience and War, Series A, Correspondence with Lewis B. Hershey, SCPC. Dyer was an assignee to CPS Camp #30 in Walhalla, MI.
43. Sibley and Jacob, *Conscription of Conscience,* 265–68.
44. French Diary, April 12, 13, 1943.
45. French Diary, May 31, June 1, 1943.
46. Clarence Pickett to President Franklin D. Roosevelt, May 18, 1943, OF 111, Folder 1941–1943, Franklin D. Roosevelt Library, Hyde Park, NY.
47. Lewis B. Hershey to Stephen Early, June 9, 1943, OF 111, Folder 1941–1943, Franklin D. Roosevelt Library, Hyde Park, NY.
48. NSBRO Minutes, October 14, 1943, Center for Conscience and War, Box 1100, SCPC; and Paul French to Lewis B. Hershey, October 14, 1943, Center for Conscience and War, Series A, Correspondence with Lewis B. Hershey, SCPC.
49. French Diary, October 14, 1943.
50. Ibid.
51. French Diary, October 17, 1943.
52. Lewis B. Hershey to Mrs. Franklin D. Roosevelt, May 5, 1944, General Hershey's Staybacks, 1945 part 1, Lewis B. Hershey Collection, Army Heritage and Education Center, Carlisle, PA.

Chapter 7

1. Sibley and Jacob, *Conscription of Conscience,* 200, 216–17.
2. Memorandum on Conversation with General Hershey—Sibley and Jacob, July 26, 1946, Center for Conscience and War, Series A, Correspondence with Lewis B. Hershey, SCPC, 1
3. Keim and Stoltzfus, *The Politics of Conscience,* 123.
4. Albert Keim, "Mennonites and Selective Service in World War II: An Ambiguous Relationship," 523.
5. *Congress Looks at the Conscientious Objector,* 34, 51–52. This is a collection of primary records from congressional publications, such as hearings and the *Congressional Record.*
6. Congress, Senate, Subcommittee of the Committee on Military Affairs, *Conscientious Objectors' Benefits: Hearing before a Subcommittee of the Committee on Military Affairs,* 77th Cong., 2nd sess., August 19, 1942, 1.

7. Congress, Senate, Committee on Military Affairs, *Conscientious Objectors' Benefits,* 77th Cong., 2nd sess., Rpt. 1583, August 24, 1942, 2.

8. *Conscientious Objectors' Benefits,* August 19, 1942, 1–2. It bears mentioning that the men still received no daily wage of any sort, and the money accrued came from the total number of months a man worked in CPS in the event of death or disability. This money was to go to their survivors/dependents, not to the men.

9. Ibid., 2–3.

10. Ibid., 6.

11. Congress, Senate, Committee on Military Affairs, *Amending the Selective Training and Service Act of 1940, as Amended, so as to Extend the Benefits of the Employees Compensation Act to Conscientious Objectors,* 78th Cong., 1st sess., Rpt. 73, March 1, 1943, 1.

12. *Congress Looks at the Conscientious Objector,* 34.

13. Congress, Senate, Committee on Military Affairs, *Conscientious Objectors' Benefits: Hearing Before the Committee on Military Affairs,* 78th Cong., 1st sess., February 17, 1943, 17.

14. Ibid., *20.*

15. Congress, House, Committee on Military Affairs, *Allowances and Allotments for Dependents of Military Personnel: Hearings before the Committee on Military Affairs,* 78th Cong., 1st sess., September 29, 30 and October 1, 5, 1943, 99–100.

16. Congress, House, Committee on Military Affairs, *Authorizing the Appropriation of Amounts Received from the Service of Conscientious Objectors for Expenditure by the Selective Service System,* 78th Cong., 2nd sess., Rpt. 1581, May 31, 1944, 1–2.

17. Sibley and Jacob, *Conscription of Conscience,* 220–21.

18. Keim, *The CPS Story,* 24–25; John O'Sullivan, *From Voluntarism to Conscription: Congress and Selective Service, 1940–1945,* 201.

19. Congress, Senate, Committee on Military Affairs, *Married Men Exemption [Drafting of Fathers]: Hearings before the Committee on Military Affairs,* 78th Cong., 1st sess., May 5, September 15–17, 20, 22–23, 1943, 137–38.

20. *Conscientious Objectors' Benefits,* August 19, 1942, 14.

21. Ibid., 8.

22. Congress, Senate, Committee on Military Affairs, *Conscientious Objectors' Benefits: Hearing before the Committee on Military Affairs,* 78th Cong., 1st sess., February 17, 1943, 2.

23. Ibid.

24. Ibid., 15.

25. Ibid., 14.

26. Ibid., 15–16.

27. Ibid., 16.

28. Ibid., 22.

29. Ibid., 23; and Sibley and Jacob, *Conscription of Conscience,* 143. The institutions responsible for the direction of these experiments come from the Sibley and Jacob citation. Imirie only cited the "National Research Council."

30. *Conscientious Objectors' Benefits,* February 17, 1943, 17–18.

31. Gingerich, *Service for Peace,* 306.

32. French Diary, September 3, 7, 1942.

33. Gingerich, *Service for Peace,* 306.

34. E. E. Miller to Mennonite College Presidents and Local College Officers, December 17, 1942, P. S. Goertz Papers, Mennonite Library and Archives, North Newton, KS.

35. French Diary, March 26, 1943.

36. *Military Appropriations Act, Statutes at Large* 57, 350 (1943).

37. Congress, House, Committee on Appropriations, *Military Establishment Appropriations Bill, 1944: Hearings before the Committee on Appropriations,* 78th Cong., 1st sess., June 10, 1943, 584–85, 587.

38. Congress, House, Committee on Appropriations, *Military Establishment Appropriations Bill, Fiscal Year 1944,* 78th Cong., 1st sess., H. Rep. 566, Serial 10762, 14.

39. French Diary, June 25, 26, and 28, 1943.

40. French Diary, July 1, 1943.

41. Lewis B. Hershey to Paul Comly French, August 23, 1943, General Hershey's Staybacks, 1943, Lewis B. Hershey Collection, Army Heritage and Education Center. Carlisle, PA.

Chapter 8

1. Selective Service to C.P.S. Camps, Administrative Directive #24, (printed in *Conscientious Objection, 137);* Lewis B. Hershey to Harry H. Vaughan, April 1, 1946, OF 111, Folder 1946 #1, Harry S. Truman Library, Independence, MO: and *Selective Service and Victory: Fourth Report of the Director of Selective Service,* (Washington, D.C.: Government Printing Office, 1948), 183.

2. *Selective Service and Victory,* 184; and Hershey to Vaughan, April 1, 1946.

3. French Diary, May 8, 30, 1945; Hershey to Vaughan, April 1, 1946, and *The Reporter,* May 15, 1945, 1.

4. *The Reporter,* June 1, 1945.

5. French Diary, June 6–8, 1945.

6. French Diary, June 15, 1945.

7.*The Reporter,* June 15, 1945, 2.

8. Ibid., 2.

9. *The Reporter,* July 1, 1945, 4.

10. French Diary, July 5, 1945.

11. French Diary, July 9–11, 1945; *The Reporter,* July 15, 1945, 1–2; and Congress, House, Committee on Military Affairs, *Preventing a Point System from Being Applied in Connection with the Release of Certain Conscientious Objectors,* July 12, 1945, 79th Cong., 1st sess., H. Rep. 904.

12. French Diary, August 8, 1945; and *The Reporter,* August 1, 1945, 1.

13. French Diary, August 28, 1945; and Lewis B. Hershey to Claude Pepper, August 8, 1945, General Hershey's Staybacks, 1945, part 3, Lewis B. Hershey Collection, Army Heritage and Education Center, Carlisle, PA. Hershey's letter to Senator Pepper states that the Selective Service issued a press release temporarily dropping the point system for CPS demobilization on July 19.

14. Robert P. Patterson to Lewis B. Hershey, June 27, 1945, Letters to Hershey, 1944–1950, Trine University Lewis B. Hershey Collection, Angola, IN.

15. Lewis B. Hershey to Robert Patterson, July 12, 1945, General Hershey's Staybacks, War Department Staybacks, Lewis B. Hershey Collection, Army Heritage and Education Center, Carlisle, PA.

16. Robert Patterson to Lewis B. Hershey, August 4, 1945, General Hershey's Staybacks, War Department Staybacks, Lewis B. Hershey Collection, Army Heritage and Education Center, Carlisle, PA.
17. French Diary, September 6, 1945.
18. French Diary, September 12, 1945.
19. French Diary, September 20–21, 25, 1945; and *The Reporter,* October 15, 1945, 1.
20. French Diary, September 25, 1945.
21. French Diary, September 28, 1945
22. French Diary, October 3, 6, 1945.
23. French Diary, October 10–11, 1945.
24. Hershey to Pepper; Lewis B. Hershey to Aime Forand, October 2, 1945, General Hershey's Staybacks, 1945, part 3, Lewis B. Hershey Collection, Army Heritage and Education Center, Carlisle, PA; and Lewis B. Hershey to Henrik Shipstead, October 2, 1945, General Hershey's Staybacks, 1945, part 3, Lewis B. Hershey Collection, Army Heritage and Education Center, Carlisle, PA. This is a small sampling of Hershey's numerous responses citing his belief that V-J Day lessened some of the criticism levied toward the Selective Service concerning CPS discharges.
25. Flynn, *Lewis B. Hershey,* 133.
26. *The Reporter,* February 1, 1946, 1, 4.
27. Flynn, *The Draft,* 89–90, 93–96.
28. French Diary, March 4, 1946.
29. Paul J. Furnas to Harry S. Truman, March 15, 1946, OF 111, Folder 1946 #1, Harry S. Truman Library, Independence, MO.
30. Hershey to Vaughan, April 1, 1946.
31. *Conscientious Objection,* 313; Flynn, *Lewis B. Hershey,* 134; Flynn, *The Draft,* 96; and Gingerich, *Service for Peace,* 85.
32. *Conscientious Objection,* 313–15.
33. Ibid., 314, 318.

Chapter 9

1. French Diary, July 11, 1946.
2. Memorandum on Conversation with General Hershey, Sibley and Jacob, Swarthmore College Peace Collection, 1.
3. Ibid., 2.
4. Ibid., 2.
5. Ibid., 3.
6. Ibid., 4.
7. Ibid., 5.
8. *Cleveland Press,* June 9, 1955. Hershey's discussions of ministerial deferments particularly apply to the experience of the Jehovah's Witnesses during World War II. The Jehovah's Witnesses sought a ministerial exemption but found it difficult to gain that classification from the local draft boards or to gain sympathetic ears at the higher levels of government bureaucracy. It was a sticking point for Hershey, NSBRO, and the ACLU that resulted in thousands of Jehovah's Witnesses being imprisoned during World War II for draft law violation. For further information,

see Kohn, *Jailed for Peace;* and Sibley and Jacob, *Conscription of Conscience.*

9. This is apparent in French's diary, particularly during the first couple of years of the war.

10. Perry Bush, *Two Kingdoms, Two Loyalties: Mennonite Pacifism in Modern America,* 73.

11. Donald Durnbaugh, *Pragmatic Prophet: The Life of Michael Robert Zigler,* 129, 185, 277; and Zigler, "The Organization and Functioning of CPS," 6.

12. Zigler, "The Organization and Functioning of CPS," 15.

13. Bennett, *Radical Pacifism,* 82; Walker, *In Defense of American Liberties,* 152; and Jo Ann Ooiman Robinson, *Abraham Went Out: A Biography of A. J. Muste,* 78, 83–84.

14. Bennett, *Radical Pacifism,* 79–85.

15. Gordon Zahn, "A Pacifist's View of Conscientious Objection," 59. For Zahn's memoirs of his time in CPS, consult Gordon Zahn, *Another Part of the War: The Camp Simon Story.*

16. Zahn, "A Pacifist's View of Conscientious Objection," 59–60.

17. Leo Crespi, "Attitudes toward Conscientious Objectors and Some of Their Psychological Correlates," 82–83.

18. Ibid., 96–98.

19. Ibid., 115–16.

20. Chambers, "Conscientious Objectors and the American State from Colonial Times to the Present," 39.

21. *Selective Service Act, Statutes at Large* 62, Part 1, 612–13 (1948).

22. Ibid., 613.

23. George Q. Flynn, "Selective Service and the Conscientious Objector," 40–41; and Keim and Stoltzfus, *The Politics of Conscience,* 127–97.

24. Flynn, "Selective Service and the Conscientious Objector," 41; and Keim and Stoltzfus, *The Politics of Conscience,* 139–41.

25. Bush, *Two Kingdoms, Two Loyalties,* 173; Flynn, "Selective Service and the Conscientious Objector," 41; and Keim and Stoltzfus, *The Politics of Conscience,* 144–45.

26. Flynn, "Selective Service and the Conscientious Objector," 41–42; and Keim and Stoltzfus, *The Politics of Conscience,* 142–44, 146.

27. *United States v. Seeger,* 380 U.S. 163 (1965); *Welsh v. United States,* 398 U.S. 333 (1970); and Chambers, "Conscientious Objectors and the American State from Colonial Times to the Present," 40–43.

28. *United States v. Seeger.*

29. Ibid.

30. *Welsh v. United States.*

31. Small, *Antiwarriors,* 109.

32. Flynn, *Lewis B. Hershey,* 273–84; Flynn, *The Draft,* 225–26, 229, 237–39; and Small, 109.

33. Flynn, *The Draft,* 243.

34. Flynn, *Lewis B. Hershey,* 289; and Flynn, *The Draft,* 244–46.

35. Flynn, *Lewis B. Hershey,* 297–99.

36. Ibid., 300–302. Some of the information on Hershey's final days comes from a scholarly discussion and tour with James Zimmerman, professor of history and administrator emeritus from Trine University (formerly Tri-State University),

Hershey's alma mater. While on a research trip to Steuben County and Trine University in August 2008, Zimmerman gave me a detailed tour of the areas where Hershey grew up, pointing out the hotel in which Hershey spent his last hours. I have also personally seen Hershey's gravestone in Arlington National Cemetery, which rivals any present in terms of size.

Conclusion

1. Sibley and Jacob, *Conscription of Conscience,* 226. Sibley and Jacob state that Lewis Kosch's Camp Operations Division denied requests, with Hershey's approval, for work in various hospitals, youth-centered projects, settlement homes in Pittsburgh, and the Pennsylvania School for the Deaf.

2. Eller, *Conscientious Objectors and the Second World War,* 26–27.

3. Various collections of Hershey's speeches can be found at the following archives: Records of the Selective Service, RG 147, National Archives II, College Park, MD; and Lewis B. Hershey Papers, Trine University, Angola, IN.

4. Cohen, *Citizens and Soldiers,* 121–25.

Bibliography

★ ★ ★ ★

Primary Sources

Archive and Manuscript Collections

Army Heritage and Education Center, Carlisle Barracks, PA.
Lewis B. Hershey Collection.
Brethren Historical Library and Archives, Elgin, IL.
Photograph Collection
Franklin D. Roosevelt Library, Hyde Park, NY.
OF 111: Conscientious Objectors (Amnesty)
Photograph Collection
Harry S. Truman Library, Independence, MO.
OF 111
Photograph Collection
Mennonite Church USA Archives, Goshen, IN.
Mennonite Central Committee Civilian Public Service Photographs, 1941-1947
Mennonite Library and Archives, North Newton, KS.
H. P. Krehbiel Collection.
P. S. Goertz Papers.
Vertical File: Conference of Historic Peace Churches (1935 – Newton, KS).
National Archives and Records Administration (Archives II), College Park, MD.
Record Group 147, Records of the Selective Service.
Record Group 407, Army, Adjutant General Decimal File, 1940-1945.
Swarthmore College Peace Collection, Swarthmore, PA.

Collected Document Group A (Paul Comly French Diary).
Document Group 25, Center for Conscience and War.
Trine University Lewis B. Hershey Museum, Angola, IN.
Lewis B. Hershey Private Papers Collection.
Lewis B. Hershey Diary.

Congressional Hearings

Congress. House. *Selective Compulsory Military Training and Service: Hearings before the Committee on Military Affairs.* 76th Cong., 3rd sess., July 10, 11, 24, 25, 26, 30, 31, and August 2, 12, 13, 14, 1940.

Congress. Senate. Subcommittee of the Committee on Military Affairs. *Conscientious Objectors' Benefits: Hearing Before a Subcommittee of the Committee on Military Affairs.* 77th Cong., 2nd sess., August 19, 1942.

Congress. House. Committee on Military Affairs, *Allowances and Allotments for Dependents of Military Personnel: Hearings Before the Committee on Military Affairs.* 78th Cong., 1st sess., September 29, 30, and October 1, 5, 1943.

Congress. Senate. Committee on Military Affairs, *Married Men Exemption [Drafting of Fathers]: Hearings before the Committee on Military Affairs.* 78th Cong., 1st sess., May 5, September 15-17, 20, 22-23, 1943.

Congress. Senate. Committee on Military Affairs. *Conscientious Objectors' Benefits: Hearing Before the Committee on Military Affairs.* 78th Cong., 1st sess., February 17, 1943.

Congress. House. Committee on Appropriations. *Military Establishment Appropriations Bill, 1944: Hearings Before the Committee on Appropriations.* 78th Cong., 1st sess., June 10, 1943.

Congressional Reports

Congress. House. Committee on Military Affairs. *Authorizing the Appropriation of Amounts Received from the Service of Conscientious Objectors for Expenditure by the Selective Service System.* 78th Cong., 2nd sess., Rpt. 1581, May 31, 1944.

Congress. Senate. Committee on Military Affairs. *Amending the Selective Training and Service Act of 1940, as Amended, so as to Extend the Benefits of the Employees Compensation Act to Conscientious Objectors.* 78th Cong., 1st sess., Rpt. 73, March 1, 1943.

Congress. House. Committee on Appropriations. *Military Establishment Appropriations Bill, Fiscal Year 1944*. 78th Cong., 1st sess., H. Rep. 566, Serial 10762.

Congress. Senate. Committee on Military Affairs. *Conscientious Objectors' Benefits*. 77th Cong., 2nd sess., Rpt. 1583, August 24, 1942.

Federal Statutes

Army Emergency Increase, Statutes at Large 40, Part 1 (1917).

Military Appropriations Act, Statutes at Large 57 (1943).

Selective Service Act, Statutes at Large 62, Part 1 (1948).

Selective Training and Service Act, Statutes at Large 54, Part 1 (1940).

Government Publications

Conscientious Objection: Special Monograph No. 11. 2 vols. Washington, D.C.: U.S. Government Printing Office, 1950.

Selective Service and Victory: Fourth Report of the Director of Selective Service. Washington, D.C.: Government Printing Office, 1948.

Selective Service as the Tide of War Turns: Third Report of the Director of Selective Service, 1943-1944. Washington, D.C.: Government Printing Office, 1945.

Selective Service in Peacetime: First Report of the Director of Selective Service, 1940-1941. Washington, D.C.: Government Printing Office, 1942.

Selective Service in Wartime: Second Report of the Director of Selective Service, 1941-1942. Washington, D.C.: Government Printing Office, 1943.

Memoirs and Interviews

Elder, Robert, and James Hattersley. *Report of Interviews with Lewis B. Hershey, General, USA (Retired)*. Carlisle Barracks, PA: US Army War College, June 9, 1975.

Frazer, Heather T., and John O'Sullivan. *We Have Just Begun to Not Fight: An Oral History of Conscientious Objectors in Civilian Public Service during World War II*. New York: Twayne, 1996.

Jacob, Philip, ed. *The Origins of Civilian Public Service: A Review of the Negotiations During the Fall of 1940 between Government Officials and Representatives of the Churches Most Immediately Affected by the Drafting of*

Conscientious Objectors. Washington, D.C.: National Service Board for Religious Objectors.
Jones, Thomas E. *Light on the Horizon: The Quaker Pilgrimage of Tom Jones*. Richmond, IN: Friends United Press, 1973.
Zahn, Gordon. *Another Part of the War: The Camp Simon Story*. Amherst: The University of Massachusetts Press, 1979.

Newsletters and Periodicals

The Cleveland Press
The Saturday Evening Post
The Reporter
Selective Service
The Washington Post

Supreme Court Cases

United States v. Seeger, 380 U.S. 163 (1965).
Welsh v. United States, 398 U.S. 333 (1970).

Other Primary Sources

Congress Looks at the Conscientious Objector. Washington, D.C.: National Service Board for Religious Objectors, 1943.
O'Sullivan, John, and Alan Meckler, eds. *The Draft and Its Enemies: A Documentary History*. Chicago: University of Illinois Press, 1974.
Stimson, Henry L. *Henry Lewis Stimson Diary*. Manuscripts and Archives, Yale University Library, New Haven, CT, 1973.

Secondary Sources

Articles

Crespi, Leo. "Attitudes toward Conscientious Objectors and Some of Their Psychological Correlates." *The Journal of Psychology* 18, no. 1 (July 1944): 81-117.
Flynn, George Q. "Lewis Hershey and the Conscientious Objector: The World War II Experience." *Military Affairs* 47, no. 1 (February 1983): 1-6.

Keim, Albert. "Service or Resistance? The Mennonite Response to Conscription in World War II." *The Mennonite Quarterly Review* 52, no. 2 (April 1978): 141-155.

—— "Mennonites and Selective Service in World War II: An Ambiguous Relationship." *The Mennonite Quarterly Review* 66, no. 4 (October 1992): 508-524.

Krehbiel, Nicholas A. "'We Felt Like We Were Serving Humanity:' McPherson County, Kansas Conscientious Objectors During World War II." *Heritage of the Great Plains* 36, no. 2 (Fall/Winter 2003): 50-64.

Kreider, Robert. "The Historic Peace Churches Meeting in 1935." *Mennonite Life* 31, no. 2 (June 1976): 21-24.

Nolt, Steve. "The CPS Frozen Fund: The Beginning of Peace-Time Interaction between Historic Peace Churches and the United States Government." *The Mennonite Quarterly Review* 67, no. 4 (April 1993): 201-224.

Books

Ahlstrom, Sydney. *A Religious History of the American People*. New Haven, CT: Yale University Press, 1972.

Barbour, Hugh, and J. William Frost. *The Quakers*. New York: Greenwood Press, 1988.

Bennett, Scott H. *Radical Pacifism: The War Resisters League and Gandhian Nonviolence, 1915-1963*. Syracuse, NY: Syracuse University Press, 2003.

Berstein, Iver. *The New York City Draft Riots: Their Significance for American Society and Politics in the Age of the Civil War.* New York: Oxford University Press, 1990.

Brands, H.W. *Traitor to His Class: The Privileged Life and Radical Presidency of Franklin Delano Roosevelt*. New York: Doubleday, 2008.

Brock, Peter. *Pacifism in the United States: From the Colonial Era to the First World War*. Princeton, NJ: Princeton University Press, 1968.

—— *The Quaker Peace Testimony, 1660-1914*. York, England: Sessions Book Trust, 1990.

Brown, Dale. *Understanding Pietism*. Nappanee, IN: Evangel Publishing House, 1996.

Bush, Perry. *Two Kingdom's, Two Loyalties: Mennonite Pacifism in Modern America*. Baltimore, MD: The Johns Hopkins University Press, 1998.

Carp, E. Wayne. *To Starve the Army at Pleasure: Continental Army Administration and American Political Culture*. Chapel Hill: University of North Carolina Press, 1984.

Chambers, John Whiteclay, II. *To Raise an Army: The Draft Comes to Modern America*. New York: The Free Press, 1987.

Chatfield, Charles. *For Peace and Justice: Pacifism in America, 1914-1941*. Knoxville: University of Tennessee Press, 1962.

Clifford, J. Garry, and Samuel R. Spencer, Jr. *The First Peacetime Draft*. Lawrence: The University Press of Kansas, 1986.

Cohen, Eliot. *Citizens and Soldiers: The Dilemmas of Military Service*. Ithaca, NY: Cornell University Press, 1985.

Cook, Adrian. *The Armies of the Streets: The New York City Draft Riots of 1863*. Lexington: The University Press of Kentucky, 1974.

Cottrell, Robert C. *Roger Nash Baldwin and the American Civil Liberties Union*. New York: Columbia University Press, 2000.

—— *Smokejumpers of the Civilian Public Service in World War II: Conscientious Objectors as Firefighters for the National Forest Service*. Jefferson, NC: McFarland, 2006.

DeBenedetti, Charles. *The Peace Reform in American History*. Bloomington: Indiana University Press, 1980.

Davis, Kenneth Ronald. *Anabaptism and Asceticism: A Study in Intellectual Origins*. Herald Press: Scottdale, PA, 1974.

Doubler, Michael D. *Civilian in Peace, Soldier in War: The Army National Guard, 1636-2000*. Lawrence: The University Press of Kansas, 2003.

Durnbaugh, Donald. *Fruit of the Vine: A History of the Brethren, 1708-1995*. Elgin, IL: Brethren Press, 1997.

—— *Pragmatic Prophet: The Life of Michael Robert Zigler*. Elgin, IL: Brethren Press, 1989.

Eisan, Leslie. *Pathways of Peace: A History of the Civilian Public Service Program as Administered by the Brethren Service Committee*. Elgin, IL: Brethren Publishing House, 1948.

Ekirch, Arthur A., Jr. *The Civilian and the Military: A History of the American Antimilitarist Tradition*. Colorado Springs, CO: Ralph Myles, 1972.

Eller, Cynthia. *Conscientious Objectors and the Second World War: Moral and Religious Arguments in Support of Pacifism*. New York: Praeger, 1991.

Estep, William. *The Anabaptist Story: An Introduction to Sixteenth-Century Anabaptism*. Grand Rapids, MI: William B. Eerdmans Publishing, 1996.

Flynn, George Q. *Lewis B. Hershey, Mr. Selective Service*. Chapel Hill: University of North Carolina Press, 1985.

—— *The Draft, 1940-1973*. Lawrence: The University Press of Kansas, 1993.

Geary, James W. *We Need Men: The Union Draft in the Civil War*. DeKalb: Northern Illinois University Press, 1991.

Gingerich, Melvin. *Service for Peace: A History of Mennonite Civilian Public Service*. Akron, PA: Mennonite Central Committee, 1949.

Goossen, Rachel Waltner. *Women against the Good War: Conscientious Objection and Gender on the American Home Front, 1941-1947.* Chapel Hill: The University of North Carolina Press, 1997.

Greer, Thomas H. *What Roosevelt Thought: The Social and Political Ideas of Franklin D. Roosevelt.* East Lansing, MI: Michigan State University Press, 1958.

Hostetler, John. *Mennonite Life.* Scottdale, PA: Herald Press, 1968.

—— *Amish Society.* Baltimore: Johns Hopkins University Press, 1993.

Howlett, Charles F., and Robbie Lieberman. *A History of the American Peace Movement from Colonial Times to the Present.* Lewiston, NY: The Edwin Mellen Press, 2008.

Huntington, Samuel J. *The Soldier and the State: The Theory and Politics of Civil-Military Relations.* Cambridge, MA: Belknap/Harvard University Press, 1985.

Juhnke, James. *A People of Two Kingdoms: The Political Acculturation of the Kansas Mennonites.* Newton, KS: Faith and Life Press, 1975.

Keim, Albert. *The CPS Story: An Illustrated History of Civilian Public Service.* Intercourse, PA: Good Books, 1990.

Keim, Albert, and Grant Stoltzfus. *The Politics of Conscience: The Historic Peace Churches and America at War, 1917-1955.* Scottdale, PA: Herald Press, 1988.

Kennedy, David. *Over Here: The First World War and American Society.* New York: Oxford University Press, 1980.

—— *Freedom from Fear: The American People in Depression and War, 1929-1945.* New York: Oxford University Press, 1999.

Kohn, Stephen M. *Jailed for Peace: A History of American Draft Law Violators, 1658-1985.* Westport, CT: Greenwood Press, 1986.

Kovac, Jeffrey W. *Refusing War, Affirming Peace: A History of Civilian Public Service Camp No. 21 at Cascade Locks.* Corvallis: Oregon State University Press, 2009

Kutulas, Judy. *The American Civil Liberties Union and the Making of Modern Liberalism, 1930-1960.* Chapel Hill: University of North Carolina Press, 2006.

McPherson, James M. *The Battle Cry of Freedom: The Civil War Era.* New York: Oxford University Press, 1988.

Mahon, John K. *History of the Militia and National Guard.* New York: Macmillan, 1983.

Miller, William Robert. *Nonviolence: A Christian Interpretation.* New York: Association Press, 1964.

Millett, Allan R., and Peter Maslowski. *For the Common Defense: A Military History of the United States.* New York: The Free Press, 1994.

Millett, Allan R., and Williamson Murray. *A War to Be Won: Fighting the Second World War*. Cambridge, MA: Belknap Press, 2000.

Moore, Albert B. *Conscription and Conflict in the Confederacy*. New York: Noble Offset, 1924. Reprint, 1963.

Murdock, Eugene C. *One Million Men: The Civil War Draft in the North*. Madison: The State Historical Society of Wisconsin, 1971.

O'Sullivan, John. *From Voluntarism to Conscription: Congress and Selective Service, 1940-1945*. New York: Garland Publishing, 1982.

Robinson, Jo Ann Ooiman. *Abraham Went Out: A Biography of A. J. Muste*. Philadelphia, PA: Temple University Press, 1981.

Sareyan, Alex. *The Turning Point: How Men of Conscience Brought About Major Change in the Care of America's Mentally Ill*. Washington, D.C.: American Psychiatric Press, 1994.

Seiverling, Richard. *Lewis B. Hershey: A Pictorial and Documentary Biography*. Hershey, PA: Keystone Enterprises, 1969.

Sibley, Mulford Quickert, and Philip Jacob. *Conscription of Conscience: The American State and the Conscientious Objector, 1940-1947*. Ithaca, NY: Cornell University Press, 1952.

Small, Melvin. *Antiwarriors: The Vietnam War and the Battle for America's Hearts and Minds*. Wilmington, DE: Scholarly Resources, 2002.

Smith, Jean Edward. *FDR*. New York: Random House, 2007.

Stoeffler, F. Ernest. *German Pietism During the Eighteenth Century*. Leiden, Netherlands: E.F. Brill, 1973.

Taylor, Steven J. *Acts of Conscience: World War II, Mental Institutions, and Conscientious Objectors*. Syracuse, NY: Syracuse University Press, 2009.

Thomas, Norman, *The Conscientious Objector in America*. New York: B.W. Huebsch, 1923.

Trueblood, D. Elton. *The People Called Quakers*. Richmond, IN: Friends United Press, 1966. Reprint, 2002.

Tucker, Todd. *The Great Starvation Experiment: The Heroic Men Who Starved So That Others May Live*. New York: Free Press, 2006.

Walker, Samuel. *In Defense of American Liberties: A History of the ACLU*. New York: Oxford University Press, 1990.

Weigley, Russell F. *History of the United States Army*. New York: The Macmillan Company, 1967.

Williams, George H. *The Radical Reformation*. Philadelphia, PA: Westminster Press, 1962. Reprint, Kirksville, MO: Truman State University Press, 2000.

Wittner, Lawrence. *Rebels against War: The American Peace Movement, 1941-1960*. New York: Columbia University Press, 1969.

Wright, Edward Needles. *Conscientious Objectors in the Civil War*. New

York: A.S. Barnes and Co., 1931. Reprint, 1961.

Ziegler, Valarie H. *The Advocates of Peace in Antebellum America*. Bloomington: Indiana University Press, 1992.

Edited Works and Book Chapters

Augsburger, Myron. "Christian Pacifism." In *War: Four Christian Views*, ed. Robert Clouse, 79-97. Downers Grove, IL: InterVarsity Press, 1981. Reprint, 1991.

Bender, Harold S. "Mennonite Origins and the Mennonites of Europe." In *Mennonites and Their Heritage: A Handbook of Mennonite History and Beliefs*, 7-77. Scottdale, PA: Herald Press, 1942. Reprint, 1973.

Bennett, Scott H, ed. *Army GI, Pacifist CO: The World War II Letters of Frank and Albert Dietrich*. New York: Fordham University Press, 2005.

Brock, Peter, ed. *Liberty and Conscience: A Documentary History of the Experiences of Conscientious Objectors in America through the Civil War*. New York: Oxford University Press, 2002.

Chambers, John Whiteclay, II. "Conscientious Objectors and the American State from Colonial Times to the Present." In *The New Conscientious Objection: From Sacred to Secular Resistance*, ed. John Whiteclay Chambers II and Charles C. Moskos, 23-46. New York: Oxford University Press, 1993.

—— ed. *Draftees or Volunteers: A Documentary History of the Debate over Military Conscription in the United States, 1787-1973*. New York: Garland Publishing, 1975.

Durnbaugh, Donald. "Early History." In *Church of the Brethren: Yesterday and Today*, ed. Donald Durnbaugh, 1-20. Elgin, IL: Brethren Press, 1986.

Flynn, George Q. "Selective Service and the Conscientious Objector." In *Selective Conscientious Objection: Accommodating Conscience and Security*, ed. Michael F. Noone, Jr., 35-55. San Francisco, CA: Westview Press, 1989.

Hoyt, Herman. "Nonresistance." In *War: Four Christian Views*, ed. Robert Clouse, 30-57. Downers Grove, IL: InterVarsity, 1981. Reprint, 1991.

Klaassen, Walter, ed. *Anabaptism in Outline: Selected Primary Sources*. Scottdale, PA: Herald Press, 1981.

Matloff, Maurice. "The 90-Division Gamble." In *Command Decisions*, ed. Kent Roberts Greenfield, 365-381. Washington, D.C.: Center of Military History, 1960. Reprint, 1984.

Millett, Allan R. "Over Where? The AEF and the American Strategy for

Victory, 1917-1918." In *Against All Enemies: Interpretations of American Military History from Colonial Times to the Present*, ed. Kenneth J. Hagan and William R. Roberts, 235-256. Westport, CT: Greenwood Press, 1986.

Smith, C. Henry. "Mennonites in North America." In *Mennonites and Their Heritage: A Handbook of Mennonite History and Beliefs*, 78-146. Scottdale, PA: Herald Press, 1942. Reprint, 1973.

Stoffer, Dale. "Beliefs." In *Church of the Brethren: Yesterday and Today*, ed. Donald Durnbaugh, 43-60. Elgin, IL: Brethren Press, 1986.

Stokesbury, James L. "The U.S. Army and Coalition Warfare, 1941-1945." In *Against All Enemies: Interpretations of American Military History from Colonial Times to the Present*, ed. Kenneth J. Hagan and William R. Roberts, 279-303. New York: Greenwood Press, 1986.

Zahn, Gordon. "A Pacifist's View of Conscientious Objection." In *Selective Conscientious Objection: Accommodating Conscience and Security*, ed. Michael F. Noone, Jr., 57-61. San Francisco, CA: Westview Press, 1989.

Film Transcripts

The Good War and Those Who Refused to Fight It. Paradigm Productions. Independent Television Services Script. Bullfrog Films, 2000.

Dissertations

Blackstone, Robert C. "Democracy's Army: American People and Selective Service in World War II." Ph.D. diss., University of Kansas, 2005.

Robinson, Mitchell Lee. "Civilian Public Service During World War II: The Dilemmas of Conscience and Conscription in a Free Society." Ph.D. diss., Cornell University, 1990.

Index